Disarming patriarchy

Disarming patriarchy

Feminism and political action at Greenham

Sasha Roseneil

Open University Press
Buckingham · Philadelphia

Open University Press
Celtic Court
22 Ballmoor
Buckingham
MK18 1XW

and
1900 Frost Road, Suite 101
Bristol, PA 19007, USA

First Published 1995

A catalogue record of this book is available from the British Library

ISBN   0 335 19057 X (pb)   0 335 19058 8 (hb)

Library of Congress Cataloging-in-Publication Data
Roseneil, Sasha, 1966–
    Disarming patriarchy : feminism and political action at Greenham /
Sasha Roseneil.
        p.   cm.
    Includes bibliographical references and index.
    ISBN 0-335-19057-X (pbk.)   ISBN 0-335-19058-8 (hardback)
    1. Women and peace.   2. Antinuclear movement—Great Britain.
3. Patriarchy—Great Britain.   I. Title.
JX1965.R67   1995
305.42—dc20   94–40164
                                                      CIP

Typeset by Dorwyn Ltd, Rowlands Castle, Hants
Printed in Great Britain by St Edmundsbury Press Ltd
Bury St Edmunds, Suffolk

Contents

Acknowledgements   vi
Map of Greenham Common   viii

1   Introduction   1

2   The origins of Greenham   14

3   The making of Greenham   30

4   The ethos of Greenham: theorizing practice and practising theory   60

5   The internal mode of action   71

6   The external mode of action   97

7   Boys against girls, girls against boys: the dynamics of Greenham's
    challenge   118

8   Transgressions and transformations: experience, consciousness and
    identity at Greenham   136

9   Conclusion: disarming patriarchy   164

Appendix I   Characteristics of the interviewees   173
Appendix II Commentary on the sample   175

Notes   180
References   197
Index   216

Acknowledgements

The origins of this book are deeply embedded in the past twelve years of my life, and many people have, wittingly or not, contributed to its creation.

First of all I must thank all the women who agreed to be interviewed about their experiences of Greenham: Carola Addington, Katrina Allen, Ann Armstrong, Sarah Benham, Penni Bestic, Lesley Brinkworth, Carmel Cadden, Sian Edwards, Lynne Fortt, Ann Francis, Liz Galst, Penni Gulliver, Rowan Gwedhen, Carol Harwood, Jenny Heron, Clare Hudson, Helen John, Helen Mary Jones, Christine King, Susan Lamb, Margery Lewis, Linda, Jinny List, Nell Logan, Ann Lukes, Pat Paris, Barbara Rawson, Barbara Schulman, Kim Smith, Leah Thalmann, Trina, Trisha, Simone Wilkinson, Vee Wright, and Bridget Evans, the woman who didn't want to be named. Ann Armstrong, Lynette Edwell and Jinny List allowed me access to their personal Greenham archives. Jane Deighton discussed court cases with me.

The following people have read and commented on earlier versions of parts of the book: Lisa Adkins, Paul Bagguley, Nickie Charles, Nicky Edwards, Carli Lessof, Kirk Mann, Carol Smart, Angus Stewart, and Sylvia Walby. I am grateful to them for the variety of perspectives which they brought to bear on the project, and the assistance this gave me in developing my ideas.

The research was supported financially by a studentship from the Economic and Social Research Council, the Metcalfe Studentship from the University of London, and a grant for transcription from the London School of Economics. Karen McMullen rescued me from despair by transcribing many of the interviews. Librarians and archivists at the following institutions have helped me in various ways to research the book: the British Library of Political and Economic Science in London, the Mid-Glamorgan County Archives in Cardiff, and the Schlesinger Library at Radcliffe College, Cambridge, MA.

From back in the early 1980s I wish to thank Anita Thistlethwaite, for suggesting that I should write about Greenham. Thank you, also, to the women with whom I had adventures at Greenham in 1983–4, particularly Rebecca Long and Liz Galst. All my parents, Wendy, Sidney, and Pat – are owed thanks for their lack of intervention when I went to live at Greenham, and together with my sister, Justine, for their support over the years. My grandmother, Margaret O'Connell, who was involved in the Committee of 100 long before I was born, has been a source of inspiration as far back as I can remember. Rebecca Johnson and Lisa Adkins have been good friends during the writing of the book.

Above all, though, thanks to Nicky Edwards, for everything.

Map of Greenham Common (Winter 1983–4)

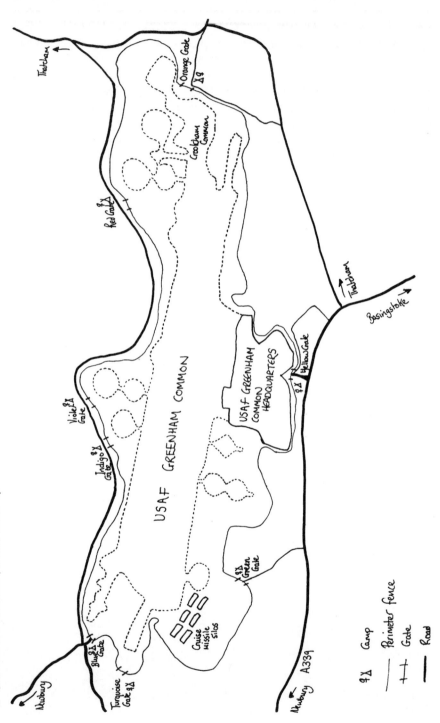

①

Introduction

To disarm patriarchy, to resist and transform relations of male domination and female subordination, must be the ultimate goal of feminism.[1] The question of how this is to be done is, therefore, one of feminism's central concerns, and is also my subject here. This book is about how, at one historically specific moment, in one particular place in the world, women acted together to confront patriarchy and to challenge militarism.

My focus is on a women's movement which began in Britain in 1981, and which mobilized more women than any other since the campaigns for suffrage of the early years of the twentieth century – Greenham Common.[2] These two words have come to represent not the United States Air Force base at which Cruise missiles were stationed between 1983 and 1991, but an instance, place, and style of feminist political action. A movement of importance both globally and in the lives of tens of thousands of women, Greenham deserves the serious attention of feminists and those interested in social movements.

My theoretical project is to contribute to the understanding of women's agency. Historically, feminist sociology has been better at exposing, naming, and analysing the structural oppression of women than it has been at theorizing and tracing the contours of women's agency and resistance.[3] In the past, there has been a tendency to portray women as 'the passive victims of a mechanistic and deterministic system' (Maynard 1990:274). Feminists have often failed to consider the implications of their own feminism, and often lesbianism, in the theories they have constructed. Surprisingly little has been written by feminist sociologists about women's movements and feminist campaigns (leaving the area largely to feminist historians), or about feminist consciousness and empowerment.[4] However, concern with women's agency has recently begun to take off within the field. And is particularly evident in the feminist tradition within cultural studies, and in work on violence against women and sexuality.[5]

In their routine daily lives, women make use of the rules and resources of a patriarchal society, and in so doing contribute to its reproduction. In the terms of structuration theory (Giddens 1977, 1984), patriarchal structures are 'both constituted *by* human agency, and yet at the same time are the *medium* of this constitution' (Giddens 1977:121); this is the 'duality of structure'.[6] The everyday practices of, for example, entertaining a husband's employer or paying income tax which is spent on nuclear weapons, in which a woman follows the rules of the social system, contribute to the reproduction of patriarchy and militarism. Individual actors are knowledgeable about their actions, not cultural dupes, but the reproduction of structures is the unintended consequence of their action. They make sense of their action and of the world around them using the discursive resources, that is, the sets of ideas and claims about truth, which are available to them. However, they are also capable of transgressing the rules and resources of society, of questioning them, and seeking to transform them by creating alternative practices and new discourses with which to understand the world.[7] This can take place at an individual level, but by acting collectively the possibility of substantial transformation of society is greatly increased.[8]

In this book I am less interested in the routine actions by which women contribute to the reproduction of patriarchy, than in non-routine, extraordinary political action, through which women seek social change.[9] By looking in detail at the case of Greenham, I discuss how it was possible for a movement of women to step outside the ongoing practices and discourses through which patriarchy is continuously reconstituted. I analyse the way in which women created this social movement, constructing a collective identity and engaging in the daily practices of maintaining its cohesion. And I examine the many different actions which they took to challenge patriarchy and militarism, in order to reach an assessment of Greenham's transformative impact.

To prefigure my conclusions, I will argue that women at Greenham posed a very significant challenge both to their first and most obvious target – the nuclear policies of the United States and NATO within Britain – and in their wider project of disrupting dominant gender relations. Greenham occupied a position of liminality, outside many of the structures of contemporary western societies – outside the heterorelational dynamic of patriarchy (Raymond 1986), outside the private sphere of women's subordination, outside the framework of male-dominated liberal democratic politics. As a women-only community, Greenham developed its own ways of working and forms of political action, and engaged in 'cognitive praxis' (Eyerman and Jamison 1991) to create new forms of consciousness and new identities. The experience of involvement in Greenham was one of empowerment and of transformation of self: housewives, mothers, and 'grannies for peace' became feminists and lesbians; isolated young lesbians discovered community; jaded veterans of left politics found renewed energy and passionate participation.

As well as a theoretical contribution to the sociology of women's agency, I provide a detailed ethnography of Greenham. Through this, I engage with criticisms which some feminists have made of Greenham. These have tended to be based on constructions of Greenham in the media and the very earliest external face presented by the camp. The features of Greenham which have most attracted feminist condemnation were its supposed maternalism and essentialism; yet these are assumed rather than investigated (e.g. Onlywomen Press 1983; Segal 1987). Few feminist scholars have written at any length about Greenham. In addition to two books by Greenham women themselves, written within the first two years of the camp's life (Cook and Kirk 1983; Harford and Hopkins 1984), there is one book-length study of media representations of Greenham (A. Young 1990), and a history of the women's peace movement, which devotes several chapters to Greenham (Liddington 1989).[10] The two major historical accounts of recent feminist politics in Britain – by Lovenduski and Randall (1993) and Rowbotham (1989) – each only devote a few pages to Greenham. This is despite the fact that Greenham activated hundreds of thousands of women, was the most visible form of women's activism (and together with the 1984–5 miner's strike of any form of oppositional politics) in Britain in the 1980s and provided the model for women's peace camps in at least eight other countries.

Unlike much that has been written about Greenham, I seek to present its complexities. I highlight contradictions and conflicts within the movement, and between and within its ethos and actions. Above all, the approach is diachronic; this is not a snapshot study of Greenham, but one which teases out processes of change over time.

In the course of the book I also contribute to sociological understanding of social movements. Focusing on an instance of collective action by women highlights problems with the gender ignorance of much previous research on social movements, and I propose a framework for the analysis of women's movements which takes seriously the patriarchal contexts from which they are forged. My approach to studying Greenham makes use of the main traditions within social movement theory, but moves beyond them, suggesting critique and synthesis.

Gender, feminism, and militarism[11]

Though western culture has long constructed women as 'beautiful souls' and men as 'just warriors' (Elshtain 1987), there is no natural or inevitable connection between women and peace, or between men and militarism. Women have historically, and traditionally, supported wars. As wives and mothers they have waved their men off to battle, and provided succour to returning soldiers, thereby contributing to the reproduction of the military (Enloe 1983, 1989). As official and unofficial military workers – nurses, drivers, telecommunications officers, prostitutes, camp followers, and soldiers – they have actively participated in armies, and are increasingly occupying combat positions in NATO armed forces.[12] Women have organized to support militarist and nationalist projects, in Nazi Germany (Koonz 1988), for example, and, more recently, in the former

Yugoslavia. And, particularly in the United States, the campaign for equality within the armed forces has been an important part of liberal feminist political agendas. Nor have all men always supported wars; the long history of pacifism, conscientious objection to conscription, and peace movements testifies to this.[13]

However, there is also a considerable history of opposition to militarism in which women *qua* women have drawn attention to the gendered social and cultural practices which sustain armed forces, defence establishments, and the activity of war.[14] There are three main discourses within which women have critiqued and protested against militarism: maternalism, materialism, and feminism.[15]

The discourse of maternalism has historically underpinned women's peace campaigning on the basis of a mother's moral and practical duty to protect life. In its early manifestations in the nineteenth century (Liddington 1989), maternalist anti-militarism remained firmly within the hegemonic discourse of 'separate spheres' (Davidoff and Hall 1987), and did not take women into the public sphere to confront the military system. However, as the ideological confinement of women within the private sphere weakened in the twentieth century, maternalism has been mobilized to legitimize women's activism outside the home. At times when there was no visible feminist movement, women's commitment to peace work tended to be framed entirely in terms of their maternal role, as was the case with the Women's Strike for Peace in the United States and the British group, Voice of Women, in the early 1960s (Liddington 1989; Swerdlow 1989). Other women's peace campaigns, such as the Women's International League for Peace and Freedom (WILPF) and the Women's Peace Party in the United States, which were founded by suffrage campaigners, have combined maternalist rhetoric with a feminist critique of the gender politics of militarism (Wiltsher 1985; Liddington 1989).

Maternalist peace activism by women has been widely criticized by feminists over the last two decades. It has been argued that maternalist women's peace campaigning is reactionary and anti-feminist, shoring up the gender division of labour and perpetuating ideas about essential differences between men and women. For instance, Simone de Beauvoir is quoted as having said: 'Women should desire peace as human beings, not as women. And if they are being encouraged to be pacifists in the name of motherhood, that's just a ruse by men who are trying to lead women back to the womb. Women should absolutely let go of that baggage' (Swerdlow 1989:225). The implication is that maternalism is 'false consciousness', an ideology imposed on women by men in order to dominate them. Undoubtedly men do benefit enormously from women's labour as mothers and homemakers (Delphy and Leonard 1992) but women's political activism rooted in maternalism cannot be written off as 'false consciousness'.

An alternative way of understanding maternalism is suggested by Ruddick (1990) and Elshtain (1985). This sees maternalism as a way of thinking that is grounded in the material reality of women's lives and work as mothers. Ruddick (1990) draws on feminist standpoint theory and argues that 'maternal thinking' arises from 'maternal practice', the work of preservation, nurturance, and training which is involved in childcare. This work is primarily, though not necessarily, carried out by women.[16] Ruddick recognizes that many mothers have supported wars, but argues that there is a clear contradiction between the violence of war and maternal work; not only the daily practice of childcare, but also the long-term aims of maternal practice are threatened by war.

Rather than being 'false consciousness', then, this argument suggests that maternalism is a discourse which resonates with many women's socially constructed material experience. It is a discourse women are able to mobilize without seriously transgressing the dominant gender relations that have structured their experience thus, but it is also a discourse which has within it the seeds of its own transformation. Consciousness is malleable and open to change and, historically, many instances of women's collective action which have begun within a maternalist framework have become increasingly feminist as women stepped outside the very roles that they were seeking to defend.[17] Such shifts from 'female' to 'feminist' consciousness (Kaplan 1982) are particularly likely to occur at times when feminist discourses are available in wider society to replace maternalism. This, I will argue, is precisely what happened at Greenham.

Women's materialist opposition to militarism has focused on the gendered nature of the actual material hardship, injury, and death which is consequent on war and preparation for wars. Whilst not in itself necessarily feminist, it has often occurred in conjunction with a feminist critique of the gender politics of militarism. The classic example of materialist opposition to war was Emily Hobhouse's campaigning for the women and children displaced by the Boer War. She argued that the 'brunt of the war' fell on non-combatants, primarily women and children, and she challenged the convention of counting the cost of war purely in terms of dead soldiers (Hobhouse 1902). Others, such as Hallowes (Cambridge Women's Peace Collective 1984), Swanwick (Liddington 1989), and, most famously, Woolf (1982), have advanced the materialist argument that to the extent that anyone gains from war, whether in terms of glory or conquered territory, it is men rather than women.[18]

From a more socialist perspective, women anti-militarists have also campaigned against 'economic war'. The WILPF, for instance, opposed the Allied food blockade of Germany after the First World War because of its effect on non-combatants (Liddington 1989), and throughout its history has made theoretical connections between high military expenditure and poverty (Foster 1989). Recent writers have pointed out that increases in military budgets invariably mean reductions in social expenditure, which disproportionately affects women as the heaviest users of public services. Militarism is seen therefore as contributing to the 'feminization of poverty' (Enloe 1981; Tobias 1985; Beneria and Blank 1989).

The explicit use of feminist discourse in the critique of militarism has taken three main courses. The first focuses on the almost entire exclusion of women from the military as an institution and from the governments which take decisions about defence and foreign policy. The argument that women therefore have not consented to wars declared by nation states was one frequently made by feminist peace campaingers of the First World War (Liddington 1989), and is still used by feminists despite the winning of formal equality of political citizenship rights.

The second theme of feminist opposition to militarism draws attention to the cultural connections between militarism and masculinity and to the gendered and sexualized discourses of militarism. Cohn (1987a,b, 1989, 1993), for example, examines the 'techno-strategic discourse' of defence-intellectuals, which serves as legitimation for the technological/nuclear arms race.[19] The language of nuclear militarism is disassociational; it is abstract, euphemistic, and sanitized, and uses blatant imagery of male sexual domination and female subordination. For example, during Cohn's participant observation of the US defence establishment, nuclear 'spasm attacks' were described as 'releasing 70–80 per cent of our megatonnage in one orgasmic whump' (Cohn 1987a:18). Moreover she heard disarmament referred to as 'get[ting] rid of all your stuff' (1987a:18), West German politicians concerned about the deployment of cruise missiles were dismissed as a 'bunch of limp-dicked wimps' (1993:236), and the masculinity of those members of NATO who disagreed with US support for Nicaraguan Contras was questioned by the appellation, 'Euro-fags'. In a similar vein, Enloe's (1983, 1989) feminist analysis of militarism argues that military systems depend on particular constructions of masculinity and femininity, and serve to reinscript hierarchical gender differences. She reveals, for instance, how military training is a socialization process designed to inculcate an aggressive, misogynist masculinity into the recruit, both in order to prepare him for the job of waging war and in order to maintain the image of 'military manhood' as the apotheosis of male virility. The latter is a fundamental part of the discourse of chivalry, which has traditionally been used to justify militarism: the idea that the military exists to protect the 'weak' (women and children) from the men of other nations.[20]

Linked to such analysis is the third strand of feminist opposition to militarism which connects militarism with male violence. This discourse has been at the forefront of recent transnational feminist campaigns for the recognition of rape as a war crime, following the widespread raping of women during the wars in the former Yugoslavia. Two main positions exist within this general theme. One of these sees war as providing an opportunity for men's sexual violence on a scale not seen in peacetime, and links this with cultural critiques of the 'manliness of war'. Exemplifying this is the work of Brownmiller (1976), which exposes the universality of rape in war and argues that war provides men with 'the perfect psychologic backdrop to give vent to their contempt for women' (1976:32). She states that the men who rape in war are 'ordinary Joes' (1976:32), who, in the male-only club of the military 'prove their newly won superiority' by raping the defeated enemy's women. The other position within this theme is the radical feminist argument, which characterizes war as a form of male violence in and of itself. Dworkin (1981), for example, conceives of war as male aggression, in which 'older men kill boys by generating and financing wars' (1981:51). She argues that older men's hatred of boys stems from their hatred of women:

'Older men hate boys because they still have the smell of women on them. War purifies, washes off the female stink' (1981:51). War is, then, for those who survive, the route to manhood, from identification with women, to identification with men and allegiance to 'the male code'. The military and its mythology of heroism, in which male violence is institutionalized, serve to develop in men 'a strong loyalty to violence', which is a necessary part of male identity. Daly (1979) takes the argument further than Dworkin, arguing the 'State of War' is in fact the normal 'State of Patriarchy', and that the enemies in the war waged by patriarchal rulers are women and life itself (1979:355). The implication of this is that the violence of war is part and parcel of the violence perpetrated by men as an intrinsic part of patriarchy. Russell (1989) draws on the work of both Dworkin and Daly and seeks to expose the 'male face of violence'. She suggests that war and nuclear militarism are the ultimate acts of male violence, in a society where masculinity is fundamentally constituted through aggression and violence.

Each of these three discourses – maternalist, materialist and feminist – will be seen to have framed, at different times, both the public voice of Greenham and the motivations of individual women. In the course of the book, I trace how the emphasis shifted between the discourses and developed in new directions, producing significant transformations in consciousness and identity at the level of the individual.

Researching Greenham

Three main sources provide the data on which the book is based; my own 'retrospective auto-ethnography', interviews with Greenham women, and documentary sources.[21]

Retrospective auto-ethnography

In effect, the research for this book began back in December 1982, when I first visited Greenham for the 'Embrace the Base' demonstration. But this was not a conventional research trip; I was sixteen, and went to Greenham wholly as a participant.[22] A year later I had left school and moved to Greenham, where I lived for ten months. During this time, I had the whole range of 'Greenham experiences' – actions, arrest, court appearances, prison, evictions, harassment from police, soldiers and vigilantes, and, above all, being part of the camp, contributing to its daily re-creation and transformation. I kept a diary only sporadically and, untrained and uninterested in the niceties of sociological research methods, I did not systematically gather 'data' on Greenham whilst there. However, my memories and reconstructions of experiences at Greenham have been plundered continually in the course of the formal research process.

Whilst 'insider research' is rarely discussed in texts on research methods, I am certainly not the first sociologist to use her personal experience and unique life history for research purposes. Long before feminists were advocating this, Mills argued that the sociological imagination thrives on inward reflection:

> [Y]ou must learn to use your life experience in your intellectual work, continually to examine and interpret it. In this sense craftsmanship is the centre of yourself and you are personally involved in every intellectual product upon which you work.
>
> (Mills 1958:196)

Similarly, Riemer claims that 'opportunistic research strategies' (1977:467), using one's own 'at hand' knowledge, unique biographies, and situational familiarities as sources of research ideas and data, can be sociologically profitable.[23] I coin the term 'retrospective auto-ethnography' (Roseneil 1993) to describe the research, to suggest that it involved the studying of my 'own people' (Hayano 1983:150), by 'looking back on events from my past life [to] observe and analyze them' (Greed 1990:147).

My own involvement with Greenham locates me as anything but the unbiased, objective observer required by the positivist tradition in sociology, or even of mainstream interpretive qualitative research.[24] Within an epistemological framework of 'fractured foundationalism' (Stanley and Wise 1990, 1993), which recognizes the contingency of all claims to truth and their inevitable partiality and situatedness (Haraway 1988), this is not in itself a problem.[25] Rather than 'bracketing' (Schutz 1967) my pre-existing experiences and politics, I sought to engage with them reflexively, to interrogate them, and to locate myself on the same critical plane as the women I interviewed and the archives I trawled. Indeed, I claim a high level of validity for my findings *because of*, not despite, my own involvement in Greenham. I do not claim that this work is in anyway definitive, but I do believe that it is better than that produced by an outsider could have been.

This said, insider research is not without problems. The most obvious of these is the danger of being too close to the subject matter, either to see the sociological significance of that which appears completely normal, or to be able to frame criticisms – the 'rose tinted spectacles' problem. Had I started researching Greenham very soon after living there, with little time for reflection, desensitization through familiarity may have been a more serious issue. As it was, beginning four years after Greenham had last been my home, I came back to the subject matter refreshed. Throughout the formal period of the research I made a conscious effort to 'make the familiar strange', to attempt to see things as if for the first time and then to compare these observations with my immediate 'gut feelings'. As far as criticizing Greenham is concerned, the proof of the pudding is in the reading – I have attempted to tell 'the truth' about Greenham as I understand it, warts and all. Here again the length of time between my living at Greenham and formally beginning the research, and my subsequent engagement with individual feminists and a feminist literature hostile to Greenham have, I believe, afforded me a certain degree of critical distance.

Interviews with Greenham women

As a loosely structured network of individuals and groups, Greenham had no membership list and hence no ready-made sampling frame from which to draw a probability sample. I therefore had to rely on my own knowledge of the social organization of Greenham by gate-based networks.[26] In sampling, I started from a small number of women I knew, most of whom had lived at Greenham between 1982 and 1985, and I worked outwards, using a 'snowball sampling' technique (Coleman 1958). I was able very quickly to move beyond women of my acquaintance by asking each woman I interviewed to suggest further possible interviewees. Of the 35 women interviewed, 25 were not known to me prior to the interview.

In order to maximize the heterogeneity of the sample, and to challenge the popular stereotypes of Greenham women (the *Guardian* stereotype of the middle-class, middle-aged, southern England mother of four, and the *Sun* stereotype of the teenage lesbian punk), I used a method of 'judgement' (Burgess 1984) or 'strategic' sampling (Thompson 1988). Based on my knowledge of hundreds of women I had met at Greenham, I formulated a list of characteristics which I hypothesized were important variables, and sampled with these in mind: age when first involved; class; gate of association; level of involvement – 'camper', 'stayer', or 'visitor'; motherhood status before involvement; occupation before involvement; region of residence before involvement; and sexual identity before involvement. I was concerned particularly to focus on women who had not been in the public eye as media-chosen 'spokespeople'.[27] Whilst the final sample is not statistically representative of the population of Greenham, it covers a very broad cross-section of the sorts of women who were involved, in different ways and at different periods in the camp's history. For a detailed discussion of the sample, see Appendices.

My insider status and knowledge had many advantages in the process of interviewing Greenham women. Already 'empirically literate', about Greenham, I could avoid the *faux pas* of the visitors and journalists who besieged the camp at its peak, and who were described, in affectionate exasperation, in the following Greenham song:

At the Peace Camp, Newbury, Berkshire
(to the tune of *English Country Garden*)

What are the questions visitors will ask us
At the Peace Camp, Newbury, Berkshire?
I'll tell you now of some that I know,
And the rest, you'll surely ask them.
'Are there many of you here?'
'Is it cold, and are you queer?'
'Where do you get your water from?'
'Would you die for the cause?'
'Do you shit in the gorse?'
At the Peace Camp, Newbury, Berkshire.

What are the questions the media will ask us
At the Peace Camp, Newbury, Berkshire?
I'll tell you now of some that I know,
And the rest, you'll read them later.
'Why did you make this sacrifice?'
'Can I talk to someone nice?'
'How does it feel now you have failed?'
'Can you pose by the gate?'
'Hurry up, it's getting late.'
At the Peace Camp, Newbury, Berkshire.

There was a high level of 'in-built, face-level trust' (Riemer 1977:474) between myself and the interviewees, and we shared a language and set of symbolic meanings associated with Greenham. Many of the women said that they would not have agreed to be interviewed by an 'outsider', with a few commenting that our shared histories of involvement allowed them to discuss issues, particularly internal conflicts, which they would not have otherwise done.[28] My membership of Greenham friendship networks also made it possible for me to interview many women whom an outsider would not have 'found'; for example, women without a high profile in the media, and those whose involvement was largely in local support groups, rather than at the camp.

The interviews, which were all tape-recorded, were semi-structured, and lasted between two and four hours. I was particularly interested to understand the relative significance to the interviewees of different events and aspects of life at Greenham, and of the issues with which Greenham was concerned. Questions about nuclear weapons were therefore asked nearer to the beginning of interviews, and I refrained from raising issues of feminism and sexuality until later, in an attempt to minimize the impact of the research framework on the subjects discussed, although, of course, this was gradually revealed in the course of the interview.

The interviews were conducted between 1989 and 1991, up to ten years after the events they describe, and my use of auto-ethnography draws on experiences of over eleven years ago. The problem usually highlighted in relation to retrospective data is the possibility of distortions in memory, due either to memory failure, or influenced by subsequent changes in values and norms, which may unconsciously alter perceptions. Thompson (1988) argues that the most significant loss of material from the memory occurs very shortly after the event (within minutes). The process of discarding continues over time, but for the first thirty-four years is insignificant compared with the immediate phase of loss. Thus there seems to be a 'curve of forgetfulness' which inevitably affects even contemporary reporting and participant observers. Thompson also suggests that the memory process depends, to a large extent, on the interest of the interviewee in that which is to be remembered.

Greenham had been a very significant part of the lives of all the women, and all were keen to talk about it. Their memories were therefore probably aided by this, together with their interest in the research. I do not, however, wish to suggest that the interviews somehow provide access to 'the truth' about Greenham. Accounts given in interviews are always and inevitably shaped by many factors besides 'memory'. An interviewee engages in an active process of constructing stories within the particular context of the interview situation. These narratives are shaped by the discourses to which she has access, and by the interaction itself, and her understanding of what she thinks is required of her. Thus, a story may be reformulated at different times, in other contexts, and to other audiences. For instance, in the light of a new feminist consciousness, many women described their husbands' attitudes to their involvement in Greenham differently from how they would have done at the time. In other cases, unhappy and disturbing experiences were not recalled as readily as more positive ones. Judicious prompting and questioning in the course of interviews, however, produced some accounts of loneliness or isolation at Greenham, and gave rise to considerably more memories of incidents of violent assault and abuse from local men and from police and soldiers than were initially volunteered.

The interviews were not so much seeking 'factual data', as the social meanings of past events and of women's experiences at Greenham. The retrospective nature of the interviews was, in itself, interesting. It granted the women a certain temporal perspective on Greenham, allowed for a longitudinal element in the study and focused both my attention and their attention on changes at an individual and a societal level. As Morgan (1977) has noted, it is only really possible to grasp the meanings of our actions and changes in our consciousness retrospectively.

Documentary sources

Various types of documentary sources were used in the research. First, I made use of my own quite extensive archive of Greenham paraphernalia, gathered over the years; this includes leaflets about actions, the irregularly produced Greenham newsletter (to which I contributed extensively in 1984), pamphlets and my personal diary. Second, I was given access to the archives of several other Greenham women, which complemented my own. Third, I consulted publicly available archives and newspaper libraries.[29]

Analysis and theorizing

Like most research, this study of Greenham did not conform to either of the ideal typical models of induction or deduction. I did not come to the project with 'an empty head' and a hypothetical 'explanation' of Greenham as the former tends to suggest. Nor was the agenda of the research entirely preset or its products untainted by my own material experiences as the latter proposes (Stanley and Wise 1990). The method of data analysis that I used owes a debt to Glaser and Strauss's 'grounded theory' (1967), although I did not follow their injunctions to the letter.[30] What my approach shared with theirs was a commitment to refining and testing theory throughout the process of data collection, so that the collection of data could be guided by the emergent theory.[31]

I began the study with a large number of ideas and hypotheses at various stages of development. These were derived from reflections on my own period of involvement and an engagement with the literatures on social movements, women and politics, and feminist theory. From there I formulated a set of research questions, which helped to focus and bound the data collection. I set out to challenge these initial ideas and tentative hypotheses to the test of the accounts of the sample of Greenham women. More hypotheses arose from the interviews, which were incorporated into subsequent interviews, and I often asked interviewees directly what they thought of a particular idea or theory. The virtue of the loosely structured, in-depth interview was that it was possible, throughout the formal fieldwork period, to continually test my latest thoughts on other women and incorporate their feedback into my evolving analysis.

This practice acted as a form of 'respondent validation' (Hammersley and Atkinson 1983; Miles and Huberman 1984) of my interpretations of the data. It acknowledged and made use of the knowledgeability and agency of the interviewees. Above all, it recognized that feminist (and other) theorizing is not the exclusive province of the academy. The production of feminist theory is a collective enterprise, closely intertwined with political praxis. I sought not to theorize *about* Greenham women, as some strange foreign species under the gaze of the colonial ethnographer; rather I wanted to theorize *with* them. Perhaps the ideal situation would have been to do this in group meetings when Greenham was at its height.[32] But given that this was no longer possible, and that the women now live scattered all over Britain and beyond, the process of analysis that I adopted seemed a reasonable compromise. Many of the women interviewed volunteered their own theories about Greenham, and about the reactions of men and of the various agencies of the state, as well as about the methodology of my research. Texts on ethnography traditionally regard the 'theorizing informant' as problematic, but I found her invaluable.[33] In many respects, interviewing Greenham women was like having a large, diverse research team with whom to mull over findings and hunches. The analysis presented here therefore draws heavily on the theoretical contributions of many women.

Ethical/political issues

Much as feminist sociologists may wish it, myself included, problems of objectification and exploitation in the research process do not just disappear because of shared experiences between researcher and researched.[34] Indeed, it is probable that my insider status, which encouraged women to be exceptionally open with me, has given me more opportunity to exploit the interviewees than an outsider could ever have achieved.[35] Moreover, at social occasions with friends, when the conversation turned to Greenham, or at 'reunions' at Greenham (which I would have gone to even had I not been doing the research), I often felt like a spy, secretly gathering snippets of information for later use. Whilst my friends knew about my research, I did not repeatedly warn them that anything they said might be taken down in writing and used as data.[36] Doing research in which one's own past life and one's friends and acquaintances are always potential sources of theories and data can be socially, as well as ethically problematic; it also means that one is never really off-duty.

However much I sought to involve the women in the research process, I have not conducted a truly *collective* piece of research. I have *exploited* and *used* the women I interviewed (and many others whom I didn't), extracting and abstracting their accounts to illustrate my own arguments. When women did not validate my ideas and theories about Greenham, when 'interpretive asymmetry' became apparent, I sometimes chose to ignore their interpretations. Whilst I have endeavoured to represent the voices of women with whom I have disagreed, and have attempted not to erase the heterogeneity of Greenham, I have retained the power of authorship. In the final analysis, it has been *my* analysis that has triumphed. This book is, ultimately, my version of Greenham.

The origins of Greenham

How can the emergence of Greenham as a mass social movement be explained? The existing sociological literature on social movements suggests two possible approaches to this question. Resource mobilization theory – the dominant tradition in the American sociology of social movements – concerns itself with the processes by which interests are mobilized within the political opportunity structure.[1] The analysis of the historical context of a movement and of the origins of the political dissatisfaction it addresses is beyond the remit of this approach.[2] This means, as Melucci (1989) points out, that whilst the 'how' of social movement formation may be adequately discussed, the 'why' is forgotten.

In contrast, the European school of 'new social movements' research prioritizes the 'why' question. Here the assumption is that attention to the historical context of a social movement is central to understanding both its emergence and its sociological significance.[3] The explosion of new movements since the late 1960s is explained in terms of changes in the structure of industrial society.

It is my contention that in order to understand the emergence of any social movement, it is insufficient to study *either* micro-level mobilization *or* macro-level social structural change. Rather, social movement research should integrate analysis of macro-, meso-, and micro-level social processes, focusing both on the enabling and constraining aspects of social structures, and on individual and collective human agency in challenging and transforming them.

The analysis of the emergence of Greenham developed in this book therefore plunders the theoretical tools of both approaches, whilst also formulating critiques of each. Drawing on, and critiquing, resource mobilization theory, I leave the examination of the actual processes by which Greenham was created to Chapter 3. This chapter examines the origins of Greenham, mapping out its broad macro-structural context and the more specific meso-level political environment and geopolitical situation of the time. In doing this I argue that the contextual framework suggested by theorists of the new social movements is of limited use for the case of Greenham. Although the women's movement is cited as a key new social movement by a number of writers (e.g. Touraine 1981, Dalton *et al.* 1990; Scott 1990), and gender is sometimes referred to as an analytic category (Lash and Urry 1987), no real attempt has been made to integrate gender into the theory of the new social movements approach.[4] Exponents of the perspective have rarely studied women's mobilizations and there has been no attention to the gendered historical context of the new social movements. This approach is fundamentally flawed by its exclusive attention to changes in capitalism, and by its failure to analyse changes in patriarchal social relations. Greenham must be studied as a *women's* movement; the specificity of women's social position and history is of vital importance in understanding why, at a particular historical moment, it arose.

The macro-structural context

A new phase of capitalism?

The belief is now widely held within the social sciences that over the last two or three decades Western capitalist societies have been entering a new phase in their development. It is argued that this transformation takes social, economic, cultural, and political forms, and that the new social movements are one expression of this new age. This macro-structural social change is called variously: the transition to postindustrial society (Touraine 1971, 1981; Bell 1974; Melucci 1985; Offe 1987), postFordism (Murray 1988), postmodernity (Lyotard 1978), 'high' or 'late' modernity (Giddens 1990, 1991), disorganized capitalism (Offe 1985; Lash and Urry 1987), programmed society (Touraine 1981), complex society (Melucci 1989), or just 'new times' (Hall and Jacques 1989). Although this plethora of terms suggests a variety of different bases of macro-structural change, there are a number of common themes running through these discussions.

The transformation of contemporary society is generally seen to be rooted in processes of global economic restructuring. The globalization of production has been accompanied by the decline in Western capitalist societies of manufacturing industry and the growth of the service sector. This, together with the burgeoning of white collar welfare state employment, and the expansion of higher education, has resulted in dramatic changes in class structure. The traditional manual working class has contracted and the 'service' class, or 'new middle class' of professional, scientific, technical, administrative and managerial workers has increased in size (Lash and Urry 1987).

These economic and social structural changes are then posited as the causes of changes in political allegiance and the development of new political cleavages. The 'old' politics of conflict over the distribution of material resources, which shaped and characterized industrial capitalism, are seen as giving way to a 'new' politics no longer polarized along class lines and no longer structured around the conflict between capital and labour (Habermas 1987a; Offe 1987). The new politics, exemplified by the new social movements, are said to stress individual needs and experiences and the centrality of personal autonomy rather than collective interests (Melucci 1989), and participation and self-expression rather than representative democracy. They seek to defend the individual against encroaching bureaucratic and technological control, par- -ticularly by the state – the 'colonization of the life-world' (Touraine 1981; Habermas 1987a; Melucci 1989). The product of the economic security of the post Second World War era, the new politics express 'post-material' values and are concerned with issues of quality of life (Inglehart 1977, 1989; Cotgrove and Duff 1981; Chandler and Siaroff 1986; Habermas 1987a; Giddens 1991). However, it is emphasized that these are the politics of a relatively narrow sector of the population; specifically, the new, university-educated, middle class of public sector, human service professionals, and students (Parkin 1968; Cotgrove and Duff 1980, 1981; Taylor and Pritchard 1980; Cotgrove 1982; Byrne 1988; Mattausch 1989).[5] As Offe sums it up, the new politics are the 'politics of a class, but not *on behalf* of a class' (1987:78).

Alongside changes in economic and social structure it is argued that there have been major transformations at the level of culture. Whether contemporary society is termed 'postmodernity' or 'late' or 'high' modernity, its predominant cultural characteristic is held to be the widespread loss of faith in the idea of progress. Science and technology, which carried modernity's promise of progress, have increasingly come to be seen as posing intense risk and danger to the planet. The advent of the nuclear era, with its 'baroque arsenal' (Kaldor 1982) and 'exterminist' momentum (Thompson 1982a) has fundamentally altered the nature of warfare. The distinction between military and civilians, combatants and non-combatants, is obsolete, and the fate of the earth is called into question (Schell 1982). Contemporary society is 'risk society', unbound by divisions of class and place (Beck 1992). As Giddens (1990:125) says:

> The possibility of nuclear war, ecological calamity, uncontainable popu-lation explosion, the collapse of global economic exchange, and other poten-tial global catastrophes provide an unnerving horizon of dangers for everyone [. . .]. The global intensity of certain kinds of risk transcends all social and economic differentials.

The formation of social movements, such as the anti-nuclear and environmental movements, to contest the sources of these dangers is therefore seen both as a result of, and as a causative factor in, science's loss of privileged status.

This conceptualization of recent changes in industrial capitalism cannot be adopted wholesale as a theory to explain the emergence of Greenham. First, in all the attention to economic restructuring, little or no mention is made by the new social movement theorists of one of the most significant economic changes of the postwar period – the mass entry of women into the labour force. The writers say next to nothing about the changing economic and social position of women. Whilst

I certainly do not wish to advance an economically reductionist account of the origins of Greenham, judging the new social movements thesis within its own terms necessitates the highlighting of this significant silence. I will go on to argue that women's increasing participation in the labour market is just one of a number of important macro-structural changes which must be considered.

Second, the new middle-class activists identified by the new social movement theorists, although present at Greenham, were not representative of Greenham women. Greenham's participants were heterogeneous in class background, many were not in paid employment, and no clear relationship existed between involvement in Greenham and social class (see Chapter 3 and Appendix II for further discussion).

Third, although the advent of 'risk society' is clearly part of the backdrop to Greenham, I question whether the loss of faith in progress that is described by new social movement theorists applies to women as a social group in the same way as it does to men. I would suggest that women stand in a different relationship to the 'project of modernity' (Habermas 1987b) from men. Whilst a long tradition of liberal feminism has struggled for women's equal participation in the project of modernity, the aim is yet to be realized. Not only have women historically been excluded from scientific careers (Harding 1986, 1991), but science has been applied by men to control women, in the home and the workplace.[6] Men's control of science and technology and the gendered nature of their benefits belie the universalism of discussions of the end of belief in progress.

Fourth, and in summation, the classification of Greenham, the recent women's peace movement, and indeed the women's liberation movement as a whole as 'new social movements' is problematic. Women's anti-militarist action and feminism are hardly 'new'. This raises the criticism of new social movement theory that it overemphasizes novelty and discontinuity, at the expense of recognizing historical precedent and continuity of political tradition.[7] In characterizing recent movements as 'new', attention is drawn to their difference from *the* old movement, the labour movement, so that the history of movements concerned with non-economic aspects of social life, for instance women's movements, peace movements, and environmental movements, is obscured. Whilst the new social movements thesis claims to be analysing 'post-materialist' movements, which are not contesting the relations of production, writers still attempt to explain the emergence of these movements by reference to changes in economic production. The fundamental problem with the new social movements thesis is that issues of economic production, albeit *changes* in economic production, are still given a primary, determining role in explaining the creation of social movements.

Whilst the changes in industrial capitalism emphasized by the new social movement writers have undoubtedly affected women, as a theory to explain the origins of Greenham, they are of strictly limited applicability. Women's political action cannot be understood through gender-ignorant analyses of changes in capitalism.

Changes in patriarchy

In order to theorize the macro-structural context of Greenham we have to go beyond the false universalism of the new social movements approach to look at changes in the structure of patriarchy. In recent years the development of a feminist historiography has posed a fundamental challenge (as yet unmet by the malestream of sociology and history) to traditional periodization of history and social change.[8] By studying a number of periods usually considered to be times of progressive change, feminist historians have shown that what counts as advance for men often has a very different meaning for women. For instance, both the Renaissance and the French Revolution may have been emancipatory moments for men, but they were not for women; indeed both led to a marked diminution of women's position in society (Kelly-Gadol 1976).

The new feminist historiography argues that the study of social change must be broadened to include changes in the social relations between the sexes and in the social position of women.

Walby (1990a,b) provides a useful reperiodization of recent social change in Britain from the perspective of women. She argues that during the twentieth century there has been a change in the form of patriarchy, away from the private model which developed during the nineteenth century, towards a public form of patriarchy. Under private patriarchy women were primarily controlled in the domestic sphere and were largely excluded from education, paid employment, and citizenship rights. Public patriarchy, on the other hand, allows women a level of freedom from the individual control of husbands and fathers, but subordinates them in the public sphere, in the labour market, and in political and cultural institutions. Walby argues that, with the transition from one form of patriarchy to the other, there is a change in the locus of control of women's sexuality from that exercised in the private sphere by husbands and fathers, to a more public form, exercised by patriarchal institutions such as the media and the state, and, I would add, by men as collective actors.

Walby identifies two key moments in the transition from private to public patriarchy. The first was at the end of the nineteenth and beginning of the twentieth centuries, when first-wave feminism achieved a number of important victories for women, such as the vote, access to education and the professions, and rights to own property and leave marriages. It is at this historical juncture that women's close friendships and relationships with each other were pathologized and cultural sanctions against lesbianism instituted through the media of sexology and Freudianism. Fadermann (1981) argues that the cause of this was the new possibility for women to live outside male control. The second moment – the product of capitalist economic expansion since the Second World War – has seen women's increasing involvement in paid employment, giving women a greater degree of economic independence than hitherto (Walby 1990a).

This change in patriarchal relations is an important part of the contextual background to the emergence of Greenham. The diminution of the legal, economic, and social power of husbands and fathers over women which is represented by this transition was a necessary precondition to women's autonomous political and social organization in the public sphere. In the nineteenth century a woman could be forcibly returned to her husband if she left against his wishes (Walby 1990a:99), as many Greenham women did, and divorce was difficult to obtain. Although there have always been women who have been financially independent of men, who have lived alone or with other women, and who have resisted the economic and cultural pressure towards marriage (Fadermann 1981; Vicinius 1985; Raymond 1986), these legislative achievements of first-wave feminism enabled large numbers of women, including working class women, to spend time or live at Greenham.

Women's mass entry into the labour market in the postwar period and the opening up of state benefits to women were also vital conditions for the emergence of Greenham. Women's increasing, if still far from complete, financial independence of men, whether derived from employment or state benefits, enabled individual women to both travel to and live at Greenham and, at the collective level, it meant that women in support groups around the country were able to raise money from other women for the camp.[9] Whilst Greenham received considerable financial support from mixed peace groups at the peak of its media visibility, it could not have survived without donations and money from women's groups and from individual, self-supporting women. This money was particularly important to the financing of the full-time participation of married women and women from overseas who were without access to state benefits or independent resources.

The macro-level transformation in the form of patriarchy during the twentieth century laid the ground for Greenham by facilitating women's relative economic and legal independence from men. However, we have to turn to the meso-level political environment to understand its more immediate context.

The meso-level context

The meso-level context of Greenham refers to the more immediate, middle-range background preconditions prevailing in the years preceding the beginning of the camp. It can be seen as being composed of two interrelated dimensions. One dimension is the nationally specific political environment, particularly that of non-institutional political action, within and in reaction to which Greenham emerged. The other dimension is that of geopolitics.[10] Like the macro-structural context, the meso-level is also gendered.

The political environment

Greenham did not suddenly arise, fully formed, from nowhere in 1981. Rather its roots must be seen, first, as stretching back through the long history of feminist anti-militarism, and, more immediately, within a particular configuration of traditions of political action and political discourses which existed in Britain in the postwar period.

The mixed peace movement of the late 1950s and early 1960s, in particular the Direct Action Committee against Nuclear War (DAC) and later the Committee of 100, established a precedent for non-violent direct action, which was to be taken up by numerous groups and organizations in the following decades.[11] The DAC organized the first march from Aldermaston to London in 1958, and later sit-downs at military bases and attempts to board the supply ship for the Polaris submarine fleet at Holy Loch (Randle 1987). The Committee of 100 spearheaded mass civil disobedience in 1961–2, including sit-downs in London and blockades and occupations of USAF bases around the country; many activists were imprisoned. The DAC's and the Committee of 100's stress on the responsibility of individuals to oppose nuclear weapons and their opposition to the parliamentarian 'Labour-path' strategy of the Campaign for Nuclear Disarmament (CND), were precursors of Greenham's ethos and mode of action in the 1980s.

Following the gradual decline of the peace movement in the wake of the Partial Test Ban Treaty of 1963, the late 1960s in Britain saw the flourishing of the New Left and the students' movement. On a smaller scale, but perhaps an even more significant intellectual precursor of Greenham – the Situationist movement – advocated a politics of the 'spectacular' disruption, and reinvention, of everyday life (Erlich n.d.; Plant 1992). The Vietnam War called forth renewed and widespread peace protest, and directed the gaze of activists towards US imperialism in the Third World. At the beginning of the 1970s the Gay Liberation Front was formed, promoting a radical, confrontational politics of the personal (Jeffrey-Poulter 1991). Also in the 1970s, provoked by the energy crisis of 1973, the environmental movement burst onto the political scene, challenging the postwar consensus on the desirability and possibility of continued economic growth.[12] Environmentalists focused particularly on campaigning against the construction and extension of nuclear power plants, and large-scale non-violent direct actions were held at Torness in Scotland.[13] Another important part of the political environment of the time, and often neglected by writers about the social movements of the 1970s, was the predominantly anarchist squatters' movement in many urban areas, especially London, which established a large number of alternative communal households. Finally, the end of the decade also saw the development of the Anti-Nazi League, and mass street protest against a resurgent National Front (Brittan 1987).

Considered together, the social movements of the 1950s, 1960s, and 1970s offered a major challenge to the military–industrial complexes of Western capitalist societies. They protested not only against particularly destructive and dangerous practices and policies, but also developed a critique of the materialism and consumption patterns of industrial societies and politicized new arenas of social life. These movements bequeathed a legacy of anti-establishment attitudes, a strong strand of anarchist hostility to hierarchies, representative forms of democracy and the state, and a belief in the legitimacy and necessity of extra-parliamentary forms of political action.

However, more important in setting the scene for Greenham than any of these movements was the women's liberation movement. The social movements of this period were permeated by underlying tensions about gender politics, and a number of writers on second-wave feminism trace its roots to the misogyny and marginalization that women experienced within the movements of the 1960s. In particular they highlight the New Left, the students' movement, anti-Vietnam groups, and communes.[14] The emphasis of these movements on personal politics and liberation served to encourage women to examine the contradictions of their experiences as part of supposedly liberatory movements.

Greenham's transformation from being a small, mixed (albeit mostly women) peace camp in its first six months, into a large, open women's community of protest can only be understood in the light of critiques and practices developed within the women's liberation movement. Above all, the women's liberation movement articulated the necessity of women-only organization and social space. Ways of working compatible with feminist principles were tried out and the women-only, locally-based, autonomous, non-hierarchical, small group emerged as the paradigmatic form of organization. A certain amount of non-violent direct action and street campaigning was a part of the movement from the Miss World demonstration in 1970 onwards, although never on the scale of the first-wave movement. Examples range from women's protests against being placed at the back of the TUC-organized mass demonstration against the Corrie Bill in 1979, which resulted in three arrests (Bassnett 1986:157), to smaller local and national women-only Reclaim the Night marches, and physical attacks on sex shops by the underground group 'Angry Women'. In addition, radical and lesbian feminist strands of the movement created the beginnings of a vibrant women's culture in most of the major cities and a number of towns throughout Britain. Women's literature – poetry, fiction, and theory – produced by small feminist publishers, plays written and performed by feminists, women's bands and discos, women's centres and newsletters, and hundreds of communal women-only houses sprung up during the 1970s. This national feminist community helped to facilitate the transmission of news about Greenham through a potentially sympathetic audience. It also served to raise the issue of women's oppression in society, and was to provide discursive resources for Greenham in its development from a maternalist politics to a feminist politics.

Militarism and nuclear weapons were not issues of great concern within the women's liberation movement in the 1970s. However, Liddington (1989) has traced the threads of feminist interest in non-violence back through this period. She highlights the impact of feminism on women working within mixed peace movement organizations, such as International Fellowship of Reconciliation and War Resisters International (WRI). They organized a women's workshop at the WRI triennial in Holland in 1975 (which met with considerable male resistance), a five-day-long women-only gathering in rural France in 1976, and then in Britain, they established the Feminism and Non-violence Study Group. From these groups a specifically feminist conceptualization of non-violence began to develop. Following the Three Mile Island incident in the United States in 1979, feminists organized together against nuclear power, and an ecofeminist position began to emerge within the environmental and women's movements.

American radical feminist theory of this period, particularly the work of Mary Daly (1979), Susan Griffin (1978), and Andrea Dworkin (1981) and the ecofeminist activism of the Spinsters and the Women's Pentagon Action (Linton and Whitham 1982; King 1983) were important in laying the ground for Greenham. The women's liberation movement was a transnational movement; not only were American feminist actions reported in British newsletters and magazines, and American writers avidly read on this side of the Atlantic, but individual women travelling between the United States and Britain brought news and experiences with them (Liddington 1989). The affinity group structure and the dramatic symbolism, theatricality, and humour of the Spinsters web at the Vermont Yankee power station and the Women's Pentagon Action encircling of the Pentagon were inspirations for later actions at Greenham.[15]

It was events on the geopolitical stage, however, that provided the immediate catalyst for the new women's peace movement in Europe.

The geopolitical context

With the revival of the Cold War in the 1980s social scientists directed considerable attention to what Mann (1987) calls 'geopolitical privacy', that is the high level of autonomy exercised by the state elite in the realm of foreign and defence policy.[16] It has been pointed out that early decisions about the development of nuclear weapons were made by small groups of senior politicians without public debate or approval, sometimes in direct contradiction of their professed policy. The Labour Party, in particular, has a record of taking nuclear decisions in secret. For example, in 1947 Attlee railroaded the decision to develop the A-bomb through a small subcommittee of the Cabinet and, during the 1974–9 Labour government, Callaghan, Healey, and Owen secretly went ahead with the Chevaline programme. What has not been so widely acknowledged, however, is that in the last twenty years real power over nuclear weapons decisions has rested not in the hands of elected politicians, but rather in those of 'small groups of people of whom most of us have never heard' (Elworthy 1989:166). These are: top-echelon scientists in nuclear weapons laboratories (Los Alamos and Lawrence Livermore in the United States, and Aldermaston and Farnborough in Britain); the 'intelligence community', which provides annual estimates of enemy military capability (in Britain, the Defence Intelligence Service within the Ministry of Defence (MOD); MI6, the Secret Intelligence Service; MI5, the Security Service; and GCHQ at Cheltenham); and the Procurement Executive in the MOD (Elworthy 1989). Kaplan's work on the United States makes a similar point. Kaplan argues that defence intellectuals, a 'small and exceptionally inbred collection of men – mostly economists and mathematicians, a few political scientists' (1984:10), clustered at the RAND Corporation, have devised and implemented the ideas underlying US defence policy.

But whilst this lack of democratic control over foreign and defence policy has been much remarked upon, the issue of gender and geopolitics has been largely ignored. If members of parliament, the media, and the electorate are excluded from geopolitical decision-making, then women as a social group experience double exclusion, being under-represented, when not entirely absent, from the 'small groups of people' discussed by Elworthy and Kaplan. It is my contention that the coincidence of the new Cold War's threat of nuclear annihilation with a vibrant women's liberation movement, which was challenging the limitations of the old liberal feminist struggle for inclusion within political and scientific elites, served to crystallize in the consciousness of large numbers of women their exclusion from the life and death decisions of the geopolitical sphere. This is a crucial factor in the contextualization of Greenham.

The end of the 1970s saw the collapse of détente between the superpowers and the beginning of a new Cold War. Although in 1977 Carter's presidency had begun with the stated aim of eliminating nuclear weapons, during his four-year term of office the arms race intensified greatly. Carter's foreign and military policy was much influenced by the well organized lobbying of the defence establishment, in particular the virulently anti-communist Committee on the Present Danger (CPD), which had been set up to defeat the Strategic Arms Limitation Talks (SALT II) (Sanders 1983; Kaplan 1984; Knelman 1985). In 1977 Carter pressed NATO to deploy the enhanced radiation, or neutron, bomb, a move which presaged the beginning of the revival of the peace movement throughout Europe.[17] Following the Dutch peace movement, CND collected over a quarter of a million signatures on a national petition against the neutron bomb. This marked the return of nuclear weapons to the political agenda after an absence of a decade and a half. Although Carter changed his mind about the neutron bomb, the CPD achieved its objective of the demise of SALT II, which was signed in June 1979 but never ratified.

Meanwhile the Soviet Union began to deploy SS-20s and the Backfire bomber in Eastern Europe and, on 12 December 1979, Carter persuaded NATO to take the 'twin track' decision. This constituted an offer to enter into negotiations with the Warsaw Pact about reductions in intermediate nuclear forces (INF) in Europe, whilst as the same time 'modernizing' NATO's intermediate nuclear forces by introducing ground-launched Cruise missiles and Pershing II missiles. The initial plan was to deploy 464 Cruise missiles (on 116 launchers) in Britain, Belgium, the Netherlands, and Italy, and 108 Pershing II launchers in West Germany, beginning in 1983 (Lodgaard 1982).[18] The public justification for the twin track decision presented Cruise and Pershing as an essential response to the new Soviet intermediate nuclear weapons, and made much of the Soviets' supposed conventional superiority.[19] However, the European governments were probably much more concerned to 'recouple' the United States with Europe, and to ensure the continued existence of the US nuclear 'umbrella' and the United States was concerned to reassert its dominant position in the Atlantic alliance.

The twin track decision marked a watershed in the development of East–West relations for two reasons. First, the new missiles were part of a new 'generation' of 'theatre', or tactical nuclear weapons which included the American

MX missile system and the Soviet SS-18 and SS-20.[20] Unlike earlier intercontinental 'strategic' nuclear weapons which could travel between the United States and the Soviet Union, 'theatre' nuclear weapons were designed for use on a nuclear battlefield within Europe (Cox 1981). Equipped with new delivery systems and terrain-contour matching guidance systems, they were to be more accurate and better able to 'penetrate' defensive systems than existing weapons. This meant that they possessed the ability to pinpoint and destroy 'hard' targets, such as command and control sites and nuclear storage facilities (Arkin 1982). The missiles were also small enough to be transported on mobile launchers, and it was claimed that they would 'blend into the countryside' to avoid detection by the Soviets.

Second, the NATO decision constituted the formal enactment of a change in US nuclear doctrine which had been evolving during the 1970s. This became apparent when, in the summer of 1980, Presidential Directive 59 (PD-59) became public knowledge. PD-59 introduced Schlesinger's 'counterforce doctrine', which said that US nuclear forces were henceforth to be aimed primarily at military targets, particularly command, control, communications and intelligence centres, and nuclear storage facilities rather than at centres of population. The implication of this was that NATO had moved from a strategy of deterrence to one that aimed to fight and win a nuclear war by means of a pre-emptive first strike. The threat of a retaliatory strike against empty missile silos is ineffectual, meaning that the plan must be to strike first. The high degree of accuracy claimed for the new missiles was the single most important technological element to the counterforce strategy (Krass and Smith 1982).

Two further developments on the geopolitical stage enhanced the growing crisis of the end of détente and served to fuel the opposition to the euromissiles. The first of these was the Soviet invasion of Afghanistan, which followed close on the heels of the Cruise decision. The US administration had already been justifying the twin track decision by reference to the Soviet Union's supposed conventional superiority, and the invasion of a neighbouring state served to reinforce beliefs in Communist expansionism and the 'red menace'. The United States responded by halting the sale of grain and high-technology products and knowledge to the Soviet Union, and by instituting a boycott of the 1980 Moscow Olympics. This latter move brought home to millions, more clearly than many other developments, the serious deterioration in relations between the superpowers.

The other crucial factor was the rise of the New Right and the accession of patriotic right-wing leaders in Britain and the United States. Both Thatcher and Reagan placed great emphasis on firm leadership, and can be seen as reacting to the social, political, and cultural upheaval of the 1960s and 1970s (Hall and Jacques 1983; Gamble 1988).

In Britain, a Conservative government was elected in 1979 on a platform of increased military expenditure, amidst allegations that the Labour Party had damaged Britain's defences (Smith and Smith 1980). A 3 per cent real increase in defence spending in the 1980 budget was accompanied by cuts in other areas of public expenditure. In the same year the new government announced the £5,000 million replacement of Britain's 'independent deterrent': the Polaris submarine-launched ballistic missile was to be superseded by the Trident system. The obvious involvement of the British government in the acceleration of the arms race had a major impact on the stirring peace movement. Perhaps even more important though were the 60 per cent rise in spending on civil defence announced in 1980 and the misconceived 'Protect and Survive' campaign. The booklets distributed by the state as part of this campaign advised, in the event of a nuclear attack, whitewashing the windows of one's house and hiding under a door propped against a wall with a substantial supply of food and a transistor radio. The effect of such public information was to massively increase public awareness of preparations for a nuclear war in Europe. Meanwhile, the Conservative revelation of the previous Labour government's involvement in the Chevaline programme to 'modernize' Polaris at a cost of £1,000 million (and against Labour Party policy) served to augment public disquiet at the secrecy surrounding nuclear decision-making. It probably also turned many in the emerging peace movement away from a Labour-path strategy for disarmament towards more radically confrontational and extraparliamentary methods.

With Ronald Reagan's inauguration as US President in 1981, the deteriorating international situation took a further plunge. Knelman argues that the Reagan administration introduced a 'quantitative and qualitative change in the dynamics of the arms race' (1985:3).[21] Long known for his outspokenness against the perils of Communism, Reagan was elected with the stated aim of 'revitalizing' the United States. This involved a two-fold plan: supply-side economics, or monetarism, and the restoration of national prestige through the strengthening of the military. The term began with the ordering of the B-1 bomber, stepping up of preparations for the deployment of the euromissiles, and sharply increased expenditure on conventional and nuclear arms. After the first three years of Reagan's presidency, defence spending had increased 40 per cent in real terms. Thirty two members of the government team had been members of the CPD and the influence of CPD thinking on Reagan's policies was clear. Anti-communist rhetoric came thick and fast from government sources and was frequently coupled with Christian fundamentalist statements about the inevitability of Armageddon. Reagan declared that Soviet leaders were not to be trusted because they 'reserve unto themselves the right to commit any crime, to lie, to cheat, in order to obtain their objective [. . .]. Communists are not bound by our morality' (Knelman 1985:30). The Soviet Union was 'the force of evil in the modern world [. . .] an evil empire' (Knelman 1985:177) and Reagan repeatedly stated his determination to drive the Soviet Union into economic bankruptcy through an arms race (Clesse 1985). Moreover, it very quickly became apparent that the administration believed that nuclear war was winnable (Secretary of Defense Weinberger), and that a nuclear war could be confined to Europe (Reagan) (Clesse 1985:54). In 1981 the *New York Times* uncovered the 'Five Year Defense Plan', which expounded a nuclear warfighting strategy for 'decapitating' the Soviet Union (Knelman 1985).

Analysing the geopolitical situation

Analysts of the new Cold War differ in the degree of responsibility assigned to the two main protagonists. The orthodox Atlanticist version of the East–West conflict, which achieved hegemony with the Reagan and Thatcher administrations saw as inevitable and irreconcilable a clash between 'freedom' and 'totalitarianism', and blamed Soviet expansionism and conventional superiority for the end of détente. In contrast, E.P. Thompson, the founder of the European Nuclear Disarmament campaign (END), developed an analysis based on the principle of isomorphism. In this, the ruling groups of both the United States and the Soviet Union are seen as 'ideologically addicted' (Thompson 1982b:171) to the Cold War, needing the other for the construction of their respective national self-identities and to silence internal dissent:

> [T]he Cold War is now about itself. It is an ongoing, self-reproducing condition, to which both adversaries are in a reciprocal relationship of mutual nurture: each fosters the growth of the other. Both adversaries need to maintain a hostile ideological posture as a means of internal bonding or discipline.
>
> (Thompson 1982b:175)

Thompson characterizes contemporary society as 'exterminist', that is, as founded on the weapons-system, and possessing an economy, a polity and an ideology/culture which support the weapons-system in its inertial thrust towards destruction.[22] Drawing on Thompson's work, Kaldor (1982) elaborates the argument that the Cold War – the 'imaginary war' – was a 'joint venture'. She argues that the elements of conflict between East and West were far outweighed by the complementarity of the two blocs. Both sides insisted on military parity, a concept always open to different interpretations and hence 'a recipe for an arms race' (Kaldor 1982:183), and neither side was prepared to tolerate within-bloc change and release its grip on the nations within its sphere of influence. The Soviet Union would not allow reform in Eastern Europe, and the United States, jolted by its declining role in the world and the humiliation of Vietnam, sought to re-establish its dominant position by imposing decisions on NATO members.

Unlike Thompson and Kaldor, Halliday (1982) sees the superpowers as fundamentally asymmetrical, and he ascribes primary responsibility for the new Cold War to the United States. For him it was US concern to regain military superiority *vis-à-vis* the Soviet Union that was the fundamental cause of the failure of détente, because NATO's version of détente rested on the assumption of continued superiority. Halliday emphasizes that the United States was seeking strategic ascendancy not just over the Soviet Union, but also over Europe, the economically threatening Japanese, and the Third World. Defeat in Vietnam and a series of revolutions in the Third World during the 1970s (Angola, Mozambique, Ethiopia, Iran, Nicaragua) seemed to signal a decline in US power on the world stage. Within the discourse of the New Right anxiety about this, and about internal problems of recession and cultural upheaval, were projected onto the rediscovered Soviet threat. As Halliday sums up his argument:

> One of the major domestic sources of the chauvinism of US public opinion in the late 1970s has been the generic sense of a lost power, in which the visibly increased economic and diplomatic freedom of action of the EEC and Japan has played its part. All-round confrontation with the USSR serves to create conditions of quasi-emergency in which the USA can reassert its superiority over the other advanced capitalist countries.
>
> (Halliday 1982:315)

Halliday's position is implicitly supported by Walker's (1993) history of the Cold War. Walker argues that Soviet President Andropov was seriously seeking conciliation with the West, pointing to repeated offers of summits, arms reductions, and a non-aggression pact. Reagan's response was his famous 'evil empire' speech, and the announcement of the Strategic Defence Initiative ('Star Wars'), which fuelled Soviet fear about US preparations for global domination. Walker's work suggests that the asymmetry of aggression between the United States and the Soviet Union was demonstrated in September 1983 when Soviet tension was so high that its air defences shot down a Korean aeroplane which had strayed into its airspace; shortly afterwards the KGB sent a 'Molinya' (flash) message to its Western offices telling them to secure all Soviet premises, ships, and aircraft against possible Western attack.

The opposing positions of Thompson/Kaldor and Halliday/Walker were each represented to some extent in the new peace movement of the 1980s. The Soviet Union was not excused its part in the arms race, and the stationing of SS-20s in Eastern Europe was condemned. However, the peace movement's immediate focus was on the NATO weapons to be deployed in US bases in Western Europe. To have intermediate nuclear weapons on European soil was regarded as making the countries involved into targets. Moreover, US warfighting rhetoric and public contemplation of a nuclear war confined to Europe was not matched by similar statements from the Soviet Union. As a debate developed about the siting of Cruise missiles in Britain, public awareness began to increase about the extent of US military activities in Britain, and a sense of subject-nation status arose, with the feeling that the twin track decision had been imposed from outside.[23]

The geopolitical processes at the end of the 1970s and the beginning of the 1980s had a profound cultural impact in Europe. On the one hand the militarism deeply embedded within the dominant culture was called upon and reinforced as a part of the project of the new Cold War. Luckham (1984) develops the concept of a hegemonic 'armament culture', which he sees as based on the fetishism of the advanced weapons system.[24] This culture functions to neutralize the premonition of danger by establishing an equivalence between the concepts of security, defence and armament, and by entering and shaping consciousness through cultural products such as science fiction, espionage novels and films, toys and computer games. In a similar vein, Walker (1987) and Chilton (1987) point to the dominant role played by 'nuclear discourse' during this period in legitimizing the nuclear arms race by establishing the demonology of the enemy and by the reification of weapons systems.

On the other hand, in reaction to the hegemony of armament culture and the anti-communist rhetoric of the new Cold War, a counter-cultural sense of malaise, of resignation, despair, and cynicism which had existed in the 1950s and early 1960s re-emerged at this time, with a vengeance. 'Nuclear fear' pervaded society. The iconography of the mushroom cloud spread through popular music and art, students held 'end of the world' parties and many people reported recurrent nightmares of nuclear war. It is hard, writing in the mid 1990s, to recapture the widespread feeling which existed in the early 1980s that the world was standing on the brink of destruction, to conjure once more the sense of urgency and the depth of despair which existed. But it is only by making the leap of imagination, or memory, necessary to do so that the context in which Greenham emerged can be fully understood.

The revival of the peace movement

In the immediate wake of the December 1979 decision to deploy Cruise and Pershing II, a peace movement began to stir in Europe. First in Norway and the Netherlands, and spreading to Britain by the spring of 1980, old networks were galvanized and new campaigners activated by anger and fear at the developments just described. The 'Appeal for European Nuclear Disarmament' was published in 1980 (END 1980), setting the agenda for the emergent END. Local groups sprung up around the country, both affiliated to CND and independent, and anti-nuclear marches were organized in Newbury and Caerwent (Cox 1981). CND membership shot up, the London office took on more staff, and in October 1981 the first mass demonstration of the new wave attracted over 70,000 people.

At the same time, small groups of women began to form women's peace groups. In March 1980 a conference was held in Nottingham on 'Women and the Military', and soon afterwards Women Oppose the Nuclear Threat (WONT) was formed in Leeds (Liddington 1989). In Scandinavia, Women for Peace collected a million signatures on a petition calling for disarmament, and organized a march from Copenhagen to Paris. Women in the Netherlands and in West Germany also set up Women for Peace groups. News was spread through the feminist press (particularly *Spare Rib*) and peace networks and newsletters, and in 1981 the Women's Peace Alliance was set up to facilitate liaison and communication between the various groups in Britain. But the numbers of women were still very small, and the public profile of the groups low until Greenham began to attract attention some months after its formation in September 1981.

This chapter has explored the social and historical context within which Greenham emerged as a social movement. Rejecting the application of the new social movements thesis to Greenham, it has examined both macro-structural and meso-level contexts, highlighting the relevance of the gender relations of macro-structural change, of the political environment and of geopolitics. In the course of the discussion of the particularity of the origins of Greenham, I have argued that the study of gender must be incorporated into social movements theory, if such theory is to be of use in the analysis of women's political action.

However, explanations at the levels of social structure, collective action and geopolitics take us only part of the way along the road to understanding the formation of Greenham. In the next chapter I turn to the explication of the micro-level context of Greenham, that is, how individuals became part of Greenham, and the processes by which the collective action and identity of Greenham were constructed.

③

The making of Greenham

Whilst it is important to locate the emergence of Greenham within its macro- and meso-level contexts, its formation cannot be 'read-off' social structures or the political environment of the time. Greenham, like all social movements, came into being and continued through the agency of human actors, whose subjective motivations must be considered. Nor is it sufficient to provide a historical description of the beginnings of Greenham. Its making was not a one-off event, but a continuous process in which women were mobilized and activated, and a collective identity was constructed and reconstructed.[1]

After a discussion of the ways in which sociologists have sought to understand the creation of social movements, this chapter examines how the camp was established. This involves an analysis of how women were initially mobilized and activated, and of the early construction of Greenham's collective identity. I then look at the re-creation and continuation of Greenham through a detailed examination of the processes by which women got involved and their motivations for so doing.

The construction of social movements

The literature on social movements can be classified into three broad groupings: social psychological approaches, the 'new social movements' approach, and resource mobilization theory. The first, the old collective behaviour approach, dominant within US social science in the 1950s and 1960s, seeks answers to questions about the emergence of social movements and individual participation in the psychologies of those involved and in the psychological functions of participation.[2] This is in contrast to the body of work concerned with the 'new social movements', discussed in Chapter 2, which focuses on macro-structural analysis of the causes of social movement emergence. Neither of these approaches addresses the processes of mobilization and movement formation, nor the construction of collective identity.

Resource mobilization theory, on the other hand, is exclusively concerned with analysing these processes.[3] It draws heavily on rational choice theory, specifically on Olson's (1965) theory of the logic of collective action. Olson assumes that individuals make decisions to participate in a collective action only when the value of the 'selective incentives' which are contingent on participation is greater than the costs to them of participation. If the selective incentives are not strong enough, 'collective incentives' which are not contingent on participation will not induce the rational person to take part; the rational person will become a 'free-rider'.[4] Fundamental to resource mobilization theory is the belief that potential participants engage in a deliberate and conscious assessment of the costs and benefits of participation.

There are three problems with resource mobilization theory. First, it operates with an extremely limited understanding of human motivation, reducing all the complexities of social action to a crudely instrumental rationality (Melucci 1988; Scott 1990). Cost–benefit analysis cannot explain why people form social movements which do not offer them 'selective incentives', or material rewards. Involvement in collective action is often motivated by political or ethical values, (in Weber's term, *Wertrationalität*), and is frequently expressive and affectual in orientation (Scott 1990).[5] Scott emphasizes the cultural benefits which accrue to those involved in social movements, giving as examples the opportunities offered by social movements for engagement in consciousness-raising, for the formation of friendships and for the experience of membership of a close-knit community.

Second, resource mobilization theory grossly overstates the strategic processes by which social movements are created.[6] It tends to assume that at the heart of a movement is a social movement organization (SMO), which engages in deliberate mobilizing activities in pursuit of a consciously formulated plan. In fact, many social movements do not have an SMO at their centre, either eschewing all formal organizations, or having so many that no overall mobilization plan for the movement is evident. Deliberate attempts at mobilization can explain only a small part of social movement construction. A distinction should be drawn between processes of *activation* and processes of *mobilization*. Processes of activation are those processes which lack deliberate, strategic and formal planning; they have an element of spontaneity and unexpectedness about them, and cannot be accounted for in the language of rational choice-inspired organizational theory. Processes of mobilization are more clearly planned, more deliberate and self-conscious, though rarely as strategic as is suggested by resource mobilization theory.

The third problem with resource mobilization theory also afflicts social psychological approaches and the new social movements school. All three ignore the central role of 'cognitive praxis' (Eyerman and Jamison 1991) and the construction of collective identity (Melucci 1989) in the creation of social movements. Cognitive praxis refers to the intellectual work of social movements, which is both constitutive of collective action and is also the product of collective action. The formation of social movements is dependent on discursive 'framing', that is, the mobilization and construction of a set of ideas within which the problem addressed by the movement is identified and action proposed to deal with it.[7] This discourse is not produced at the outset, once and for all; rather, it evolves gradually and is constantly revised in the course of action.

The creation of a common discursive framework is one dimension of the building of a collective identity. Collective identity is further produced as relationships are established between the actors taking part in a movement. This leads to the enhancement of shared meanings, increases the motivation to participate and contributes to the development of emotional investments in the action (Melucci 1988:343).

Narratives of the beginnings of Greenham

The histories that have been written of the beginning of the women's peace camp at Greenham share a descriptive orientation to the subject and do not address the sociological questions about movement formation that I have raised above.[8] Liddington (1989), for instance, identifies the Women for Life on Earth walk from Cardiff to Greenham as the 'brainchild' of one woman – Ann Pettitt. She tells the story of Ann's life before she had the idea to organize the walk, tracing the origins of her concern about nuclear weapons to her earlier concerns about pollution and nuclear power (1989:222–4) and showing Pettitt's integration into, and leading role in, anti-nuclear networks and groups in mid Wales. The description that follows of how the idea for the women-led walk from Cardiff to Greenham took off concentrates on the involvement of a handful of named women.

This named-but-ordinary women approach to historical reconstruction is a popular method of writing women's history, but is one that is problematic. Locating the origin of a major social movement in the thoughts and actions of less than half a dozen women wrenches the movement from its wider social, political, and cultural context. Whilst Liddington does trace the history of feminist campaigns against militarism and thus provides some historical background, explicit analysis of the processes by which Greenham was created is also required.

The Women for Life on Earth walk: Cardiff–Greenham Common

The idea for the women-led walk from Cardiff to Greenham Common, from which the women's peace camp developed, had its roots in pre-existing anti-nuclear networks.[9] The suggestion arose amongst a group of women who were involved in the Carmarthen Anti-Nuclear Campaign, which was originally an anti-nuclear power group but in 1981, like many anti-nuclear groups, was turning its attention to nuclear weapons. They read news about the walk from Copenhagen to Paris organized by the Scandinavian Women for Peace in *Peace*

News, and were struck with the idea of a similar march in Britain (Liddington 1989:223–4). The title 'Women for Life on Earth Peace March 1981' was chosen, and it was decided to walk to the United States Air Force base at Greenham Common, near Newbury, Berkshire, which was to be the first site for Cruise missiles in 1983.

The march was mobilized in a more deliberate fashion than was the case with later events in the life of the camp. The initiators (named by Liddington as Ann Pettitt, and later, Lynne Whittemore, Carmen Kutler, Angela Phillips, and Liney Seward) tapped into networks throughout the south west of England and Wales, particularly those along the route of the walk. Four main sorts of groups were contacted in the preparation for the march: peace and anti-nuclear groups; women's peace groups, both old and new; women's liberation groups; and mixed political organizations not specifically concerned with peace issues.[10] The initiators made extensive use of their personal knowledge of individuals who were likely to be sympathetic to the march, writing to dozens of acquaintances to solicit support or participation. Those who offered help or who got involved were a heterogenous collection of people who could be described as sharing a counter-cultural orientation and an opposition to nuclear weapons; they included an anarchist–feminist artist, a Christian feminist, a woman involved in a peace centre, a woman who owned a radical bookshop, a woman from the Centre for Alternative Technology in Wales, a man from Crèches against Sexism, a radical midwife, a woman Quaker, a woman from the Liberal Party, and an anarchist–feminist band, the Poison Girls.[11]

The other main way in which participants were mobilized was through the media, both mainstream and alternative.[12] The walk received advance publicity in the *Sunday Times*, *The Guardian*, *Cosmopolitan*, the newsletter of the Women's International League for Peace and Freedom, and *Peace News*.

The provision of resources was both mobilized and activated, that is, both deliberately sought out and offered spontaneously, from sympathetic individuals and groups. National CND was approached for financial assistance and agreed to lend the march £250. Money was also donated by several mixed peace groups, by Cambridge WONT, and by individuals. Anti-nuclear groups in towns on the march route through Wiltshire, Avon, and Berkshire were asked to provide over-night accommodation and evening meals, and Berkshire Anti-Nuclear Campaign's Women's Group agreed, at Ann Pettitt's request, to organize the reception of the march at Greenham. Individuals offered to drive luggage and to provide an Elsan toilet for the rally at Greenham.

Thus it can be seen that whilst much of the mobilizing work was done by a small group of women, and in particular by the one woman whose idea it had first been, the walk only came to fruition through the mobilization and activation of pre-existing social and political networks. The media, both mainstream and alternative, also played an important role in spreading information about the march.

This leads to the question of mobilizing ideas: how was consensus mobilized and what was the nature of the discourse developed to frame the issues around which participants were mobilized? The key document used to mobilize potential walkers was a press release written in July 1981.[13] This statement fulfilled all three of Snow and Benford's (1988) core 'framing' tasks. First, it identified the problem in need of changing: 'the deadly peril in which we are put by the escalating nuclear arms race', and specifically, the installation of Cruise missiles at Greenham, which places 'the whole of South Wales and the south of England right into the front line for utter destruction in any nuclear exchange'. Second, it proposed a solution to the problem: 'peace through disarmament'. Third, it called for action to achieve disarmament: by joining the march. So, whilst the statement was a 'fear appeal', highlighting the proximity of the manufacturing and storage of nuclear arms to the daily lives of the population, it proposed positive remedies, which Klandermans (1988) suggests is necessary to mobilize participants.

Most importantly it conveyed and sought to create a shared identity between women, to encourage participation and to raise awareness of the dangers of nuclear weapons. In this respect the statement used, whether self-consciously or not, a strategy of minimizing the differences between those already committed to participate (of whom there were 35) and those it addressed as part of the mobilizing potential.[14] In all it made six references to the fact that the women involved had children and were concerned about their children's future, and referred to them as 'ordinary people' and 'unknown women'. Thus the identity which the statement sought to create was one based primarily, though not exclusively, on motherhood. However, all three of the traditions of women's opposition to militarism were apparent in the mobilizing discourse of the march: maternalist, materialist, and feminist.

Maternalist opposition to nuclear weapons was expressed in terms of women's role as carers and nurturers:

> Most women work hard at caring for other people – bearing and nourishing children, caring for sick or elderly relatives and many work in the 'caring' professions. Women invest their work in people – and feel a special responsibility to offer them a future – not a waste land of a world and a lingering death. Through the effects of radiation on the unborn and very young children, women are uniquely vulnerable in a nuclear war.[15]

This call to women as mothers echoed the Women's Strike for Peace in the US and Voice of Women in Britain in the 1960s, which opposed nuclear weapons and testing on the grounds of the damage to children's health. In its reference to women's work and 'investment' in caring it suggests too a materialist maternalism. A broader materialist opposition to nuclear weapons, again specifically addressed at women, was also articulated:

> Women bear the weight of cuts in public expenditure – fewer social services, nurseries, less provision for the elderly and infirm, cuts affecting schools.[16]

Finally, the statement addressed the gender politics of militarism from within a liberal feminist discourse about women's exclusion from political life:

[M]ost women have played no part in the decisions and delusions that have brought the world to a position where a few people hold the lives of all of us in their control.[17]

In addition, under the heading 'Why Women?' the first reason given for the march being led by women was one of gender equity in the peace movement and the public sphere:

> The march is led by women to show everyone that women are active and prominent in the peace movement. Men are welcome as supporters, but most of the speakers at meetings and events along the route will be women – some of them already known to the media, most just the unknown women who will be coming on the march to tell the world what they think of our society's priorities.[18]

It is interesting to compare the themes of this statement with the Unity Statement of the Women's Pentagon Action (WPA), which was written a year earlier by women anti-nuclear activists in the United States.[19] The WPA statement also expressed fear about the future, and fulfilled the three framing tasks identified by Snow and Benford (1988). It too demonstrated opposition to militarism based on maternalism, materialism, and a feminist analysis of the gender politics of militarism. However, it differed from the WFLOE statement in the extent of its commitment to feminism, its explicit attention to differences and commonalities between women, and its concern with issues of race, class, sexuality, and disability. Moreover, it drew attention to the connections between militarism and male violence against women. Whereas the WPA statement sought to create a collective identity between participants through the acknowledgement first of differences and then of commonalities, the WFLOE statement tended to assume a unity between women on the basis of the capacity to bear children and of traditional gender roles.

The leaflet handed out to bystanders on the march itself actually dropped all explicit reference to the women-led nature of the walk, and with it any mention of the gender politics of militarism. Instead it appealed unambiguously to concern for children and fears about nuclear war. On one side the leaflet posed the question, 'Why are we walking 110 miles across Britain, from a nuclear weapons factory in Cardiff to a US base for "Cruise" missiles in Berkshire?' The other side featured a photograph of a seriously disabled baby, and the following words:

> This is why. The mother of this baby was exposed to radiation from the nuclear bomb dropped on Hiroshima. 200,000 were blasted and burnt to death. She survived, but her baby, like many others, was born dead and horribly deformed.
>
> The younger you are, the more likely you are to be damaged by radiation from nuclear weapons. As well as deformities in the unborn, this causes cancers and leukaemia.

In addition, there was an ungendered reference to the cost of nuclear weapons. The fact that the feminist politics which were expressed in the initial mobilizing statement were dropped from the leaflet, the public face of the march, highlights the ambivalent nature of the relationship between the march and the early camp and feminist politics.

Of the women interviewed in the research, two had taken part in the Cardiff–Greenham march. How had they been drawn into participation in the march, and why did they get involved?

Helen John heard about the march through Welsh anti-nuclear networks in which she had got involved when proposals were announced to site nuclear waste near her home. This threat seemed to undermine her attempts to give her children a clean and healthy environment, which had been her aim in moving to Wales. She was a former nurse and in 1981 was a housewife looking after her five children. Framed within a maternalist discourse of concern for her children, her immediate motivation for joining the march was:

> [B]ecause I really did believe that women had an enormous impact that they could and should make. And also I was aware that you couldn't constantly just keep writing letters and complaining because it wasn't achieving anything.
>
> (Helen John, 34, camper)[20]

Margery Lewis, in contrast, was relatively isolated from political and counter-cultural networks. She saw *The Guardian* article about the march by Jill Tweedie and was attracted by the idea of taking part. She had a long history of involvement in anti-nuclear politics, having taken part in the Stockholm Peace Petition in 1951, and having been a founding member of a women's anti-testing group in Loughton, Essex, in the late 1950s and involved in the establishment of CND. Her participation in the Aldermaston marches was, in retrospect, less than she would have liked; she had four children whom she looked after whilst her husband went on the march, and she was only able to visit for the day. After she and her family moved to Cardiff from London she found little political activity that engaged her, and spent her free time walking. In 1981 she was 64, with no paid employment and her husband had recently died. Whilst her interest in Greenham lacked the maternalism of Helen's, she was not a feminist.

> *Margery:* I wrote to Ann Pettitt and said, was it a feminist thing or was it a religious thing? And she rang me up and she said, no.
> *Sasha:* It's not feminist, it's not religious?
> *Margery:* No, it's people just like you. And so she said, so help me organize it from Cardiff. So then a man here had done an awful lot of work and he was going away and I took over from him, and I got thoroughly involved.
> *Sasha:* So what was it when you saw this article that caught your interest?
> *Margery:* Well, there hadn't been anything like that. There had been the Copenhagen march. And in a way it presented a challenge to walk a hundred and twenty miles.
>
> (Margery Lewis, 64, visitor)

These extracts from interviews with women who were part of the march suggest two refinements to the discussion of mobilization thus far. First, they illustrate contrasting routes into involvement with the march: membership of social and political networks is an important factor in encouraging involvement, but it is possible for a relatively isolated individual, when supplied with the necessary information by the media, to be activated. However, this was also facilitated by the length and depth of Margery Lewis's prior commitment to anti-nuclear politics, which provided her with some political skills and a degree of confidence in her political efficacy (McCarthy and Zald 1973, 1979). In addition, the fact that her letter to enquire about the march was responded to by a telephone call and a request to take on a major organizational role (liaising with the police) from one of the instigators, undoubtedly provided an extra, personalized pull into participation.

Second, the interviews suggest that the reasons given by participants for their decisions to get involved rarely match the way the issues are framed in mobilizing material or publicity such as leaflets. Motivation is complex and embedded in each individual's personal circumstances and biography. It should not be assumed that the women who took part in the march did so because of a complete congruence between their pre-existing beliefs and those expressed in the march's mobilizing statement, nor indeed that they adopted the discourse of the march later. Statements from women who were on the march, published in Harford and Hopkins (1984:10–13) underline the diversity of motivations amongst them. Effie Leah, for instance, described how she felt 'things had altered. The weapons were piling up and I began to feel I needed reassuring by being with other people' (Harford and Hopkins 1984:11). She made no mention of maternalist, materialist or feminist reasons for her involvement; rather it was just a sense of wanting to do *something*. Liz Stoker admitted that she was not well informed about the issues and saw the march as a way of learning about them. But above all, having been ill, she saw the march as a physical challenge (Harford and Hopkins 1984:12). Ev Silver was motivated by her terrifying fears of a nuclear war (Harford and Hopkins 1984:12). Only Jayne Burton was explicit that she was attracted to the march because it was woman-led, having experienced men's domination of her local CND group (Harford and Hopkins 1984:12). All this suggests that the discourse of the march, whilst in its public face primarily maternalist, lacked a coherent unifying theme, and that women were attracted to take part for a variety of different reasons.

The establishment of the camp

The ground was laid for the setting up of the camp by the creation of a strong sense of collective identity during the march. Margery Lewis described it thus:

It was an incredible march for there being no bad feeling and no schisms, and we were all, I felt, pulling together. I thought it was great from that point of view that we were what seemed like a homogeneous group and we were bonded. There was a good feeling.

(Margery Lewis, 64, visitor)

During the march there were a number of long, intense meetings in which every-one was encouraged to participate, and which served to draw people together. The shared experience of nine days of walking and evenings spent socializing together provided the basis for the decision to continue the action on arrival at Greenham Common.

Although the march attracted some advanced media coverage, reporting of its progress through south Wales and south west England was largely confined to a handful of local papers.[21] This was despite the issuing of press releases to local and national press and broadcasting companies. Women on the march had anticipated extensive coverage, and indeed some believed that it should be led by women solely to attract publicity.[22]

I think why we had it women only (well of course we did have some men on it) was because we thought that it would attract more attention [. . .]. But we felt we weren't making any impact at all. And there we were, women. We were different. We were women, and we were pushing babies, and nobody had done this before, and nobody thought it was outstanding. We thought we were absolutely amazing [laughs], but nobody agreed with us. So as we got nearer to Greenham, that's when we had the idea of chaining ourselves to the fences, to make some impact, because we were just making no impact at all.

(Margery Lewis, 64, visitor)

So, it was the lack of media attention to the march, which had only ever been intended as a one-off, nine-day event, that sparked the anger that led to the establishment of the camp. The idea for four women to chain themselves to the fence of the base to press the demand for a televised debate with the Secretary of State for Defence arose towards the end of the march, and was a self-conscious reference to a protest tactic of the suffragettes. Having been discussed at a meeting in which everyone was encouraged to express her opinion about the proposal, consensus was reached that it should go ahead despite anxieties about possible arrest. The four women who came forward to chain themselves left Newbury for Greenham ahead of the rest of the march early on Saturday 5 September 1981. More work was done contacting the press, and when the march and supporters from the local anti-nuclear group, Newbury against the Missiles, arrived at the base later that day, reporters and photographers were there. A rally was held that afternoon, and the base Commander came out and said that as far as he was concerned, they could stay there as long as they liked:

So it was at that moment, it was about six o'clock on the Saturday night, that we decided we would just stay there. It hadn't been planned. That's just literally what happened.

(Helen John, 34, camper)

That evening 39 people decided to camp outside the base to support the chained women. On Sunday local people brought camping equipment, as the marchers had none with them. This immediate provision of resources by anti-nuclear sympathizers in the locality, together with those that were donated in the weeks that followed, was crucial to the continuation of the camp. Although many marchers had to leave in accordance with their earlier plans, enough stayed so that by the end of the first week, those who were there decided to continue the camp indefinitely, and to march to the CND rally in London in October. Despite numerous further written requests and considerable correspondence with BBC and ITV producers, no televised debate occurred.

What is important to note, then, about the establishment of the camp was its spontaneous nature. It had never been imagined by those who mobilized for the march to Greenham that a peace camp would be set up when they arrived. Moreover, in the first week of the camp, donations of basic equipment, bedding, tents, and food arrived without having been requested or deliberately mobilized by those who were staying there. Networks of peace and women's groups sprang into action, sending telegrams and letters of support and money, and as the weeks passed and news of the camp spread, particularly after the speech by Ann Pettitt at the 24 October CND rally in Hyde Park, visitors increased.[23] The naming of the camp 'Greenham Common Women's Peace Camp' also occurred haphazardly. The 'Women for Life on Earth' tag for the march had never been uniformly applied, with some leaflets headed 'Women's Action for Disarmament', and both ebbed away once the camp was set up. The words 'Women's Peace Camp' were painted in purple, green, and white (suffragette colours) on pieces of board one weekend by a woman who was visiting the camp; no formal decision was ever taken to call the camp thus, but it stuck (Harford and Hopkins 1984:19).

The women-only decision

Although the walk to Greenham had been initiated and led by women, and although the camp was called a 'Women's Peace Camp', until February 1982 a small number of men were involved. By the early 1980s the principle of autonomous women-only organization was well established within the women's liberation movement, but remained extremely controversial beyond its boundaries. During the first six months of the camp, many feminists visited Greenham and left very quickly on discovering that it was not women-only (Harford and Hopkins 1984:32). Over the months there was considerable discussion of the issue of women-only versus mixed actions, but matters finally came to a head when women living at the camp organized their first women-only meeting. This decided that all future actions should be women-only, that only women should live at Greenham, and that the camp should always attempt to deal with women representatives of the authorities and women journalists.[24] The men living there at the time were asked to leave, and it was suggested that they might camp on another part of the Common.

This was an epiphanic moment and represented the first major point of conflict over the collective identity and political direction of Greenham. Whilst a few women had gone into the meeting wanting a women-only outcome, most only reached the decision through the process of the discussion. In the course of explaining the decision afterwards and repeatedly, in different contexts, to different audiences over the years, a variety of reasons were given. Some argued that only women should take part in actions to ensure that they remained non-violent. Experience of the violence and aggression of some of the men who had been living at Greenham suggested that women were less likely to be violent. Some also believed that the police were less prone to using violence against women protesters, and therefore the camp should be women only in the run-up to the threatened eviction. Others, more explicitly feminist, took the position that for only women to deal with the authorities was more than a tactic to avoid violence; it was a symbolic action drawing attention to the gender politics of militarism and its support from the state. This was often coupled with the argument that working within a women-only environment was empowering and would build women's confidence and strength. Finally, others argued that men were a drain on the camp, had not taken responsibility for their share of the domestic labour, and were pushing women back into traditional housewifely roles.

The men who were asked to leave responded angrily, one exacting revenge by picking up an axe to chop down a shelter, another, a non-violence trainer, throwing a pot of water over a woman; but they all departed. However, the women-only decision was called into question and debated in many more meetings at the camp before it became firmly established as one of Greenham's guiding principles. Some of the women who had been on the initial march to Greenham, but who had not chosen to live there, attempted to overturn the decision, arguing that it was divisive, would weaken the peace movement, and that men should be encouraged to be non-violent and to change, rather than being excluded.[25] Ann Pettitt, in particular, believed that her vision had been betrayed and continued to actively oppose the policy for many years, often bringing her male partner to camp on the Common in their van. The conflict, in part, turned on the question of who 'owned' Greenham, and who therefore could decide on its direction. As such it presaged later tensions and splits and between those living at Greenham and those who did not (discussed in Chapter 5). Ultimately, the decision was upheld by force of numbers. The resolve of women living at Greenham strengthened as they experienced their increasing sense of personal power in a women-only environment, and as the decision became well known within anti-nuclear and feminist networks, the new women who came to Greenham were more prepared to accept it; indeed, many got involved only because it was women-only.

The creation and re-creation of Greenham

The march to Greenham, the establishment of the camp and the early creation of collective identity were only the first stages in the making of Greenham. There was no inevitability about the continued existence of Greenham even after the decision had been made at the end of the first week to stay indefinitely. Greenham was a process in creation, the collective action of all those who became involved over the years. It took the form it did because thousands of women made individual decisions to go to Greenham and to become part of its re-creation.

Getting involved in collective action is itself a process, not a one-off decision. Women usually went to Greenham for a day, in the first instance, and later decided to continue and increase their involvement. Many women moved from visiting the camp, to staying there and then to living there, or from visiting directly to living there, and then later from living there to just staying occasionally. Thus in the discussion that follows, 'getting involved' refers to the process by which women actively became part of Greenham, in various ways and to differing degrees, often over an extended period of time.

The context of getting involved

The sociological literature on movement formation suggests that there are a number of factors influencing the mobilization of individuals into involvement in collective action. These include membership of social/political or counter-cultural networks and exposure to media reportage. In addition, new social movement theorists have argued that membership of the new middle class, state employment, and higher education are correlated with movement participation (see Chapter 2). To this Offe (1987) adds that 'peripheral groups', those who are outside paid employment and whose time is flexible – primarily middle class housewives, students and the unemployed – are particularly likely to get involved in social movements. Similarly, resource mobilization theorists suggest that one of the most important resources required by an individual if she is to participate in collective action is discretionary time (McCarthy and Zald 1973; Freeman 1979).

To what extent did these factors apply to the women interviewed in this research? What were the contexts within which they decided to get involved with Greenham, and what were the constraints operating upon them to structure and limit the form of their involvement? How did they come to make the decision to participate and why did their participation take the form it did?

The context of paid employment
At the time of getting involved with Greenham 14 of the 35 women interviewed were engaged in some form of paid employment, and 21 had no paid employment, being dependent either on state benefits, on a husband or, in one case, on her parents (Table 3.1).

Seven of the fourteen women were in regular full-time paid employment at the time of getting involved, and of these three became campers, three became stayers, and one a visitor. Six of those in regular full-time employment were employed by the state, as is predicted by the work of Mattausch (1989) (though the majority of women interviewed were clearly outside the 'state class'): two social

Table 3.1   Employment status at time of getting involved

Employment status at time of getting involved	Number
Unemployed	8
Regular full-time paid employment	7
'Housewives'/carers	6
Self-employed	4
Regular part-time paid employment	3
Extended travelling	3
Retired	2
Full time education	2
Total	35

workers, a teacher, a Youth Training Scheme trainer, a student nurse, and a park-keeper; the other woman was employed in the voluntary sector by Women's Aid. Another three of those interviewed had regular part-time employment, in two cases by choice in order to combine employment with the pursuit of artistic interests (pottery and writing). One of these women worked for a co-operative language school as a tutor and administrator, one as a secretary and the third as a care assistant; all three became campers. Four women were self-employed as freelancers or worked for agencies: a graphic designer, a translator, a journalist and a private nurse. Of these one became a camper and three stayers.[26]

A number of the women in paid employment mentioned in their interviews that they were dissatisfied with their jobs, or that they were looking for 'something more' in their lives. This contributed to their readiness to get involved with Greenham. For example, Barbara Rawson, who worked part-time as a care assistant said:

> I was fed up with work, which was quite difficult because I was working for another supervisor who I didn't get on with and we hadn't a thing in common, and all that was building up, and I thought, well, if I go to Greenham that will all go away for a bit, and then I can see.
>
> (Barbara Rawson, 52, camper)

Table 3.2   Relationship between employment status and level of involvement

Occupation	Camper	Stayer	Visitor
Paid employment (includes regular full-time employment, part-time employment and the self-employed)	7	5	2
No paid employment	12	7	2
Total	19	12	4

Vee Wright had been working as a residential social worker in a job which left her hardly any free time. Then, on getting divorced, she moved to a residential job, in a new town, which whilst very time consuming, allowed her considerably more time off than she had enjoyed previously:

> [T]hat was the point at which I wanted to start doing other things. I wanted to have a life outside of work [. . .] I went in to that situation really looking for other things to do with my life apart from just work.
>
> (Vee Wright, 25, stayer)

Penni Bestic was working on a freelance basis as a graphic designer when she was smitten by the urge to go to Greenham. She took the opportunity of the end of a contract to make the decision to go to live there.

> I was at the Plaid [Cymru] conference and we knew that they were going to take the fence down [Halloween, 1983]. A whole group of women at this conference all knew about it, and Sian came back and said, it's down. And all the women just let out this huge great whoop. And all the men were sitting there, going, what's happened? And we just said, the fence has come down at Greenham. And they said, why didn't you tell us? They turned to their wives and said, why didn't you tell us? It was just tremendous. I just decided I was going to go there. I had a contract at this place I was working, and they said, do you want to renew your contract, and I said, no.
>
> (Penni Bestic, 31, camper)

Of the 21 women who had no form of paid employment at the time of getting involved, two were in full-time education: one on a post-graduate course, one a sixth former; both became stayers. Five women were 'housewives', of whom two became campers and three stayers, and another was an unpaid carer (of an elderly relative) and became a visitor.[27] Two women were pensioners, one becoming a stayer and one a visitor, and eight were unemployed, all of whom became campers.[28] The three non-British women who were interviewed were all travelling at the time of getting involved, two of them having come to Britain specifically to be involved with Greenham. They had previously been a doctor, a student, and a freelance journalist/film-maker; two became campers and one a stayer.

Information about the occupational status of the women interviewed provides some contextual background to decisions to get involved and to the level of involvement chosen, though it should be borne in mind that the number of women in each category is small (see Table 3.2). At an aggregate level, women who were in paid employment were no less likely to become campers than those without any paid employment. However, part-timers were more likely to become campers than those in full-time work and than the self-employed. Being in full-time employment did not make it impossible for a woman to live at Greenham (the YTS trainer and the Women's Aid workers gave up their jobs, and the social worker first negotiated nine months unpaid leave and then left her job entirely). Women who worked as freelancers or for agencies, such as the graphic artist, the nurse and the journalist, were able to organize their work to make their involvement as campers or stayers possible.

No woman interviewed cited her commitment to her job as a reason for not being more involved with Greenham; reasons given fell into two categories – caring responsibilities and other forms of political commitment (either to anti-nuclear work in their own area or to other forms of politics). However, two caveats must be made to this. First, women whose work commitments were great enough to severely hinder their participation were unlikely to find themselves represented in the sample, which was biased towards campers. Second, it may be the case that some women felt unable or did not wish to acknowledge that the demands of their job, rather than political commitments, restricted their level of involvement, as the latter would have been more ideologically acceptable in the environment of Greenham.

There was a particularly noticeable relationship between being unemployed and becoming a camper. A number of women who were unemployed at the time of becoming involved spoke of how their lack of regularized ties facilitated their decision to move to Greenham. Rowan Gwedhen, for example, was clear about how her unemployment and other life circumstances were related to her readiness to move to Greenham:

> I was living in a shared house with a couple of women who were lovers and I think that wasn't working out too well, and I was on the dole, and I'd only been in London for about 6 months. I hadn't found my feet. I didn't have a lot of reason to stay in London [. . .]. I didn't give anything up to go to Greenham.
>
> (Rowan Gwedhen, 24, camper)

However, the relationship which appears to have existed between being unemployed and becoming a camper must not be assumed to be causal. The women who were unemployed did not all have complete flexibility of time, and were not all unencumbered by domestic ties; two had children, one a baby and one of school age, yet both became campers. Nor were the circumstances and decisions about involvement of the group of 'housewives' uniform; one had grown-up children and became a camper, and four had young children, of whom one became a camper and the other three stayers. It is interesting that, despite having young children, none of these women confined their involvement to being visitors. Clearly then, as well as being shaped by a context of employment/non-employment, each woman's involvement with Greenham occurred within a specific domestic context.

Lesbian and heterosexual contexts and domestic responsibilities

The process of getting involved with Greenham was also influenced and constrained by a woman's sexuality and domestic circumstances. Twenty women were heterosexual at the time of getting involved; eighteen were involved in long term relationships/marriages.[29] Fourteen were lesbians (Table 3.3).

The majority of women interviewed who were lesbians at the time of getting

Table 3.3 Sexuality at time of getting involved

Sexuality	Number of women
Heterosexual	20
Lesbian	14
Don't know	1
Total	35

Table 3.4 Sexuality at time of getting involved and level of involvement

Sexuality at getting involved	Level of involvement		
	Camper	Stayer	Visitor
Heterosexual	8	9	3
Lesbian	10	3	1
Don't know	0	1	0
Total	18	13	4

involved became campers (Table 3.4). In general the lesbians were younger than the heterosexual women, and tended to have fewer constraints on participation. Of the eight women who were unemployed, six were lesbians, and all of them became campers. None of the lesbians had children at the time, did not have to negotiate involvement with a resentful male partner and were therefore more emotionally 'open' to the affective incentives of Greenham. In addition, as will become evident later in the chapter, the lesbians often experienced a strong 'pull' into involvement because of the lesbian identity of the camp.

In contrast, heterosexual women were less likely to become campers and more likely to be stayers and visitors. Involvement in heterosexual relationships often imposed constraints upon participation in Greenham. One form of constraint common amongst the heterosexual women interviewed was anxiety about their partner's feelings of exclusion and the possibility, or actuality, of deterioration in their relationships as a result. Several women said that they felt torn between their relationship with their male partners and Greenham, and that they made conscious decisions to limit their involvement to occasional stays at Greenham, or to stop living at Greenham, in order to placate their partners (see Chapter 7 for further discussion of the response of male partners to Greenham).

The other main constraint on the involvement of heterosexual women was childcare.[30] Fourteen women (none of them lesbians) interviewed had children at the time of getting involved (Table 3.5), though only seven had children under the age of 18.[31] Four of these women became stayers and three became campers (including the only woman with a child under five). Whilst some of these stayers

Table 3.5   Number of children at time of getting involved and level of involvement

No. of children	Camper	Stayer	Visitor	Total
0	13	6	2	21
1	1	0	0	1
2	2	4	1	7
3	1	2	0	3
4	0	0	1	1
5	2	0	0	2
Total	19	12	4	35

were prevented from becoming campers because of childcare problems, all managed to arrange childcare for periods of several days, or even a couple of weeks at a time, to enable them to be spend time at Greenham, and, in some cases, to go to prison. Most relied on help from male partners, whilst a few made use of extended kinship networks. However, childcare often became the issue around which husbands' or male partners' hostility to the women's involvement with Greenham was expressed. A number of the women with school-aged and younger children described how they had to engage in delicate negotiations with their male partners about childcare, which, in retrospect, they understood as being more about soothing the men's egos than about the actual practicalities of childcare.

Pat Paris's circumstances illustrate well the constraints imposed on hetero-sexual women's involvement by both childcare responsibilities and the attitudes of male partners. At the time of the 'Embrace the Base' demonstration in December 1982, Pat had just given birth to a premature baby and was living in rural Wales with no personal transport.

> I couldn't do anything but stay put; I was completely grounded and we hadn't got any transport [. . .] I can remember quite clearly, I think it was four o'clock, that they finally linked all round the base. And the point that happened, I was sitting in almost darkness in this kitchen, breast-feeding this baby, with this other woman sitting opposite me breast-feeding her baby and the pair of us streaming tears because we could hear women singing behind the news report, and we weren't there. We were stuck in this kitchen, immobilized with these children. I can remember that being a real emotional thing, the frustration of not being able to do anything because you were stuck with these kids and there were all these thousands of women miles away.
>
> (Pat Paris, 33, camper)

However, she later moved to Nottingham and got involved in the Women for Peace group. When her daughter was eighteen months old and she had stopped breast-feeding, she negotiated an arrangement with her partner in which he would look after the child for four days a week whilst she was at Greenham. She would then return home and take charge of childcare for the next four days, before going back to Greenham. This arrangement allowed her to live at Greenham over a period of two years, but during this time constrained her level of involvement:

> I felt I wasn't in a position to decide that I would go to prison rather than pay a fine because I had to ask him to look after her. It was so awful. It was like an unspoken thing. It's all right if you go, but don't expect me to do more than I'm already doing. The one time I did get arrested somebody rang him to tell him, and his first comment about it was 'bloody stupid woman'. Then he said, 'oh no, I didn't mean that'. He suddenly realized he was talking to another right-on woman who might tell me. So I used to legal observe.
>
> (Pat Paris, 33, camper)

Political and social orientations

I argued in Chapter 2 that, at a collective level, the origins of Greenham can be traced back into the political environment of social movements, groups, and campaigns that were part of the 'cycle of protest' (Tarrow 1983) of the 1960s and 1970s. It was out of this political environment that many of the formative ideas and modes of action of Greenham emerged. It was also within this context that many of the women interviewed were first constituted as political actors. Their political beliefs and orientations were shaped in this world, in both a positive and a negative sense. Moreover, past activism provides individuals with political and organizational skills, some sense of political efficacy, and, very often, solidarity networks which draw past activists into new involvements (McCarthy and Zald 1973, 1979).

All except five of the women interviewed had been involved, in various ways and to varying degrees, in political activism prior to Greenham. The range of campaigns with which they had been associated is shown in Table 3.6. One important point to be noted is that few women had been actively involved in the women's liberation movement prior to Greenham, although many said that they had been interested in feminism.

The women who had been politically active before Greenham can be divided into two groups. The first, smaller group of women regarded their involvement with Greenham as the logical extension of their existing political activism, and tended to see little or no tension between the two. The second, much larger group saw their involvement with Greenham as related to and emerging from their prior involvements, yet constituting, for various reasons, a considerable break with their political past.

Examples of those who saw Greenham as part of a continuing set of political commitments were Nell Logan and Sian Edwards, who were two of the seven women interviewed who had been active in political parties. Nell Logan had been an active trade unionist and member of the Communist Party since the age of

Table 3.6   Previous political involvements[33]

Political campaign/movement	Number of women
Peace movement (1979–)	17
Political parties	7
Plaid Cymru	3
Communist Party	2
Labour Party	1
International Marxist Group	1
Peace movement (1950s/1960s)	5
Environmentalism/anti-nuclear power	5
Women's Liberation Movement:	
Women's Aid	4
Reclaim the Night Marches	3
Women's health/reproductive rights	2
Student politics	3
Anti-apartheid	2
Trade unions	2
Alternative/Left journalism	2
Anti-Nazi League	1

14 when she began work as a weaver in the Lancashire cotton mills. She had been a union organizer during the weavers' strike in the 1930s, supported the anti-fascists in the Spanish Civil War, and campaigned against nuclear weapons in the 1950s and 1960s. For her, Greenham was part of a lifetime's commitment to fighting capitalism, fascism and imperialism.

> I've had all these experiences, you see, and it's made me like I am, I think. Because I've seen poverty and I've seen people in the weaving strike really down and out, and I can't forget it [. . .]. I thought this [deployment of Cruise] is just the last straw, that they're going to use such hardware that would cause such destruction and so much destruction afterwards [. . .] How can they? It's all American imperialism.
>
> (Nell Logan, 71, stayer)

Sian Edwards, who joined Plaid Cymru at the age of 13, also saw Greenham as an extension of her existing political activities:

> The nuclear issue has always been a very strong policy with Plaid, it's a very pacifist party [. . .]. And Greenham seemed such an amazing way of actually doing something, and I was also obviously very influenced by the Welsh

influence on it, that there were so many women from Wales [. . .]. At the Plaid women's section we put a motion to conference about opposing cruise and general anti-nuclear things, and as a practical thing that we as a women's section were going to maintain a presence at Greenham at weekends.

(Sian Edwards, 33, visitor)

Illustrative of the larger group who regarded Greenham as a considerable break with their previous political and social orientations were Penny Gulliver, Kim Smith, Carol Harwood, and Pat Paris. Penny Gulliver had been active in student politics both at further education college and then at drama school, and had been involved in Anti-Nazi League demonstrations and worked as a volunteer for Women's Aid. She had also been out as a lesbian since she was 17, but did not connect her left-wing politics with her sexuality until she got involved with Greenham.

All my politics were 'issue' politics, you know, and to do with class. I would have said that I was a feminist, but I still had a gap between the things that I thought were women's politics and sexuality and stuff, and issue politics, you know, important politics.

(Penny Gulliver, 22, camper)

Kim Smith had been involved in the International Marxist Group at university, and in trade union politics when she worked in the civil service, but had become disillusioned with the left. Greenham represented for her a different and more effective form of political activism.

I'd been working in the civil service in Ipswich [. . .] and I was involved in trade union things and various claimants' rights groups, and I'd just had a gut full of it [. . .]. I didn't believe anymore that things could be changed from the inside, which was my naïve belief when I joined the civil service [. . .]. Whereas Greenham I thought was actually going to achieve something.

(Kim Smith, 25, camper)

A number of other women had become aware of patriarchal practices within the political groups and social networks of which they had been members, and this predisposed them to involvement with Greenham as a women's initiative.[33] For example, Carol Harwood, who had been active in the Committee of 100 in the early 1960s, had learnt from her experiences as a young pregnant woman in a male dominated movement.

I mean even back in the sixties I knew that there was something absolutely flawed about any political movement that was mixed unless men changed their ideas [. . .]. I knew that there was something really radically wrong with politics because I knew that men were playing their own power games within radical and left wing and peace politics.

(Carol Harwood, 36, stayer)

Pat Paris's experience of the counter-culture of the 'hippy scene' had raised her awareness of the problems of patriarchal practices in supposedly 'alternative' environments, and predisposed her towards Greenham as a women-only protest.

> I'd spent quite a lot of time on the hippy scene, so although I wasn't political, I was quite alternative. And so I'd seen unconventional mixed living, and I knew that women in teepees had a harder life than women in council houses, by and large. It was no joke getting the water at 6 o'clock in the morning from frozen wells and streams, and dealing with shitting babies in the middle of the night. I couldn't see what was alternative about it, from a woman's point of view.
>
> (Pat Paris, 33, camper)

Of the five women who were interviewed who reported no previous political experience, four were twenty years old or younger, suggesting that their lack of previous political experience was a function of their age. All five either had friends who were involved with Greenham or were part of a loose counter-cultural environment in which there was a general disapproval of nuclear weapons. Jinny List's mother had a friend (Pat Paris) who was very involved in her local Women for Peace group; Trina worked with a group of lesbians and feminists who regularly visited and talked about Greenham; Trisha described herself as a punk, who, like her punk friends, was opposed to nuclear weapons and militarism; Sarah Benham was the daughter of liberal minded teachers who were opposed to nuclear weapons; and Leah Thalmann, although describing herself as 'apolitical', was involved in a counselling network and was friendly with a woman who had set up the Derby Women for Peace group.

In addition to having been involved in political activism themselves, eleven women spoke of the formative influence of having grown up in homes where radical politics of various kinds were frequently discussed. Two of the older women's mothers had been suffrage campaigners, and five women had parents or grandparents who had been Labour Party (or Independent Labour Party) activists. Two women had parents who had been involved in the peace movement in the 1960s, and had been taken on anti-nuclear demonstrations as children.

Other women, who had not necessarily been surrounded by political discussion as children, none the less saw their childhood experiences as important in forming their political consciousness. Bridget Evans, for instance, was brought up as a Protestant in Northern Ireland.

> In some respects it's impossible to grow up in Northern Ireland without being politically aware and I think I was politically aware from the age of 13, 14 and that process has continued all my life [. . .]. My politics are different from my family's – they are Northern Irish Protestants, and are liberal unionists, but they're definitely not republicans. Whereas I'm a republican, but I'm also a socialist, definitely. And a womanist.
>
> (Bridget Evans, 23, camper)[34]

Carmel Cadden saw her childhood, as the daughter of an Irish Catholic serving in the British army in Africa, as a formative influence on her later politics.

> I remember always being uncomfortable about being a white person belonging to the army, when we ourselves were not part of the army. We didn't fit in with the other white people. We would go to the Catholic church where all the black people went and very few other white people.
>
> (Carmel Cadden, 30, stayer)

However, it was not the case that every woman who got involved with Greenham had grown up in a radical or highly politically aware environment, or saw the beginnings of her political consciousness in her childhood. Four women described their parents as conservative or ultra-conservative, and four women said that politics were never discussed at all at home. Many of these women had only became interested in politics as students. It is certainly significant that eighteen of the women interviewed were educated to degree level or above (see Appendix II), given that higher education tends to contribute to an individual's sense of competence to make judgements about political issues (Offe 1987:88).

Routes to Greenham

Greenham's attempts to mobilize women for particular events or just to spend time at the camp never constituted a strategy; rather they were haphazard, irregular, and often the product of a notion mooted around the fire and then carried out by whoever wanted to get involved. The best example of something approximating deliberate and concerted mobilization by women at Greenham was for the 'Embrace the Base' action on 12 December 1982 and the 'Close the Base' blockades the next day, but even this was very different from the picture of mobilization painted by resource mobilization theorists. It consisted of sending a letter to everyone on the various different mailing lists of supporters which had been compiled since the Cardiff to Greenham march. The letter asked every recipient to send copies to ten friends. Posters were designed, printed, and distributed, and local women's peace groups began organizing coaches to Greenham. The widespread publicity created a momentum for the two days of action, producing a sense amongst those who were part of the networks reached by the chain letters and the posters that something important was happening. The provision of transport by CND groups and women's peace groups in almost every city and town of any size throughout England, Wales, and Scotland made participation easier (in the language of resource mobilization theory, 'reduced the costs of participation'). Moreover, the clearly delimited nature of the commitment required encouraged many to participate who shared the worry that they had to leave home entirely to be involved with Greenham.

Many of the women interviewed, however, had not been drawn to Greenham through such mobilization efforts. Their involvement tended to have been activated primarily by the enthusiasm of a friend, whose encouragement for them to come along on a trip to the camp or to a local meeting served to replace the deliberate outreach work of women at Greenham.

But whether women were mobilized or activated, what was overwhelmingly important was personal contact with others who were already involved with Greenham. Whilst a number of women recalled the inspiration of reading about or seeing Greenham in the media, this alone did not offer a clear route into involvement. The liberal press tended to idealize Greenham women, presenting them as heroines and martyrs to the cause of world peace, with the effect that other women tended to feel admiration rather than identification with them.

> I'd got this picture [from the media] of very adamant women, I suppose, very tough [. . .] An attractive picture, a desirable picture of strong women being very cold and putting up with dreadful things for world peace and a vision of a better humanity. But I couldn't fit myself into that because I was so normal [laughs].
>
> (Jinny List, 20, camper)

> [W]e heard about Greenham through the press [. . .]. I thought they were amazing, the women early on, and when you would see interviews with them, you would feel very much in awe of them, and feel guilty that you weren't doing more. You read stories about people leaving their husbands and children and jobs and I felt, I ought to do that. And I suppose in the early days you felt, I couldn't, it would be so hard.
>
> (Ann Armstrong, 44, stayer)

Both Ann and Jinny only became involved with Greenham themselves when they developed social or political connections which mediated their participation.

In contrast to being introduced to Greenham by the media, being inspired in the first instance through a social or political group or by an individual friend, provided women with a social context in which to think about Greenham and with encouragement to get involved. The enthusiasm of friends who were involved made Greenham seem more accessible, and having a friend already at Greenham, or someone to go to Greenham with, tended to make experience of arriving at the camp less frightening. On a practical level, women generally are less likely than men to own cars and to be able to drive, and so membership of a group which could hire a minibus and find a driver was an important facilitator of involvement. Many of the women interviewed had rarely travelled long distances around Britain alone and confessed to initially having been daunted by the prospect of getting to Greenham.

Personal contact with women who were already involved with Greenham enabled women to identify themselves as the sort of women who could go to Greenham, and smoothed the path to involvement. For instance, Jenny Heron had been 'a silent female member' of her local CND group:

> But then a Greenham woman came to talk to the Socialist Workers' Party, and some of us from CND went down to hear what she had to say. She was

very quiet and spoke very softly and you had to strain to listen to what she said, but she was saying about all the marvellous things that they were doing for International Women's Day for Disarmament in Leicester, and I think we came away thinking, if someone as quiet and unassuming as that can do those marvellous things, then we can too. So we started a Women for Peace group, and organized a march and [. . .] made up leaflets.

(Jenny Heron, 30, camper)

Carmel Cadden's experience of hearing a Greenham woman talk about the camp was similar; she felt an immediate sense of identification with the woman, and could therefore imagine herself involved with Greenham:

I'd heard about Greenham in the October. There was a very big CND march, October 1981, just after the women had gone to camp. It was Ann Pettitt who spoke [. . .]. She has a high quavering voice, a bit daunted by a quarter of a million people, or whatever, and she really inspired me [. . .]. And I was just riveted. I thought, that sounds incredible, I must go, I'd really like to go down there and see what it's like [. . .]. And she sounded so ordinary. She wasn't a professional speaker. She was just like any woman.

(Carmel Cadden, 30, stayer)

Another woman, whose knowledge about Greenham had been limited to newspaper reports until she met someone who was very involved with the camp, described how information from a personal contact made it possible for her to go to Greenham for the first time:

I had the idea if you went to Greenham you had to throw everything in and go and commit yourself. I wasn't ready to do that [. . .] Then I was talking to another woman in Derby who was quite committed and she said, no, you can just go and visit and spend a day there and see what it's like [. . .]. Anyway, when she said this, I thought, all right, I will go.

(Leah Thalmann, 53, camper)

Reasons for getting involved

A wide variety of motivations for getting involved with Greenham were described by the women interviewed. Most women explained their involvement in terms of a number of different factors, and indicated that their reasons also changed over time. I have identified five predominant explanations given in the interviews both for women's initial involvement and for staying involved.

Concern about nuclear militarism

The initial interest in Greenham of most (though not all) of the women interviewed was rooted in their concern about nuclear weapons, in particular the siting of Cruise missiles in Britain and the escalation of the arms race from the end of the

1970s. This motivating factor was expressed in various ways. A number of women spoke about how they were haunted and obsessed by their fears about a nuclear war. For some nuclear fear took the form of anxiety about the future of their children or grandchildren, and was articulated within a maternalist discourse:

> I had got involved because I did feel that the world was about to end if somebody didn't do something [. . .]. I had these terrible dreams about what would happen if my children were at school and nuclear war broke out. My whole life was absorbed in this fear that my children, not even that they might die, but that they might actually live and I might be crawling around in some half-life state.
>
> (Simone Wilkinson, 36, stayer)

The explanation given by Susan Lamb for her involvement resonates with Ruddick's (1990) notion of the contradiction between maternal practice and the effects of militarism. She was impelled to get involved with Greenham by feeling that her work as a mother, specifically teaching her children about the value of honesty, was directly threatened by nuclear weapons:

> The thing that triggered me into doing something was my daughter [. . .]. We are in the flight path for Heathrow and every plane that went over, she said, 'Mummy, mummy, they're going to bomb us'. The only way I could calm her fears was to tell her lies, which is not what I want to be doing. So I had to face my own bloody fears about it. So about a week later there was the first resurgence of our CND group and they held their first meeting and I went. It was through that we became involved with Greenham.
>
> (Susan Lamb, 28, stayer)

Pat Paris' motivation also centred around concern about her child, though it was less directly expressed in terms of nuclear fear, and also involved a materialist opposition to military expenditure:

> I had Rowan not long afterwards [the Falklands war], and because she was so small and hovering it concentrated my attention wonderfully on death and destruction. And there was an incredible shortage of equipment in the premature baby unit – they hadn't got incubators [. . .]. I mainly started to get involved at that level. I was very irate about the amount of money that was being wasted on nuclear weapons.
>
> (Pat Paris, 33, camper)

The maternalist expression of concern about nuclear weapons was, however, by no means predominant. Others, particularly younger women, experienced fear for their own future, and were engulfed in depression and despair:

> I felt like the world is going to explode at any minute and why am I going to college? I mean, why go on with your life in this normal way when you feel like the world is about to blow up?
>
> (Liz Galst, 20, camper)

I remember when Reagan was elected I was still at university and we had an End of the World party because that was how we felt. I mean everybody just got roaring drunk for two days because we really felt like that was it, that none of us were going to live to see the end of our twenties.

(Helen Mary Jones, 23, visitor)

Many described how they felt that conventional anti-nuclear campaigning – joining CND, signing petitions, and going on demonstrations – was insufficient to meet the gravity of the situation. They were searching for more effective ways of expressing their opposition to the nuclear arms race. Greenham provided an antidote to their sense of powerlessness to affect the arms race:

[I]t seemed obvious that things were heading towards annihilation, if they went on [. . .]. I was feeling very frustrated, and I was looking for an outlet or a channel. You go on marches or join CND and never feel that you are quite getting anywhere. That's why Greenham seemed to offer a real channel.

(Carmel Cadden, 30, camper)

However, not all the women interviewed were initially well informed about the state of the arms race. Some only became aware of the issue because of the protests at Greenham, and others, who had a gut-level opposition to Cruise, gained the knowledge to underpin and argue their opposition through their involvement with Greenham. For a few women, the issue of nuclear weapons was never the major motivation for being at Greenham.

A women-only movement and community
As a women-only protest and community, Greenham exercised a powerful pull to involvement for many women. This is a clear illustration of the centrality of expressive, affective, and cultural motivations for involvement in social movements. Every woman interviewed whose participation dated from after the decision for the camp to become women-only said that she found the women-only policy an important attraction. For some this was because they could feel a sense of ownership and participation in a women-only environment which they did not in political actions with men. Most said that they would not have got involved with Greenham had it still been mixed:

The fact that it was women only made me feel that I could have a chance to operate freely [. . .]. I wouldn't have got involved if it hadn't been women-only. It was that strong, really.

(Carmel Cadden, 30, camper)

The fact that it was a women-only camp was really important. If it had been a mixed camp I wouldn't have entertained the idea of going down and staying [. . .]. I wouldn't have lived at an anti-nuclear camp if there had been men there. So that was a big deal.

(Penny Gulliver, 22, camper)

For many women – both campers and stayers who returned for weekends regularly over the years – the social side of Greenham, being in a women's space and developing close friendships with women, became increasingly important:

I think more reasons for being there emerged. I think the main reason, to protest about Cruise being there, was always there, but I think the other reasons just happened. It was about being very fond of and being very close to women.

(Barbara Rawson, 52, camper)

Sasha: Did your reasons for going back to Greenham change?
Vee: Yes, yes.
Sasha: How?
Vee: It was still just as strongly about nuclear weapons, I mean that never ever went away for me. I was very clear that was why I was there. But I suppose I was also going to Greenham because it was women-only. And because of what Greenham stood for, not just in terms of the nuclear stuff, but because of what it stood for in terms of being a women-only place.

(Vee Wright, 25, stayer)

First of all it was incredibly noble, getting rid of Cruise missiles, and towards the end of the time, now, I just go there to be with other women who are like-minded. I go for a holiday.

(Ann Armstrong, 44, stayer)

A lesbian community
The fact that Greenham developed into a strongly lesbian community was also an important factor in attracting women to the camp. After the first six months as a mixed camp, when there were few lesbians living there, and fewer still who were 'out', Greenham rapidly became an environment in which lesbianism was the norm. The more lesbians who went to Greenham, the more it attracted. It was a place where women could live as lesbians twenty four hours a day, without feeling they had to suppress aspects of their identity, and where they were able to be openly affectionate with each other, both in friendship and sexually.

A number of the women interviewed cited the predominance of lesbians at Greenham, often together with the women-only policy, as a major reason for their involvement:

I was heavily against nuclear weapons [. . .] but I became more involved in that sort of thing once I'd got to Greenham, rather than the other way round, of people being involved in that sort of thing and discovering women when they got to Greenham. It was more to do with it being women living in that way, for me [. . .] I would never have dreamt of going there if men had still been there [. . .] I wasn't involved with men at all. I'm a cradle dyke.

(Rowan Gwedhen, 24, camper)

The women weren't the only reason I was there, but they were certainly a big attraction [laughs . . .]. For the first time in my life I felt I'd found a place where I fitted in and whatever I was was OK, and the same as the others.

(Jinny List, 20, camper)

Some women, particularly those who were in the process of, or on the verge of coming out, identified, in retrospect, the lesbianism of the camp as drawing them to Greenham:

[I remember] being quite shocked when [Jane] said that quite a large percentage of the women there were lesbians. That hadn't twigged at all. I'd had a two-year relationship with a girl at school, but I was so completely closeted, to myself as much as to anyone else, and just hadn't made the connection at all. And it was obviously one of the reasons I was being so strongly drawn to it, because the place was heaving with dykes [laughs].

(Sarah Benham, 17, stayer)

The pursuit of personal change

Greenham was a place in which women engaged in significant projects of self-transformation. Many went to Greenham primarily to oppose Cruise missiles, with no conscious notion that they would be fundamentally changed by the experience (this is discussed further in Chapter 8). In retrospect, however, several of the women who were interviewed came to believe that they had been seeking personal change, and that this had been a major reason why they had got involved with Greenham.

Leah Thalmann, who took nine months unpaid leave from her job as a social worker in order to go to live at Greenham, exemplifies this:

I was saying to myself I went for political reasons, but I'm not sure. I'm not saying I didn't, but I'm not sure that there weren't other reasons that were just as important to me that at the beginning I didn't know I was there for, but later on I realized I had been there for. Yes, it was much wider than just the political issues; it was all part of a huge time of change for me.

(Leah Thalmann, 53, camper)

'Saving the world is really fun'[35]

Finally, perhaps the most important reason why women chose to get more involved with the camp, returning to stay at frequent intervals or deciding to live there, was because they liked being there. However earnest her initial motivation, every woman interviewed who had been a camper or a stayer talked of how much she enjoyed the humour and excitement of Greenham. Being part of a vibrant, ever-changing community, in which affective bonds were strong, was experienced as extremely enjoyable, far outweighing the occasional misery of cold feet and damp sleeping bags.

> My reasons for going were that I thought I ought to go, because I felt that other people were doing something that I ought to be doing and I shouldn't be leaving this to other women to do [. . .]. I kept thinking, I must go. But when I was there it was really different because I really loved it [. . .]. I loved all the excitement and I loved to do all the actions and all that. It was great. And mixing with a big group of women which I'd not done before. I really had a good time and liked it and enjoyed it. And that's why I stayed [. . .]. I stayed because I liked it, and I did feel that it was important as well. My mate Trina says, everyone gets this amount of excitement in their life, and we had all ours in one year, and it's all downhill now.
>
> (Penny Gulliver, 22, camper)

The theme of recaptured, exuberant child-like fun, often physical, dirty, and unfeminine, appeared in many interviews. At Greenham women felt able to play in a way that women generally are not able to; rough and tumble sports, adventure holidays, and being part of a gang are activities socially defined as masculine, primarily the prerogative of boys, but open to adult men as well. In many ways, women freed themselves from the conventions governing feminine behaviour at Greenham:

> We enjoyed ourselves so much. Sometimes it was awful and unpleasant – wet and cold and boring. It was also incredibly exciting, and you had the attention of the world, and my god, what power [. . .] I thought it was sometimes like we were living in an Enid Blyton novel. It was like Five Go Mad at Greenham. How many tins of pineapple chunks shall we eat today? Lashings of Christmas pudding. Cop-baiting. For me it was a licence to go mad. And that was also what kept it going as well.
>
> (Penni Bestic, 31, camper)

> It was all your childhood fantasies, playing cowboys and Indians, goodies and baddies. Making a little home out of branches, and building a little fire and cooking a little supper. It was every tomboy's dream. On top of which we were also being outlaws [. . .]. Running around in the bushes in the dark, with boltcutters down your trousers, and ducking and diving.
>
> (Rowan Gwedhen, 24, camper)

> I was really playing out a lot of childhood adventures. I used to like playing in woods when I was a child and I used to like stories about Robin Hood, because they all lived in the woods. And I think I always had a vision of how lovely that would be, to just live in the woods among the trees. And I think a

lot of that was what I was doing. Living in the woods, with a group of people and doing things that were great fun. I loved cutting the fence.

(Leah Thalmann, 53, camper)

Other women emphasized the exceptional energy which they felt at Greenham, the sense of collective and personal power and exultation.[36] This was enhanced on occasions of mass gatherings, but many women said that they felt that Greenham was a special place at all times, often drawing on a spiritual language to describe their experiences:

[T]here was just something very magical about it [. . .]. It just seemed to have that extraordinary energy there. If I'm honest, it wasn't just about the politics, it was about the women's energy.

(Penni Bestic, 31, camper)

This variety of motivations for involvement, as expressed in the retrospective interviews, was recognized by women at Greenham at the time, and was seen to be a strength of the movement. A positive value was placed on diversity, and Greenham had no party line or set of aims and objectives which were supposed to guide everyone's actions. Whilst Greenham had a deadly serious project of opposition to Cruise, the women who composed Greenham were anything but instrumental in their actions, and placed great importance on affective motivations and actions.

To conclude, in recognition of the limitations of the three main schools within social movements research, this chapter has advanced a fourth mode of analysis, which synthesizes the useful insights of each of the others, whilst attempting to overcome their respective weaknesses. This has involved building macro–micro linkages by focusing on the processes by which Greenham was made by human actors, who were located within specific social and historical circumstances. I have underlined the importance of considering subjective motivation, as is suggested by social psychological approaches, and affective and emotional motivations, in contrast to the rational choice framework of resource mobilization theory. I have also drawn attention to a distinction which should be made by social movement researchers, between processes of mobilization and processes of activation, in order to stress the spontaneity and lack of strategic planning which is often crucial to understanding a movement. Finally, I have traced the beginnings of the formation of collective identity and have looked at the cognitive praxis of a social movement in formation, to highlight the centrality of these to movement creation.

The ethos of Greenham:
theorizing practice and practising theory

That feminism is both theory and practice is something of a truism within feminist circles. But what does this often-stated but rarely explored assertion mean? How does feminism provide theories and practices that challenge patriarchy? How is feminism to be practised, and how is that practice to be theorized? How do theory and practice feed into each other? The following three chapters attempt to grapple with these questions through the lens of Greenham.

As was the case in early women's liberation groups, theory and practice at Greenham existed in a feedback loop, and to separate them out as I do in the following chapters is to impose upon them a fictive distinction. Theories and ideas brought by women to Greenham from other movements and bodies of political thought influenced the way Greenham operated. At the same time the practices of living day-to-day in a women's community in opposition to the nuclear state and of taking action against the base gave rise to theories and ideas about how Greenham should work, which in turn influenced further action. This was the 'cognitive praxis' of Greenham: the intellectual work of a social movement, the creation of the knowledge, ideas and consciousness which constitute both its cognitive identity and one of its most important achievements and legacies (see Eyerman and Jamison 1991). This chapter explores the theory of practice, or ethos, which was thus produced, and Chapters 5 and 6 focus on Greenham's practice itself.

The formation of the ethos

Action at Greenham was guided by a distinctive ethos, or moral and political framework. This ethos was never consciously and explicitly formulated by women at the camp or those involved in the wider Greenham network, and was relatively loose and informal. There were no meetings specifically devoted to writing it down in the form of rules, guidelines or policies.[1] The process of cognitive praxis through which it developed was gradual. It began on the Cardiff to Greenham march, but continued to evolve through the discussions of politics that were embedded in daily life at the camp.[2] The ethos was not spelt out to newcomers, but they would become aware of it as they spent time at Greenham.[3] Indeed, questioning Greenham's ethos demonstrated 'outsider' status at Greenham, and its acceptance was a sign of group membership, of being a 'Greenham woman'.

Greenham's ethos was no less real for being unwritten and implicit. It constituted a powerful moral discourse about the practising of feminism that shaped and constructed life at Greenham, providing continuity as women came and went, and forming part of the core collective identity of Greenham. The ethos was, therefore, both constructing of and constructed through action at Greenham; it was an implicit theory of political action, demonstrating the duality of theory and practice at Greenham.

Each of the women interviewed was asked whether she thought that there was an ethos, or a set of principles or ethics, underlying life at Greenham. All agreed that there was, and all of the principles which I discuss were mentioned by some of the women, though campers and stayers tended to give fuller accounts of Greenham's ethos than did visitors. Many women also pointed out that the ethos was informal, but none the less binding because of this:

> As far as rules were concerned, there was that [vegan food only at Turquoise Gate], and not having men there after dark. There were lots of things, but a lot of them were unsaid and it's just how we lived. We didn't say, we're not going to vote on things, or we won't do this if one person's unhappy about this.
>
> (Penny Gulliver, 22, camper)

> *Sasha:* Do you think that there was a set of ethics or principles at Greenham?
>
> *Penni:* Yes [. . .] that everyone has their own opinion. That was the big ethic. There were the obvious ones, about violence in the camp and about always talking, always trying to talk things through [. . .]. But there were no agreed principles in the way that there have been within the women's movement, the seven demands of the women's liberation movement [. . .]. In a sense, the ethic of Greenham was, there are no rules, although I suppose there was one rule: no men.
>
> (Penni Bestic, 31, camper)

> [. . .] communal living, shared responsibility, anti-authoritarianism, feminist principles. Basically everyone not having to do any more than they wanted to but keeping the place ticking over. Taking some sort of responsibility for your own actions, that was a pretty essential one [. . .]. There were certain things that were acceptable and certain things that weren't acceptable, and you were aware of them whether they were said or not, like for example, we have no leadership. That was said all the time. It wasn't acceptable to go round saying, I am a leader, or she is a leader.
>
> (Sarah Benham, 17, stayer)

The accounts of Greenham's ethos which were given by the women interviewed tended to place emphasis in different areas. This diversity of understandings and interpretations does not mean that the ethos was not an essential part of Greenham's collective identity. Rather it is illustrative of both the informality of its creation and transmission, and of one of the key elements of the ethos that *was* universally recognized: respect of women's differences/individuality. It was wholly consistent with the ethos of Greenham that women had a variety of understandings of it.

The creation of the ethos was influenced primarily by four main strands of political theory and practice: radical feminism, anarchism, non-violence, and ecofeminism. Amongst the women living at Greenham during its first year, which was the period during which the ethos largely developed, there was a history of involvement or familiarity with each of these bodies of thought and traditions of action.[4] In particular, I draw attention to similarities between the ethos of Greenham and the principles of the women's liberation movement (as set out by a group of radical feminists (York *et al.* 1979, reprinted 1991)) and of anarchism. In all, I identify eleven principles which together constituted the ethos of Greenham.

The ethos of Greenham

Women-only, autonomous and pro-woman

The Women's Liberation Movement has to be independent from men. A women's movement has to work out its own independent political strategy. There can be no men in the movement in any way [. . .]. We have been divided for so long, sisterly solidarity is important, especially in relation to men. This means always taking the woman's side, and not being dismissive of each other.

(York *et al.* 1979:310)

The principle that Greenham was women-only was fundamental to the collective identity of the camp, as it had been a basic principle of consciousness-raising groups within the women's liberation movement. As discussed in Chapter 3, this principle was not established until February 1982, and provoked considerable conflict. However, after a short period of time, the opposition to Greenham being women-only was expressed away from the camp, and Greenham operated as a women-only community and a social movement without internal challenge. Men were allowed to visit the camp (with the exception of Green Gate, which was an entirely women-only space), during the hours of daylight, but were always asked to leave before darkness fell.

It was considered important that Greenham was women-only for a number of reasons. First, there were the specific and immediate reasons elaborated in Chapter 3 which had led to the decision to become women-only in the first place, and which were passed down through the 'generations' of Greenham women: in particular, that some of the men who had been living at Greenham had behaved violently to the police and, after the women-only decision, to women; and that they had not pulled their weight within the domestic division of labour. It was generally thought not that men were naturally inclined to commit violence and naturally disinclined to wash up, but that their social conditioning made this likely, and that the social conditioning of women meant that they tended to intervene to calm violence and to clear up the detritus of daily life. So, making and keeping the camp women-only was seen as a way of undermining these dominant forms of gender relations and preventing their performance at Greenham.

Second, the women-only principle came to be regarded as important because it emphasized that action at Greenham was autonomous, directed and performed by women without the influence of men. In the tradition of radical feminism cited above, it was believed that women have to liberate themselves, and that this can only be achieved by women deciding for themselves how to do this. It was also thought to be a significant symbolic demonstration of women's non-compliance with the nuclear policies pursued by governments of men.

Third, the women-only principle was also seen as a pro-woman position, which challenged dominant cultural values which prioritize men's needs over women's, and which hold as illegitimate women's attention to, and pleasure in, each other.

One of the most frequently repeated points made by feminist critics of Greenham was that being women-only does not make a campaign feminist: 'Women are together without men in the Women's Institute, in the launderette too' (Mohin 1983:22); 'My mother is part of a group of women who work for Life and a member of the WI; does that make her or those groups feminist?' (Bishop 1983:32). The answer to Bishop's question has to be no. It is certainly true that the Women's Institute and the Women's Royal Voluntary Service are women's organizations which are not feminist. It is also the case that some of the thousands of women who went to Greenham accepted its women-only 'policy' from within a discursive framework of women's role as social carers (like the WRVS). However, Greenham's women-only 'policy' was very different from that of the WI or the WRVS. At a collective level the decision to become women-only was taken in response to problematic male behaviour, in a context in which feminist arguments about the positive benefits for women of working in an environment without men were expressed and accepted. Greenham was not feminist *because* it was women-only, but became women-only as it was becoming feminist.

Non-violence

It was a principle of Greenham that no violence should be used either in daily life at the camp or in the course of actions, even when faced by violence from police or soldiers. This principle can be seen as having its roots in the commitment to non-violence of Gandhi, and later of the civil rights movement in the United States.

Violence was rejected as a mode of power, not just at the macro-level, between nation states, but also between individuals. Moreover, this commitment was specifically feminist and involved a recognition of the (socially constructed) differences between men and women's relation to violence – the fact that men are far more likely than women to use interpersonal violence, and that women suffer huge amounts of violence at the hands of men. Contrary to critical commentary about Greenham (e.g. Alderson 1983:12), there was a firm belief that men's violence, individual and collective, could be prevented, and that it was not biologically determined. Women were not believed to be 'naturally non-violent' as Alderson suggests. Rather, non-violence was seen as a political principle, to be consciously chosen and actively pursued, which challenged the widespread legitimacy of the use of force and violence in society.

In using the term 'non-violence' to designate this principle I do not wish to invoke the whole panoply of 'principles of non-violence' enumerated by Kirk's discussion of Greenham (1989a,b). Kirk lists these as assertiveness, enjoyment, openness, support and preparation, flexibility of tactics, resistance, personal responsibility, the value of diversity, non-hierarchical organization and decision-making, and communication, co-ordination and continuity. Many of these were features of Greenham's organization, and did not have the status of 'principles'. To subsume them all under the label 'non-violence' stretches the meaning of the term in a way which obfuscates the question of violence.

The implications of the principle of non-violence were the subject of considerable debate at Greenham. In particular, before a new action was done for the first time, such as cutting the fence, there was often lengthy discussion about whether it was likely to provoke violence from police or soldiers, or whether is was in itself a violent act (see Chapter 6 for further explanation). The question of whether non-violence constituted an adequate or appropriate politics for all situations was also much debated. Few women were absolute pacifists, and many firmly supported the armed struggles of revolutionary movements such as the African National Congress, the South West African People's Organization, and the Sandinistas. However, it was none the less universally accepted that action at Greenham should be non-violent.

Anti-hierarchical and collective

We reject hierarchy and the 'star' system. No one person or group can speak for the whole movement.

(York *et al.* 1979:310)

Like the women's liberation movement principle quoted above, Greenham's ethos was that there should be no leaders or hierarchies. In particular, hierarchy based on the length of time women had been at the camp, and the ranking in terms of commitment of those who lived there, and those who stayed or visited was opposed. It was frequently stated that 'every woman is a Greenham woman, no matter how long she has been here'. There was no 'qualifying' time for membership, and even those visiting for the first time were encouraged to contribute to discussions and decision making.

It was believed that all decisions affecting the camp should be taken collectively, openly, and by consensus. This meant that there was a commitment to talking through problems and decisions, often exhaustively. The attempt was made to air all sides of a debate, to allow everyone to speak, and to reach decisions about which everyone was happy. The philosophy of majoritarian democracy, in which minorities are expected to accept the decisions of the majority, was rejected and votes were never taken, even about the most controversial issues and after meetings which had lasted for hours or even days.

The opposition to hierarchies and the principle of collectivity were, however, difficult to put into practice, and Chapter 5 explores the extent to which this was achieved.

Respect for diversity and individuality

The principle of respect for differences between women and for each woman's individuality involved a recognition that women came to Greenham with different experiences, personal circumstances, politics, interests and talents, and that they therefore involved themselves in different ways. Greenham had no party line, and it was expected that women should allow others to express their opinions, ideas and creativity as and when they wished.

Some of the women interviewed described this principle as one of tolerance; others said that at Greenham every woman's contribution and opinions were considered valid. Whatever the precise formulation, a consistent problem arose as a result of its inherent relativism as a moral principle. Conflict occurred when some women called upon Greenham's respect for diversity and individuality to support opinions and behaviour which others found problematic. The principle meant that it was difficult to challenge such opinions and behaviour, and tended to result in the stronger, louder and pushier women getting their way.

The principle was fundamentally one of radical individualism, and was generally conceptualized as being about respect for the choices and action of individuals. Within this framework, individual action tended to be abstracted from its context within the systematic structuring of power along the lines of race, ethnicity, class, or sexuality. However, this way of interpreting action was controversial within Greenham, and many women argued for a less individualist analysis, and a respect for difference which recognized that individuals are differently positioned within social structures. Conflict erupted particularly about money, between women who argued that their needs or desires for money should be respected, and those who responded that their ability to demand that money came depended on their self-confidence, which was the product of white middle class privilege. This and other problems arising from the ethos of respect for difference and diversity are discussed further in Chapter 5.

Personal responsibility and personal autonomy

Small local groups, where women can create trust and solidarity, are the microcosm of the way we want to change society. Each woman must be assumed to take responsibility.

(York *et al.* 1979:310)

Derived from anarchism, the principle of personal responsibility and personal autonomy was vital to Greenham. It was believed that each woman should take personal responsibility both for her own actions and for changing the world, and, as an autonomous individual, that she alone should take all important decisions about her life. The existence of Greenham was premised on the notion that individual women should take it upon themselves to oppose the deployment of Cruise, and should withdraw their consent from military decisions which had been made in their name but to which they had not been party.

This principle is rooted in a belief about the importance of individual agency in the production, reproduction, and transformation of society. Acceptance of personal responsibility and autonomy was seen as a refusal of victimhood, and as a refusal to cede power to the state. It was also linked to the absence of formal rules and regulations to guide behaviour, which were deemed both unnecessary if every woman takes personal responsibility for doing what is appropriate and required, and an infringement of the autonomy of the individual.

At Greenham this principle meant not placing the onus for action on others, and acting on one's beliefs or on seeing what needed to be done. Thus women were expected by each other to act according to their own desires and conscience, accepting that their actions had consequences, and not to wait for leadership. It also meant that when speaking at meetings or to the media as a Greenham woman, there was a principle that each woman was speaking only for herself, and not as a representative for the camp as a whole.

Communality

The flip side to the emphasis on personal responsibility and autonomy at Greenham was an ethic of communality. There was a strong emphasis on sharing. The tasks of daily living, such as cooking, washing-up, collecting wood, repairing vehicles, would be shared, not according to a rota or the strict rotation of roles, and not involving everyone at once, but informally and according to individual wishes. Most of the necessities of life were consumed collectively and individual possessions tended to be kept to a minimum. Communal life was highly valued and involved the exchange of life stories, the retelling of histories of the camp to newcomers, the giving of emotional support, and participation in communal entertainments, such as singing and dancing.

There was, however, constant tension between the individual and the group, the principle of personal responsibility and the principle of communality, which I explore in the next chapter.

Caring for the environment

An ethic which arose gradually through the experience of living outdoors at Greenham, and which was refracted through the discourse of ecofeminism, was that of caring for the local environment. Ecofeminist ideas were brought to Greenham by individual women (particularly American women who had been involved in the Women's Pentagon Action) and in the writings of Mary Daly and Susan Griffin, which were widely read at the camp. Living in the open, on a beautiful piece of common land (at least for those at Green and Orange Gates) made women increasingly aware of the effect of their presence on the ecology of the area. The experience of having to deal directly with the waste products of one's own existence for the first time, without running water, sewage systems, and regular refuse collection, also impressed upon women the importance of environmental issues. Combined with the ethic of personal responsibility, this created an impetus for each woman to attempt to minimize her impact on the environment. Thus the camp generally used biodegradable detergents, exercised care not to damage trees or to leave traces of its presence on the Common, and, in the planning of major actions, considered the implications for the eco-system of the presence of large numbers of women.

Openness to change: flexibility and reflexivity

It was also an ethic of Greenham that each woman as an individual, Greenham as a collectivity, and all actions at Greenham should be open to change, that they should be flexible and reflexive. Decisions, routines, patterns of behaviour, and plans should not be set in stone, but rather should be amenable to reorientation as circumstances changed and as new ideas emerged. Ways of working and behaving should be continually questioned, and modified in the light of such challenges. After actions, for instance, there were often 'de-briefing' meetings, at which the action could be discussed and evaluated, to feed into the planning of future actions. This principle of self- and collective monitoring also encouraged the processes of transformation of identity and consciousness which are discussed in Chapter 8, by valuing personal change, rather than seeing it as a sign of weakness.[5]

Enjoyment and counter-martyrdom: the pleasure principle

Whatever we do we mean to enjoy ourselves while we do it.

(York *et al.* 1979:311)

If I can't dance, it's not my revolution.

(Emma Goldman)

The ninth principle that I have identified as guiding action at Greenham was that it should not involve suffering or martyrdom, and that, as much as possible, it should be enjoyable. Like the other principles this was not consciously formulated at the outset, but arose gradually to become a fundamental part of the Greenham philosophy of action. In the tradition of situationism, it can be seen as a response to the deadly seriousness of the global situation and to the pomposity and earnestness of many in the mixed peace movement. Above all, though, it arose in reaction to the liberal press's portrayal of Greenham women as ordinary housewives and mothers heroically making sacrifices to save the world for future generations, and to the constant stream of visitors arriving at Greenham to thank the women for saving the world on their behalf. Many women wanted, quite deliberately, to overturn the patriarchal model of femininity which constructs self-sacrifice, altruism, and vulnerability as feminine virtues (Hoagland 1989:246). They sought to demonstrate that their involvement with Greenham was anything but self-sacrificial and altruistic. As I argued in the previous chapter, the experience of living at Greenham was, much of the time, great fun.

Humour was an important part of life at Greenham, and often took the form of self-mockery, irony and parody. One of the best examples of this was Gill Booth's song: '*Down at Greenham on a Spree*':

Down at Greenham on a spree,
funded by the KGB,
dirty women squatters in the mud.
Mostly vegetarians,
except when we're devouring men,
foreigners and other kinds of crud.

Mr Andropov provides us with our vodka,
Mr Castro makes sure we're kept in dope.
All the women here are outside agitators,
who can't see that Ronald Reagan brings us hope,
                          brings us hope.

What a bunch of layabouts,
who don't know what it's all about,
how we need deterrence for the best.
Lighting fires and burning toast,
bringing Communism close,
threatening the safety of the West.

In the bushes a cache of guns is waiting,
with sealed copies of Karl Marx in plastic bags,
                          in plastic bags.
All our children live in misery with rats and
                          deprivation.
But what can you expect from queers and hags?

Down at Greenham on a spree,
funded by the KGB,

laughing, singing, dancing in the rain.
Nowhere signs of sacrifice,
making do or being nice,
and most of all we're not accepting pain.

Cos we're trying to be done with games and problems,
with hypocrisy, dishonesty and fear.
So, don't be getting shirty,
Cos it's us that's getting dirty,
And because of us
We'll all be here next year.[6]

Valuing the 'non-rational' – affect, emotion, intuition, spirituality

It was a principle of Greenham that the realm of the 'non-rational', which is traditionally suppressed or excluded from consideration in politics, should be accorded significance as a source of adequate knowledge in decision-making and in daily life.[7] Thus, an integral part of discussions about how life was organized at the camp and of planning actions was attention to the feelings of the women involved. Some women invoked a language of feminist spirituality and magic, whereas for others the 'non-rational' was confined to more material aspects of expressive behaviour. In addition, caring and affectionate relationships, including physicality, between women were valued as a source of strength and pleasure.

This re-valuing of the 'non-rational' was a self-conscious attack on the Western philosophical dualisms of reason/emotion, mind/body, male/female, which, as many feminist philosophers have pointed out (e.g. Griffin 1978, 1989; Lloyd 1984), systematically devalue the side of the dualism which is constructed as female. Most women at Greenham were not implying women are *naturally* more emotional, intuitive, or closer to nature than men, but were pointing out that the 'non-rational' was an important realm of human experience, and that it should be admitted as a resource in political action. Here again Greenham was drew on ecofeminist ideas. Some women were also influenced by feminist/matriarchal spirituality, and carried out rituals at Greenham.[8] Other women, however, rejected this interest in spirituality and there was much ridiculing of 'cosmic' practices and ideas.

The inseparability of means and ends

It is plain that the goal of the revolution today must be the liberation of daily life. Any revolution that fails to achieve this goal is counter-revolution. Above all, it is *we* who have to be liberated, *our* daily lives, with all their moments, hours and days, and not universals like 'History' and 'Society' [. . .]. There can be no separation of the revolutionary process from the revolutionary goal.

(Bookchin 1971:44–5)

No revolution can ever succeed as a factor of liberation unless the MEANS used to further it be identical in spirit and tendency with the PURPOSES to be achieved.

(Goldman 1924, in Woodcock 1977: 161)

The summative principle operating at Greenham was one which stated the inseparability of means and ends.[9] Derived from the anarchist/situationist tradition, in which the re-invention of everyday life is considered a revolutionary act (Erlich n.d.), it held that the route to social change is as important as the desired goal, not just because the means determine the end, but also because the present matters in and of itself. Thus process was valued, and unlike in traditional left-wing politics, personal change, non-oppressive organizational structures and, above all, women's liberation were not to be deferred until 'after the revolution'. New tools – new ways of working – were believed to be required for the project of dismantling patriarchy and building a society free from domination and violence. The notion of the inseparability of means and ends was in direct opposition to the hegemonic military discourse of the period of the new Cold War. As discussed in Chapter 2, this held that peace in Europe could only be guaranteed by the acquisition of a new generation of nuclear weapons and preparation for war; in other words, the means (an arms race, with consequences for public expenditure, and the risk of accident) justifies the ends (maintenance of the geopolitical status quo).

These eleven principles constituted an ethos which bound together, across time and space, the thousands of women who were part of Greenham. Loose enough to be stretched almost to breaking point on occasions, and manifesting a number of internal tensions, it was none the less deeply embedded in the collective identity of Greenham and shaped the form taken both by its daily internal life and by its outward-facing actions. It is to these that I now turn.

⑤

The internal mode of action

The political practice of Greenham can be thought of as composed of two faces, an internal and an external one, and as directed at two primary goals. The internal mode of action is 'the way individuals act together to constitute a collectivity' (Offe 1987:70) and the external mode of action, is 'the way [social movements] confront the outside world and their political opponents' (Offe 1987:70).[1] There were two main goals implicit in women's action at Greenham; first, to effectively challenge nuclear militarism (Cruise missiles in particular) and patriarchal social relations, and second, the essential prerequisite of the first, for Greenham to re-create itself. Both modes of action at Greenham contributed to these two goals. The practices of daily life underpinned the community of the camp *and* provided a challenge to patriarchal ways of living and forms of political organization. At the same time, Greenham's outward-directed actions caused disruption and trouble for the forces they opposed and served to renew the commitment and energy of the women involved and to draw new women to the camp.[2]

   This chapter focuses on the internal mode of action, whilst Chapter 6 is concerned with the external mode. However, this is more a heuristic device than a real distinction; the two faces of action were actually deeply entwined, in the way that public and private spheres of social life are now recognized by feminists to be (e.g. Pateman 1989). Greenham's confrontation of the outside world depended on the way that women worked together to constitute a strong collectivity, and the confrontation with the outside world affected how women worked together and the form of daily life. Moreover, the living and working together of women at the camp was not a 'private', internal matter; it took place in public space, was open to any woman to join, and, to a large extent, to anyone to view. This said, distinguishing between internal and external action is a useful tool with which to organize the discussion of the practice of politics at Greenham.

Throughout this chapter I place particular emphasis on the ways in which a collective identity was forged in the face of significant differences between the women who constituted Greenham. Tension, debate, and conflict are recurrent features of social movements, and unity and solidarity within them are fragile constructions. Greenham was no exception to this, and conflict arose around a number of issues, both internal to the organization of Greenham and relating to broader social divisions. Most of these are familiar as arenas of conflict within the women's movement, in other social movements, and in collective living situations: money and the control of resources, hierarchy, class, and race. Conflict was part of the on-going life of Greenham, and without downplaying its significance, particularly to women who felt personally attacked, excluded, or ignored, it is important to recognize that conflict can be constructive and can result in positive change.[3]

Organizational structure

To write about the organizational structure of Greenham is something of a contradiction in terms. In comparison with conventional forms of political action, and even in comparison with other social movements, Greenham was 'structureless'. There were no institutionalized procedures, no formal decision making processes, no executive committees, no membership lists, no officers, no annual general meetings, no head office. But having no *formal* structures does not mean that there were no identifiable patterns in the organization of social life at Greenham or in the workings of the wider Greenham network. Life and action at Greenham and within the network *were* organized in particular ways in a regular enough manner to be considered to be structured.[4] None the less, the organizational structure of Greenham was extremely supple and dynamic.

In order to understand the social organization of Greenham it is important to appreciate that Greenham was a network of individuals and groups throughout Britain and beyond, which existed without a tangible physical location, as well as being a women's peace camp, which occupied a physical site outside the airbase at Greenham Common. After an initial consideration of the structure of the Greenham network and its relationship to the camp, the main body of the discussion concerns the internal mode of action of the camp.

The structure of the Greenham network

Gerlach and Hine's (1970) classic description of the structure of social movements as 'segmentary, polycephalous and reticulate' captures well the organizational features of the Greenham network. Those involved frequently depicted the Greenham network as a spider's web: a non-hierarchical, intricate pattern of individuals and groups, joined together by almost invisible yet strong connecting threads.[5]

The network was composed of dozens of local groups (one or more in almost every town and city in England, Wales, and Scotland). The groups were completely autonomous and were not arranged hierarchically ('segmentary'). Each group had connections back to the camp, which was at the hub of the network; those connections were sustained by frequent visits of women from local groups to the camp, by the newsletters produced by women at the camp and sent to contacts around the country to be photocopied and passed on, and, after the arrival of Cruise, by an elaborate 'telephone tree' (see Chapter 7). The camp acted as a clearing house for information within the network.[6] Although there was no information officer, and only very occasionally even a noticeboard (any large piece of wood invariably ending up on the fire before long!), some women at Greenham took it upon themselves to act as conduits for news.

> I saw Greenham as being a focal point of information, and I used to spend quite a lot of time talking to people who'd come there, trying to keep up with what was happening in other places so that people could know what was going on. At that stage it was very much a centre of what was happening, and people were coming down for weekends, and I felt that if I was a more permanent person there, one of the things I could do was talk about what other people were doing and different actions that people were doing, so that it would be passed around.
>
> (Katrina Allen, 31, camper)

The network had no overall control centre, and ideas for actions were generated both at the camp, in local groups, and at regional meetings of local groups (it was 'polycephalous'). Over time the connections between local groups became stronger, information was increasingly communicated between groups by telephone and by newsletter, and did not necessarily pass through the camp. Thus there were web-like connections between local groups themselves, and between local groups and the camp ('reticulate'). Above all the network was sustained by personal relationships between women, and the pleasure that women took in each other's company; friendships existed between women who lived at the camp and women in local groups, and between women involved in different local groups, which facilitated information exchange and a sense of collective identity.

Like the network as a whole, local groups tended not to have a formal membership or to demand fees. Local groups varied in size, from about six (at the beginning in Northampton) to over several hundred (in Manchester in 1983), with many towns and cities sustaining groups of between 30 and 50 active members during 1983–4 (e.g. Nottingham, Merseyside, Cardiff, Derby). Some of the larger groups decided to divide into smaller neighbourhood groups when they got too big for discussions and decision-making to involve everyone, and there were groups in most London boroughs.[7]

There was no single model followed by the local groups. Some called themselves 'Greenham Support Groups' and focused particularly on raising money and providing resources for the camp, arranging visits to Greenham and publicizing Greenham in their locality. Other groups were 'Women for Peace' groups and were less Greenham orientated in their actions.[8] In general, all the local groups tended to focus less on the camp over time, and instead developed their own particular interests. South London Women for Peace, for instance, developed connections with women's groups in Eritrea, whilst Liverpool Women for Peace focused on the nuclear plant at Capenhurst, and the Portsmouth group took to the sea in boats to protest against naval nuclear militarism.

The local groups generally had close connections with other networks of activists in their localities. Many of the groups held their meetings in women's centres and advertised themselves in women's newsletters, and usually included members who were involved with the local women's refuge, rape crisis or lesbian lines. Other groups, such as Merseyside Women for Peace, had close connections with the mixed peace movement, and would use the local CND group's office and resources. The larger groups that did not meet in a women's centre tended to hire church halls or community centres for meetings, whereas the smaller groups would meet in individual women's homes, on an informal system of rotation.

The ethos of the local groups which comprised the Greenham network was very much that of Greenham as a whole, as I have described it already. The groups were always women-only and, despite any connections they may have had with other organizations, were autonomous. They had no leaders and were self-consciously anti-hierarchical; if one woman facilitated a meeting, at the next meeting someone else would take that role. The atmosphere of meetings was informal and everyone was encouraged to participate, usually by adopting a pro-cedure common in consciousness-raising groups where each woman was given the floor in turn. There was a strong emphasis on group bonding and the emotional and affective aspects of the collectivity, and the articulating of emotions was encouraged. Conflict, however, was not entirely absent, and often centred around the political direction of the group. This was particularly the case as the women who had been involved longest became more feminist and global in consciousness, and began to turn their attention towards issues other than nuclear weapons in Britain.

There were also tensions between women who lived at the camp and those who were involved in the wider network. Despite the ethos of Greenham, which valued every woman's contribution and deplored hierarchies between women on the basis of the level of their involvement, several of the women interviewed stated that they believed that this ideal was not always met in practice. Sarah Benham, who became a stayer after having lived at the peace camp at Faslane, recalled attending a meeting about the women's peace movement at which women from Greenham and from other peace camps were present:

> I just remember Greenham women looking a certain way, having very much a Greenham look about them, and acting in a self-important way, and talking about 'Camp' [. . .], and I was thinking, there are Rosyth and Faslane, these are both camps, but we don't talk about them as 'Camp'

[. . .]. There was a real arrogance: we are where the women's peace movement is at, and that was never really challenged.

(Sarah Benham, 17, stayer)

Visitors tended to be much less critical of the women who lived at Greenham than
stayers, and all of the visitors interviewed suggested that their experience of feeling
'outsiders' was inevitable, given that they were not partaking in the daily life of the
community. Those who spent time staying at Greenham were more inclined to blame
the insularity of the campers, and their lack of real commitment to challenging insider/
outsider hierarchies. However, many women who lived at the camp were aware of the
existence of these, and there was considerable debate both about how to make all
women feel welcomed and involved, and about the extent to which Greenham should
be the focus for women's peace actions (discussed further in Chapter 7).

The structure of the camp

The women's peace camp at Greenham was an elective, co-resident yet fluid and
ever-changing community.[9] Whilst the symbolic community of Greenham
stretched far beyond the camp, encompassing thousands of women in the Greenham network, the camp had a materiality as a community based in the spatial
proximity of its members.[10] Moreover, the fact that women at the camp made
their daily lives together, rather than just coming together for meetings or to do
actions, was fundamental both to the challenge that Greenham posed to the forces
against which it was ranged and to the transformations of consciousness and
identity which involvement produced (see Chapter 8).

In order to understand the organizational structure of the camp it is necessary
to have a picture of the geography of the air base (see map). The base had a
circumference of 9 miles, with a total of eight gates (plus a pedestrian gate) along the
perimeter, and a number of gaps, which were sections of fence which could be rolled
back to allow vehicular access. At the time of the first major gathering at the camp –
the Equinox Festival on March 21 1982 (in which men were still involved) – some of
the gates were given names: New Age Gate, Forgotten Gate, Religious Gate, Artists'
Gate, Music Gate. The idea behind this was to encourage the involvement of
different sectors of the 'alternative scene', by identifying particular places for them
to gather at the festival.[11] However, the Equinox Festival had not been popular with
many of the women at the camp, who focused their energies on the women-only
blockade the next day, and before long the gates were renamed using the colours of
the rainbow: Main Gate (Yellow), Green, (Turquoise), Blue, Indigo, Violet, Red,
Orange. It was these names which stuck, though very quickly they came to refer not
to the gate itself but to the camp at that gate and even the Ministry of Defence police
adopted the names. When new camps were established at places where there had
been no gate in 1982, they were named using this 'colour scheme'. Woad Gate was
the name chosen for the camp outside the new gate positioned between the old
Indigo Gate and Violet Gate when, in 1985, the layout of the gates on the north side

of the base was altered to allow easier access for the Cruise missile convoy. Emerald Gate was the camp set up in 1984 between Green and Turquoise; although there was no gate at this place in the woods, it offered a good view of the missile silos and was important for monitoring activities within the base.

For the first 16 months in the life of Greenham there was just one camp – outside the Main Gate, which was the only gate in daily use. The camp varied in size during this period from a low of about five women to over fifty, with numbers swelling into the hundreds during the March blockade in 1982 and into the thousands during the weekend of the 'Embrace the Base'/'Close the Base' action (December 12–13) in 1982. The month that followed the huge success of that weekend saw an enormous amount of media coverage of Greenham, particularly after the silos action on 1 January 1983, in which women climbed into the base and danced on the missile silos. In the wake of these two actions and all the related reportage, large numbers of visitors and a constant influx of journalists made life at Main Gate hectic and often tense for the women living there. The number of campers was steadily increasing, and although women had started building benders and pitching tents in the clearing away from the area immediately in front of the gate, the land was becoming crowded.

So on 20 January 1983, a small group of women moved themselves, their possessions, and some basic cooking equipment to the woods near Green Gate to set up a new camp. Women who were involved in the setting up of Green Gate explained their motivation in terms of the problems of living at Main Gate. Main Gate was becoming too crowded and was too much in the public eye, and they wanted to live somewhere quieter, without the constant intrusion of male visitors and the press. The physical environment at Green Gate was much more pleasant; the camp was in the woods, about two hundred yards from the fence, and was a quarter of a mile up a quiet country lane from the busy A339. From its establishment, Green Gate was entirely women-only. Men were not accepted as visitors, and were turned away first by notices by the path leading to the camp from the lane and, if they persisted, by women from the camp.

In July 1983, during a huge influx of women for the week of the July blockades, two more new camps were set up – at Blue Gate and Orange Gate. Women had camped at both these places during periods of large actions on a number of previous occasions, but it was not until this point that a conscious decision was taken by women committed to living at Greenham to have camps there. The final phase of expansion was in December 1983, shortly after the arrival of the first missiles and during a month in which there were day-long demonstrations of over 50,000 women and hundreds of women staying; camps were set up at Violet Gate (7 December 1983), Red Gate (12 December 1983), Turquoise Gate (18 December 1993), and Indigo Gate (31 December 1983). By this time, there were two main reasons for setting up new camps. First, there was the issue of size. There were so many women now living at Greenham that there was not the physical space for everyone at the existing gates, and the existing gates had become so large that daily life was made more difficult – not everyone was able to sit around the fire, it was impossible to cook for everyone over one fire, and the anonymity of large numbers was tiring and stressful. Second, following the arrival of Cruise, many women believed that it was important that there was a presence of women protesting outside every gate. Activity within the base had heightened enormously, and more of the gates were being routinely used by civilian and military personnel. Having camps right around the base extended the impact of the protest against Cruise, and also enabled women to monitor the operations of the base, in anticipation of military exercises.

However, once camps had been set up at all the gates, this structure was not set in stone; as circumstances changed, so the structure changed. Although there remained camps at Yellow Gate and Blue Gate until the base was closed, the other camps came and went over time. Orange Gate and Green Gate existed for longer than Violet and Indigo/Woad, and Turquoise, Red, and Emerald Gates had the shortest existence. From mid-1984 onwards, these six gates would be set up, and closed down, as and when there were women at Greenham who wished to spend time there. The geographical location of each of the gates and their relative significance to the operations of the base influenced the survival of some camps and the closure of others. Yellow Gate and Blue Gate were, for a long time, the two most important entrances and exits to the base, and were located closest to main roads. This meant both that women had easier access to these gates from Newbury, and that more passers-by would see camps at these gates. The north side gates (Red, Violet, and Indigo/Woad), in contrast, were passed only by a narrow road, and had very little land on which to camp. This meant that they were less comfortable gates at which to live; women were closer to the fence and to the soldiers, and hence to harassment, and had less privacy. Green Gate occupied by far the most tranquil and beautiful location, but when numbers dwindled at Blue Gate, women at Green would tend to feel it more important to keep a presence there, and so would move to Blue. The camp at Orange Gate was also far enough away from the fence for women to be afforded some respite from the attentions of the soldiers, but by 1986 women from Orange Gate moved to Yellow and Blue in order to keep them open.

The organization of Greenham into a series of different gates had two main positive outcomes, which fed into the reproduction of the camp. First, it made it possible for women at the camp to live in small groups, which made daily life easier and affective bonds stronger. Second, existence of different gates was one of the most important ways in which the many differences between women at Greenham were managed, so that the heterogeneous mixture of women involved were able to live together reasonably harmoniously. These two consequences are worth considering in some detail.

Gates as a small group structure

As the camp at Main Gate grew in size during 1982, pressure increased on the women living there, and the ethos of collective living was put under strain. As new women arrived it became difficult to maintain a sense of equal and shared involvement in both the chores of daily life and in decision making. The close bonds of friendship and shared experience between women who had lived together through intense periods of activism, which provided much of the cement holding the camp together, were diluted as the camp became larger. The setting up of new camps at other gates facilitated a renewal of small group bonding, at least until they too grew substantially in size.

Rowan Gwedhen explained why she took part in establishing a camp at Red Gate at the end of 1983:

> I wanted to leave the Main Gate. I couldn't cope there any more. It had got too big [. . .]. [W]hen I moved there, it [. . .] was like a little women's land. It got bigger and bigger. It got so big that you didn't like all the people. And it got to the point where we had bender city over one side, quote 'long term' [. . .]. So me and Mary went and set up Red Gate [. . .]. For me it was about getting away from Yellow Gate. It was about, it was actually about creating a nice place again and getting back to the thing about women's land and community [. . .]. And it was all about making a nice environment and eating good food. I don't mean being vegan, I mean eating well [. . .]. And we made these lovely benders, and we had a guest bender. And I actually made this big fitted kitchen. There a bit of old concrete at Red Gate, and we hung polythene from the trees. I think we actually *bought* wood. And I made this wonderful kitchen with worktops and shelves and everything [. . .]. Basically I think me and Mary were in a fucking mess. I didn't want to leave camp. I wanted to stay at camp. By then there'd been actions and prisons and evictions, and 20,000 people living in a goldfish bowl at Yellow Gate.
>
> (Rowan Gwedhen, 24, camper)

Many women also reported that there was an inverse relationship between the size of the group and the extent of communality in the organization of domestic labour at Greenham:

> Smaller camps were nicer. And in some ways it was easier to work in the smaller group, to get things like the shopping and the cooking done. You did actually end up working better together, whereas in a big camp, it was just come and help yourself to things. It was more difficult to get things done.
>
> (Carola Addington, 29, camper)

Gates and the management of difference

There was never a conscious policy to set up camps around the base in order that women could live in groups of women with whom they shared some significant characteristics. Rather, this was an unintended consequence of the increased number of gates in 1983. The establishment of Green Gate, as I have already explained, occurred in order to reduce the pressure on women who had been living at Main

Gate – on both those who left, and to some extent those who remained. But it was a certain type of woman who moved to Green Gate in its early days, and this set a precedent for how Green Gate was to develop. Green Gate tended in future to attract women who shared some of the preferences and characteristics, such as a desire to be in a completely women-only space and the lesbian feminist politics, of many of those who were already there. A similar spiralling effect occurred at the other gates, and very quickly the gates developed quite distinctive characteristics. There was, however, only one gate which was explicitly set up on the basis of difference, where everyone choosing to live there was expected to conform; Turquoise was deliberately set up by vegan women from Blue Gate, and was designated a vegan zone.

A favourite pastime at Greenham, and one of the topics discussed spontaneously by almost every women interviewed (including all the campers and stayers) was the construction of typologies of the characteristics of the different gates and of the women who lived there. This was always 'tongue in cheek', but was revealing, none the less, about how differences of class, age, eating habits and, above all, sexuality were played out at Greenham.

Bridget Evans, a Blue Gater, explained:

> There was an image to the different gates, and I think that women often went to where they felt they would be most comfortable. So once Blue Gate had a reputation for being like the Scallies' Gate and the, you know, Piss Artists' Gate and the Frivolous Gate, and it was also the Young Gate and the Lesbian Gate, the Working Class Gate, then that in turn tended to attract more women. And we were the Tough Gate. We were on the front line [. . .]. We were right on the side of the road, we were right beside quite a busy gate, in terms of things that went in and out of the base, and we were right by the houses as well.
>
> (Bridget Evans, 23, camper)

Another Blue Gate woman, Jinny List, affectionately contrasted her own gate with the others:

> *Jinny:* There were a few women who moved around and never really stayed anywhere but seemed to fit in everywhere, but they were few and far between. I did spend one night at Yellow Gate by accident [. . .] and it was very different. Very, very different.
>
> *Sasha:* How would you characterize it?
>
> *Jinny:* I probably would say, more grown up. More serious. Blue Gate had a hell of a lot of fun. We had a passion bender in the woods and stuff.
>
> *Sasha:* And what went on there? [laughs]
>
> *Jinny:* Lots of passion – occasionally, and not for a very long time. It got ripped down by the bailiffs and we didn't rebuild it. And we had a television made out of a cardboard box, with a piece of wire for an aerial, you know [laughs]. There was an element of this is a game and we are all

going to play this game and we're going to enjoy it. And we were quite near the pub, and there was quite a lot of drinking, definitely. And that attracted me too. I knew that if I turned up roaring drunk, or got roaring drunk, or whatever, nobody would say anything. It was fairly normal. And I knew that there were women at Green Gate who didn't drink. I don't know who they were, but I'd heard this rumour. And I knew I wouldn't be happy there. And there was this thing that Green Gate was dead, dead cosmic, you know. And I didn't get to know until much later women who lived there, and I think that's probably incorrect [. . .]. Orange Gate was religious, which initially it may have been. The Quakers used to go to Orange Gate. That put us off. Yellow Gate was dead serious, and you'd be in trouble if you did anything naughty. There was a real 'them' - Yellow Gate.

(Jinny List, 20, camper)

Carmel Cadden painted a picture of the particularities of Violet Gate by comparing it with Blue, which resonates with the descriptions given by Bridget and Jinny:

Violet·Gate, because we sat in the mud on a slope by the side of the road, had no illusions of grandeur. In fact, we prided ourselves on being matter of fact. Each gate got its own personality. Like Blue Gate, Blue Gate were terribly disorganized, there were a lot of young anarchists and punks. They always used to have a lot of dogs around and they were all into having a lot of booze and dope. Not all the time [. . .]. Violet got a reputation for being obsessed with eating and basically having a good standard of living. One of the women had a badge saying we were the right-off gate because we were so ideologically unsound. Because we allowed everything. Also the other thing about Blue Gate was that it was quite seriously vegan, and Green Gate was quite mystical, cosmic. And so Violet Gate kept up this image of being interested in eating and having a good time [. . .]. We had such a mixture of women, we had extreme lesbian separatists, who would freeze the moment any bloke came anywhere near – we all did a bit really – and we'd have all the way through to heterosexuals, like me, [. . .] who'd found at least one of them bearable. But that never seemed to get in the way of our personal friendships.

(Carmel Cadden, 30, camper)

These comments show, however much laced with humour, that there were firm perceptions that the gates were composed of quite distinctive groups. Blue was young, lesbian, anarchic, working class, and women there drank and smoked dope. Green was 'cosmic'. Violet was a mixed gate of heterosexual women and lesbians, but women there shared an interest in eating well. Orange Gate was thought to be composed of older, more middle class women, many of whom stayed for fairly short periods of time, and who had been involved in earlier peace movements. Yellow Gate was the home of the 'old-timers', and was seen as a centre of power. In fact, it was not actually the case that all the lesbians, or all the young women, or all the working class women at Greenham lived at Blue Gate, nor that all the women at Green Gate were interested in feminist spirituality. There were women living at each of the gates, often many women, who did not fit the characterizations quoted above.

Whilst there was some accuracy in these generalizations, what is particularly significant about the extracts above is that they demonstrate the widespread existence of a discourse at Greenham which constructed the gates as different from each other in important respects. In the case of Blue Gate, for example, this meant that working class women living there felt an enhanced sense of identity and community with the women around them, and were able to distance themselves from some of the aspects of Greenham which they found oppressively middle class. Similarly, many women, aware that Greenham was often thought of as 'spiritual' and 'earth-motherly', and rejecting that aspect of Greenham, were able to construct the 'cosmic' as other, by locating it at Green Gate. There were two women, both visitors, who in the course of their interviews expressed disapproval of the behaviour and high visibility of lesbians at Greenham, and sought to disassociate themselves from the 'militant feminism' (which is frequently a euphemism for lesbianism) of some of the women. They were, in part, able to do this by pinpointing gates which they did not visit as the problem, and thus separating themselves from those features of Greenham which they disliked.

For instance:

We [her women's peace group] always went to Orange Gate. We remained attached to Orange Gate [. . .]. It was one of the bigger camps, and there was land there. It just got established, that's all. Just like the Essex people always went to Red, you know [. . .]. It got very divisive, and Blue Gate became very much, . . . there was just a group of feminists, very, very militant, who were, you know, there were one or two people who were very disturbed, which made it a very difficult place to be [. . .]. Anything like that is bound to attract people who are going to use it psychologically, you know, the situation, to work out their own problems. So there were people there who did that. But that's just a slice of life. Some people made an issue of it. I don't because I think it's wrong.

(Ann Lukes, 52, visitor)

Our early march [from Cardiff to Greenham] was a homogeneous crew with definite clear knowledge of where we were walking to and what for, but I think there was just a lot of different opinions at Greenham. That was its interest, in a way – that each camp had perhaps different ideas about things [. . .]. Red Gate was always a very welcoming gate, and Orange Gate was always a comfortable gate. Blue Gate was always full of young people, who I felt uncomfortable with [. . .]. I felt when the strident feminists were there, that they blocked out the others [. . .]. That's why I never went to Green Gate.

(Margery Lewis, 64, visitor)

Conflict over power and resources which existed at Greenham was often formulated in terms of the disproportionate power and influence of Yellow Gate. Jinny List, for instance, saw Yellow Gate as 'more grown up', 'more serious', 'the grown-ups with money', and Carmel Cadden described it as 'quite remote', 'raised up from an ordinary level'. As the first camp at Greenham, outside the main entrance to the base, Main Gate was the home of many of the women who had been at the camp longest. The post was delivered to Main Gate, the standpipe for water was at Main Gate, and Main Gate was the first, and often only, port of call for journalists and visitors. This meant that women from the other gates had to visit Main Gate to collect water each day, and that resources, in the form of donations of money, food and clothing, tended to accrue there. So whilst women at other gates were always aware of what went on at Main Gate, some of the Main Gate women of long standing never visited the other gates, and were perceived as behaving as if Main Gate was still the entirety of Greenham. The symbolic changing of the name of the gate from Main Gate to Yellow Gate took place at the end of 1983, in an attempt to de-centre Yellow Gate within the camp as a whole. The name change was enthusiastically embraced by women from the other gates, and most of the women at Yellow Gate attempted to alter their vocabulary. But a handful of women resisted, either deliberately, or because they did not consider the issue important.

So, on the one hand, the establishment of a number of gates served to create physical and discursive space for the management of differences between women at Greenham, and in so doing strengthened the camp. On the other hand, it also opened up lines of fracture within the camp, above all between Yellow Gate and the rest of the camp. This will be seen later in the chapter when I discuss conflicts which arose over the use of money and the issue of hierarchy.

The reproduction of daily life

As a community, Greenham's continuation depended on the ongoing re-creation not just of collective identity, but also of its material existence. However, the routines of domestic life and the ways in which resources were organized were more than just the means to this end; they constituted another plane of the political project of Greenham.

Domestic labour

Whilst many of the features of the organization of domestic life at Greenham were constrained by circumstance, above all by being outdoors, women at Greenham sought to transform the processes and practices of women's traditional sphere of work. Outside the physical confines of a house, and, most importantly, outside the normative expectations of patriarchal relations, women experimented with alternative ways of organizing the reproduction of daily life.

The first way in which the practice of domestic labour at Greenham challenged the conventions of late twentieth century Western societies was in its organization at the collective level; most of the basic tasks of daily survival were carried out by individuals on behalf of a non-kin group. The communal organization of domestic labour was not exclusive to Greenham, having been advocated by feminists since Charlotte Perkins Gilman (1903) and practised by socialist, feminist and anarchist communes and collective houses quite extensively since the Second World War. However, the second significant feature was that these chores were performed by particular individuals according to their choice, not determined by a rota, as is the normal practice in communal living arrangements. This meant that women were able to work when they wanted to, at the tasks at which they wanted to work, rather than either having to do everything or to do a particular job at a particular time not of their choosing.

Third, domestic labour was not accorded any more importance than other contributions to the life of the camp (such as singing or having ideas for actions), and hence was only given attention and time sufficient for its conduct to the most basic level. In other words, women at Greenham spent as little time as possible on those domestic tasks which require constant repetition and which have little satisfaction attached to their achievement.

In part this was sensible adaptation to the environment at the camp. To attempt to replicate standards of cleanliness and tidiness considered normal in houses would have been impossible. The leaves and dust could never all be swept away, the ground could not be prevented from turning to mud when it rained, there could never be storage places for all the crockery and food. When there could be no permanent shelters, standards had to be different. But applying different standards to domestic labour was also a political action. Under patriarchal domestic relations, housework has low status as an occupation, but is often fetishized by women, particularly those without access to the world of paid employment, and carried out to a standard that is much higher than the requirements of hygiene and comfort require.[12] In these circumstances, the further downgrading of the status of housework (if it were possible to downgrade it further) could be regarded as an attack on the women who perform it. However, in a women-only community, to re-position in importance women's traditional labour is an attempt to reconstruct gender identities, and is to make 'gender trouble' (this phrase is coined by Butler (1990)). It should also be pointed out that if Greenham had really been as committed to an essentialist, maternalist project, which reinscribed patriarchal gender relations and identities, as has been suggested by some feminists (for example, Onlywomen Press 1983), then domestic work, as women's traditional sphere, should have been accorded far more importance than it was. Instead, there was an attempt to minimize the investment of time and energy in routine chores, in order to free women to engage in more enjoyable and politically significant activities.

The absence of running water, electricity or gas at Greenham returned many of the routine tasks of the reproduction of life to those of a pre-industrial age. Water had to be fetched (albeit in plastic containers, and by car or van), for those not at Yellow Gate, wood gathered from the woods and common, and then chopped and stored, fires had to be laid and tended throughout the day, washing–up had to be done in bowls with water boiled over the fire, and shitpits had to be dug and covered. Other tasks were those of twentieth century Western life writ large: shopping in Newbury for between four and fifty women, to cater for vegans and lacto–vegetarians and then cooking for the same number, but over an open fire. These jobs would be done by whoever chose to do them, with women tending to do those at which they were particularly skilled, or which they enjoyed. If someone hated cooking, it was unlikely she would ever raise a knife to a carrot; if she found digging two foot deep holes in the ground too strenuous, she would not take charge of the shitpits. Those jobs requiring skills which women are not traditionally encouraged to acquire – chopping wood and car mechanics, for instance – tended to be accorded the most status, but, as part of the ethos of openness to change, skill-sharing by those who had such skills and the learning of new skills by those who did not, was common practice. Women who had not done a particular task before at Greenham would tend to join in when it was being performed by an 'old-timer', and would learn the ropes; this was particularly the case with tasks such as cooking, which required the adaptation of old skills to new circumstances.

Underlying this informal system of domestic labour at Greenham were several of the principles discussed earlier in the chapter. Every woman was expected to take personal responsibility for the collective reproduction of life at Greenham, to see what needed to be done, and to do it. In the spirit of non-hierarchy, there was no centralized allocation of duties. However, differences in interest, aptitude, experience, and temperament were respected, and women's decisions not to do particular work were rarely challenged. The other side of the principle of personal responsibility was that women were expected to take responsibility for *not* doing work as much as for doing it, to make sure that they did not become 'martyrs to the washing-up'. In other words, women were expected to exercise agency in the realm of domestic labour, whether this meant undertaking work or refusing it. For some women, particularly older women who were mothers and/or wives, realizing that they could make a choice about whether or not to do such work was a transformative experience. Helen John, for instance, who had been a housewife prior to her involvement with Greenham, spoke of how she had to make a conscious decision not to take on too much of the domestic work, and then found the low priority given to domestic work at Greenham liberating:

> For all the time I was there, I stopped having, you know, a council house mentality. I gave that up because a lot of the other women who were in my age bracket, they cracked up because the younger women – and the younger men who were there initially – I mean, these women were good housewives, you know, would wash all the dishes and go to bed at night and be horrified when they woke up in the morning and found them all covered with mud and filthy and everything'd been used and nobody'd washed them. And I very quickly decided I hadn't come there to mother people, that if they wanted to get up and have dirty cups and saucers, that was great, that was

their decision. It wasn't my responsibility. So it freed me from a lot of that. And you know, it's like cutting a big knot around your neck. I was away from that.

(Helen John, 34, camper)

In a similar vein, Leah Thalmann described how she stopped taking on too great a responsibility for domestic work:

Sasha: Do you remember whether you felt happy about the way work was done and chores were divided?

Leah: I found it rather strange at first. I can remember an experience, before I was living but when I came to stay early on at Yellow, and there was a group of women eating somewhere down by the road, and they had lots of dirty pots and cups lying on the ground. I went over to them and said, 'would you like me to wash up?'. They looked at me amazed: 'you don't have to do that sort of thing'. I crept away, feeling really awful [. . .]. And when I went to Yellow, I used to do the washing-up. It was incredibly squalid. I used to do mounds of washing-up in all this mud. All the while I was doing it, more women came and put dirty dishes down, and cups and things, and plates full of food, and there were cakes being trodden into the mud. I thought, this is terrible. I've got to do this washing-up, why does she have to come and just dump? It was endless. This seemed to be the sort of chore I could do – I felt capable of doing this particular chore. I'd wash up endlessly. I don't think it was until I went to live at Green Gate that I realized that you didn't have to be like that. I still often did the washing-up, but I realized that you didn't have to, and that I was choosing to. If I wanted to wash-up eighty mugs – and if you remember we had that mug tree with eighty mugs on it – then I was choosing to do it. I think I realized one night when I was lying in my tent and I knew that the shit-pit was virtually overflowing, and I thought, god, somebody has got to build a shit-pit, nobody's going to do it, and we're not going to have a shit-pit. Then at dawn I woke up and I heard this noise and it was women digging a shit-pit. It didn't have to be me. All the chores still get done, and you can choose what you want to do, and that is quite a revelation. That was really good. I still did the washing-up quite a lot, but I chose to do it. I didn't have this resentment about it. That was amazing.

(Leah Thalmann, 53, camper)

The women interviewed in the research were overwhelmingly of the opinion that the organization of domestic labour at Greenham was successful. Many commented that it worked much better at Greenham than in communal houses in which they had lived, before or since. This was generally explained in terms of the fact that Greenham was outdoors and therefore 'different', removed from many of the pressures associated with traditional expectations of daily life. It was considered inevitable that the anarchy of the system led to some women doing more domestic work than others, with a few women doing very little. The value placed on personal responsibility and individual autonomy was such that these problems were seen to be outweighed by the benefits of the flexibility and freedom inherent in the system.

> *Sasha:* Chores, did you feel that they got done fairly evenly?
> *Penny:* No, but they got done. Blue Gate didn't seem to worry about that kind of stuff so much. Every so often we'd have a clean-up. But when we were being evicted everyday, the bailiffs would just do it for us. We just used to leave the rubbish out [laughs].
>
> (Penny Gulliver, 22, camper)

> I think the communal living worked really well. Sometimes I'd notice that certain women didn't do anything, but there was always some contribution that they made, whether it was singing or, they would have an outstanding contribution they would make in a different way. I felt it worked really well, and I liked the idea that you contribute what you feel like, when you feel like contributing.
>
> (Jenny Heron, 30, camper)

The fact that deprioritizing domestic labour meant that the camp was often untidy, strewn with unwashed dishes and half-eaten stews in pans annoyed some women, but only two believed that domestic work should have been a higher priority at Greenham. One of these women was Nell Logan, who as a life-long member of the Communist Party disliked the anarchy of Greenham and believed that the untidiness made a bad impression on the outside world. She explained differences in attitudes to domestic order in terms of age:

> Jane and I and Ursula, we were older you see, and we were going round picking all the papers up. We didn't like the mess that went on. Some of them were young, they thought it was a picnic, in a way. And it wasn't. It wasn't a picnic, by any means. We did tidy up, and we had to do that because we didn't want visitors coming and seeing all the mess, you see. It was all right. People would pass remarks about it, but then, I'd say, I'd rather be in this mess than in that mess in there [the base].
>
> (Nell Logan, 71, visitor)

The other woman who found the lack of emphasis on 'housework' at Greenham problematic was Pat Paris. She became aware of the mess around her at Blue Gate only when she brought her young daughter to stay at the camp, and she was the only woman interviewed who spent significant periods of time at the camp with a child. This suggests that the high level of tolerance of the relative disorder of domestic life at Greenham may have existed, at least in part, because there were few young children around whose health and safety had to be considered.

> Of those of us who ran around clearing up, it was people like me and Chris who had kids and homes and knew if you left the lid off the jar long enough,

then all these flies got in and you'd be poisoned. Little things like health hazards. I took Rowan once and that was the first time I ever really looked at Blue Gate and thought, oh my god. It was in the summer. The kitchen was on pallets somewhere. There were knives covered with all sorts, knocked onto the floor, picked up, put back. All those tins that had been opened, with sharp edges, and I just saw Rowan, two and a half, and I thought, she's going to be killed here, and if she's not going to be poisoned, she'll be cut to pieces. That was the weekend that I really lost my rag and we had one of our meetings, and I said, 'I can't go on. I'm not going to be able to bring Rowan'.

(Pat Paris, 33, camper)

Although the mundane chores of daily life were not prioritized at Greenham, considerable energy and imagination was expended on activities which were less traditionally designated as female. Some of these tasks were essential to the reproduction of life at the camp, such as the building of shelters, whereas others contributed to making the place more comfortable. The building of benders, until rendered pointless by the frequency of evictions, required considerable skill if the structure was to be water- and windproof. Newcomers, living at first in tents or under communal shelters, would often help longer-standing campers to build benders, thus acquiring the necessary skills before attempting their own. Once built, many women embellished their benders, lining the inside with blankets for warmth, placing wooden pallets on the floor, building bookshelves, and even bedframes which were filled with straw. At various times at each of the gates, large communal shelters were built, to protect women from the elements whilst sitting around the fire or for communal sleeping. Such building, using only sheets of plastic, saplings still rooted in the ground, wooden poles and string was a significant feat of rudimentary engineering, and was experienced as a major personal achievement by many women who had never before engaged in manual labour.

During periods of time when evictions were infrequent a number of women, particularly at Green Gate, devoted themselves to making furniture from scrap wood and bundles of sticks. Women at Blue Gate built a mobile kitchen on pallets and wheels, in order to be able to save food from the bailiffs, and Liz Galst at Indigo Gate built a bender on an old supermarket trolley base, which could be wheeled away during evictions. At Green, Blue, and Orange Gates earth ovens were built in order to bake cakes, breads, and puddings. Other women made grills for the fire and sandwich toasting implements from pieces of the fence which they had cut down. At Green and Blue Gates showers were rigged up from trees, and for a period of time at Green Gate women exercised their creativity digging shit-pits in the shape of women's symbols, peace symbols and doves.

Participation in domestic work at Greenham, whether of a routine or a more extraordinary nature, was a crucial component of the building of collective identity. At the individual level, it was a route into feeling part of the camp, and enabled women to feel that they could contribute something of value; this was particularly important in making the transition from being a visitor, to becoming a stayer or a camper. At the collective level, working together on tasks, from cooking a meal to building a bender, resulted in a shared sense of achievement and group bonding.

The organization of resources

The organization of resources is an essential task for any social movement, but assumes additional importance when these resources do not just provide the basis for the external action of a movement, but are also the basic necessities of a community. The resources employed at Greenham can be divided into two categories: personal and collective.

Personal resources were those belonging to individual women, of which they took personal charge and which they generally bought for themselves. In some cases personal resources were given by visitors who wished to 'sponsor' an individual, and occasionally they were bought by the camp for an individual. This latter circumstance occurred when, for example, an individual was unable to afford an essential item of clothing or piece of equipment, or had lost such an item whilst at camp, usually to thieves or bailiffs. Most women's personal resources at Greenham consisted of a small income, usually from state benefits, a rucksack of clothes and some bedding. Some women, particularly visitors and stayers, also owned tents and some cooking equipment, which they would use close to their tents to provide for themselves and the group with which they were visiting, as it was expected that women visiting the camp or staying for a few days on occasions of mass actions would come self-sufficient. Finally, a small number of women owned vehicles which they brought to Greenham. These vehicles often became essential to the life of a particular gate, not just for shopping and collecting water, but for loading with everyone's personal possessions and all collective equipment during evictions.

There were five main collective resources used at Greenham: money, food, wood, equipment, and transport. Collective resources were primarily either donated to the camp, or purchased by the camp using donated money. As Greenham had no formal membership and no subscription system or fee, it relied entirely on voluntary donations for its communal funds. The total value of monetary donations during the lifetime of the camp cannot be calculated, because there was no accounting procedure; there were numerous bank accounts over the years, and many donations were made in cash and spent without being banked. However, during the peak years of activism, income from donations was substantial. The inflow of money depended in part on the amount of news coverage Greenham was receiving, and increased immediately after high-profile actions and court cases, and at times when the government was making concerted efforts to malign the camp. During the period when I was a signatory to the main camp bank account (1984), between £100 and £5000 a week of donations were deposited. This was, however, an exceptional period, when Greenham was much in the news and Cruise had recently arrived. At other times, donations were considerably lower, and often non-existent. Monetary donations came both from individuals and from groups, particularly CND and peace groups, and trade union and Labour Party branches. Money was raised through collections, raffles, jumble sales, and the showing of anti-nuclear films. Amounts varied from £1 notes sent in by pensioners and schoolchildren, to substantial donations of several thousand pounds by famous singers.

Non-monetary donations were also an extremely significant source of camp resources. Food was commonly brought to Greenham by visitors, particularly at Christmas, when there was sometimes so much food that it was passed on to local women's refuges. From mid-1984 onwards, as evictions became a regular feature of life at Greenham, a daily 'food run' was established by women from around the south of England, who operated a rota. Every day, in the late afternoon or early evening, hot meals were brought to the camp. As there was no way of knowing exactly how many women would be at the camp on any one day, there was sometimes too much and sometimes not enough to go round; but the knowledge that there would always be a meal relieved women of some of the stress which accompanied frequent evictions.

The other major resource which was donated on a regular basis was wood, an essential of life at Greenham. During and after the miners' strike of 1984–5, groups of striking miners also donated sacks of coal, in a gesture of solidarity. Other practical donations, often specifically requested in response to questions about what was needed at Greenham, included sheet plastic, thermal underwear, sleeping bags, tents, pallets, Gore-Tex survival bags, and boltcutters, for cutting the fence. Most of the crockery, cooking utensils, pots, and pans used at Greenham were also donations. During the winter of 1983–4, there were also dozens of sackfuls of clothing donated to the camp. Finally, most of the vehicles which were owned by the camp (although in an individual woman's name) were donated to Greenham by individual supporters.

Although it is possible that Greenham could have existed solely on the resources brought to it by the women who lived and stayed there, without donations life would have been considerably more frugal and difficult, and many of the actions taken against the base would have been impossible. For almost all of the British women who lived at the camp, state benefits were their only personal source of income, and it was only because of the then still relatively lenient regulations regarding eligibility for unemployment and supplementary benefits that they were able to live at the camp. Many women were registered as unemployed in their home towns, returning to sign on every fortnight, and hence received the full benefit. Those who signed on in Newbury received a reduced payment, as 'non-householders' until, on appeal in 1983, this was increased. State benefit at this time, not yet eroded by a decade and a half of Conservative Government, was adequate for women to live on at camp, if their expenses elsewhere were minimal or non-existent. However, it was not sufficient to allow women to provision themselves with all the equipment necessary for life at Greenham. Thus the communal funds were used to supplement the contributions made by individual women to the food kitty, for vehicle tax, insurance and petrol, and to buy essential equipment which was not donated, particularly building materials for benders and ladders, boltcutters, locks, and paint for actions against the base.

The collective ownership of such resources served to strengthen the collective identity of the camp by giving it a material existence above and beyond the individual women who were there at any time; camp vehicles, benders, and action equipment would remain at Greenham when individual women left. Between 1983 and 1985 there was a store of clothes, cooking equipment, bedding, and building materials on a piece of land, 'The Sanctuary', from which women could not be evicted.[13] Women could help themselves from this store as needed; this enabled women who arrived without the necessary personal resources to live at Greenham, and was a stock from which collective and personal resources could be replenished when things were lost to the bailiffs during evictions.

Even more important to the creation and recreation of collective identity was the communal consumption of food at Greenham. Breakfast, lunch, and snacks were eaten by individuals at whatever time they desired, and were usually prepared by those individuals themselves, though sometimes small groups would cook breakfast together. The evening meal, however, was a communal occasion, at which everyone living at the gate gathered around the fire and shared the meal which had been cooked on the fire or brought by a 'food run'. This tended to be the only time of the day when all the residents and women staying at the gate came together, and was a time at which news would be exchanged. After dinner there were hot drinks, and often singing or the telling of stories for several hours. This ritual served to bind the women of a gate together, to integrate newcomers, as well as providing everyone with at least one hot meal a day, which was vital, particularly in the winter.

Conflict over resources

Whilst the collective consumption of resources generally worked to strengthen the camp, conflict flared about the way in which money was to be spent and around the rather fuzzy line which sometimes existed between personal and collective resources. In general, each woman's personal resources were respected as such and considered her business alone, although individual's cars would sometimes come to be considered 'camp vehicles', at times against the owner's wishes. However, the use of the collective resources of the camp to provide for individual women often generated conflict. Requests from individual women for money from the camp to replace damaged, stolen, or evicted possessions such as boots, rucksacks, and sleeping bags were rarely contested. What did generate disagreement were demands for money for purposes which some women considered unessential, extravagant and an improper use of camp money. Examples of such requests were for the replacement of a camera, damaged during an eviction, for money to go on a two-week holiday abroad as a rest from Greenham, and for the payment of large telephone bills which had been run up by women from the camp. Controversy particularly arose when the same small group of women made repeated demands for money.

Conflict about the use of money began early in the camp's history. During the first year and a half there was no clear system for collective decision-making about money. There were a number of different bank accounts in the name of the camp, each with different signatories. Money was deposited in these accounts fairly haphazardly. Problems arose when it became apparent that the account with the largest balance could only be accessed by women who no longer lived at Greenham, and who were therefore able to exercise a veto over expenditure. These women were asked to hand over control of the account to women living at Greenham, but refused. They refused also to withdraw money to pay for locks which women wanted for an action at the base, arguing that the proposed action was violent and against the ethos of Greenham.

These events brought the issue of the control of money to a head, and a meeting was held at Greenham to discuss the matter.[14] The outcome of the meeting was the establishment of regular money meetings, at which requests for money from individuals and for camp expenses, such as petrol and equipment for actions, could be discussed openly. Each week one woman was to take charge of paying donations into a single camp account, and she would also make one withdrawal, after the money meeting, to meet the agreed expenditure. In order to prevent a concentration of power in one woman's hands, this role was to circulate each week, and there were to be several signatories to the new account, so that vetoes could not be exercised by individuals over collective decisions.

The system of weekly money meetings clarified to some extent the process by which money was handled at Greenham, but it did not eliminate conflict. During 1984 money meetings became the site of considerable disputation, which was often expressed in terms of hierarchies within the camp and between gates. Early in 1984 it was decided, after pressure from the other gates, that money meetings should not always be held at Yellow Gate, but should take place each week at a different gate. This was an attempt to deal with a perceived aggregation of power at Yellow Gate, particularly amongst women who had been at the camp for a long time. A small number of women from Yellow Gate were requesting and receiving considerably more money for personal use than anyone else. Sometimes these women offered no justification for their requests, and others felt unable to challenge them. When women from other gates spoke out, often diffidently at first, against requests which they regarded as unwarranted, money meetings erupted into shouting matches. Women asking for money saw that they were being blocked and accused those questioning them of being puritanical and middle class in their attitudes to money. Meanwhile, many of the women who were reluctant to agree to the money being spent were in fact working class, and saw the issue as one of power and hierarchy, not class. They believed that it was women who had been at the camp longest and who were the most self-confident who tended to ask for money.

Other women who were unhappy about camp money being spent on what they considered luxuries were those who were completely financially dependent on the camp; these were women who received 'camp dole' because they were ineligible for state benefits, usually because they were not UK residents. These women argued that their continued involvement with Greenham was threatened by the misuse of resources, and that money should be saved to ensure camp dole could be paid in the future. Yet another group of women who entered the fray were concerned about accountability to those who donated money to Greenham, and believed that money should only be spent on collective resources to support the needs of the camp. A further group argued that money should be redistributed to other campaigns, particularly in the Third World, once the basic needs of the camp had been met.

To summarize, conflict about money coalesced around a number of specific questions:

1 Whether individual women's requests were legitimate, that is, over the definition of 'needs'.
2 Whether individual or collective needs should come first.
3 Whether money should be spent as and when it was available, or whether there should be forward planning and saving of money for periods when donations were more scarce.
4 Whether the camp should be accountable for how donations were spent, or whether the ethos of autonomy meant that however women there chose to use it was legitimate.

The issue of money exemplified the tension which existed within the ethos of Greenham between the principle of communality and the principle of respect for differences between women. It also provided occasion for the expression of conflict about hierarchies which existed despite Greenham's commitment to oppose them, and demonstrated disagreements in political analysis and priorities.

The eventual outcome of a series of heated money meetings was the devolution of control of money to the gates. Each week money was distributed to a representative from each gate, roughly on the basis of the number of women living there, plus camp dole for those who claimed it. Each gate was then left to decide how to spend its money itself. This meant that decisions about expenditure could be taken in smaller groups, amongst women who knew each other well and were therefore more likely to trust each other and feel mutually accountable in their requests for money. As a result of this decision, the distinctive character and interests and concerns of the women living at each gate could be reflected in spending decisions. For instance, women at Orange Gate, who had been particularly disturbed by what they perceived as wastefulness and extravagance at Greenham, decided to redistribute much of their weekly income to other women's projects and campaigns, in Britain and around the world, which they believed were not receiving as much financial support as Greenham. Eventually the whole problem of money faded away; as the camp became smaller and donations fell off there was less to argue about.

Conflict about another vital collective resource, camp vehicles, also arose from time to time, although never on the scale of the arguments about money.

Disputes centred around two issues: the control of vehicles, and the way in which they were used. As Greenham had no formal legal existence as an association, club or company, camp vehicles had to be registered and insured in the names of individual women. As these women had to have driving licences, they tended to be older and were likely to be middle class, and they had usually been at the camp for a considerable length of time. In order to reduce insurance costs and to limit wear and tear on vehicles, there was an attempt for a period to designate certain women as 'camp drivers'. However, problems arose when these women were not around and journeys had to be made (to collect water or to go shopping), or when camp drivers made extended personal journeys in the vehicles. Some women believed that the camp drivers had too much power to determine the way such chores were conducted. At the same time, those women with skills in car mechanics thought that some camp drivers used the vehicles carelessly and failed to maintain them properly. This was seen by some as a misuse of donated resources.

The main problem concerning vehicles, however, was the shortage of women with driving licences. This became particularly acute at the north side gates from 1984, because vehicles were needed to store the contents of the camps during evictions to prevent the bailiffs seizing everything. At Blue Gate, where the average age was lower than elsewhere, there were frequently times when there was no one present who could legally drive a vehicle. Usually a woman from another gate would come to their aid and drive everything away in the Blue Gate van, but sometimes women without full licences had to do this. This left the few legal drivers at the camp often feeling unable to leave the camp, even to go into Newbury for a few hours.

The problem of hierarchy

In the course of this chapter I have already indicated how hierarchies were perceived to exist both between the camp and the wider network and within the camp itself, despite an ethos of anti-hierarchy, and the conscious adoption of techniques to oppose their formation.

In part, hierarchies were constructed by external factors. The press, in particular, would not accept that Greenham had no leaders, and so pinpointed a small number of women who had been involved with the camp for a considerable length of time, and who had previously given interviews. Sarah Bond, for instance, in the *Daily Express*, identified four women as 'the gang of four who pull the strings'.[15] This had the self-perpetuating effect of sending the press in search of the same women repeatedly, and also meant that these women would be asked to speak at conferences, rallies and meetings. Another effect of media concentration on 'leaders' was that visitors often wanted to meet these women, rather than anyone else; they wanted to talk to a 'real Greenham woman', and invariably asked everyone how long they had been there in order to find the woman most qualified to discuss the camp.

Most of the women highlighted for media attention attempted to deflect it, sometimes refusing interviews and suggesting journalists talk to other women, but undoubtedly being a 'peace personality' had its attractions. Its downside was, at times, a certain degree of hostility from other women living at Greenham, who believed that the women concerned should have done more to disabuse journalists of the notion that they were the leaders. If anything, the influence of these women within the camp declined in direct proportion to the amount of attention given to them by outsiders.

The hierarchies that were seen to be 'real' within the camp were not so much concerned with the few women suggested by the press or visitors to be leaders, because women living at Greenham knew that they were not. Rather, they were the hierarchies and inequalities of power which were formed on the basis of length of involvement, level of involvement and, more intangibly, personal and cultural resources. So, for example, women who had been living at the camp for a long time, and who therefore had knowledge about its history and had been part of major actions (such as the silos action), and who had perhaps been feminists prior to Greenham were particularly likely to be respected within the camp. Penni Bestic explained it thus:

> I think there were women who were leaders [. . .]. Well, no, leaders is the wrong word. More like catalysts [. . .]. They were women who were very, very strong, very bright. I think if they wanted something to happen, then it would happen. It would be very unusual if it would happen without their consent.
>
> (Penni Bestic, 31, camper)

The terms 'delegates' and 'minions' were coined, jokingly but pointedly, to highlight these inequalities:

> There was the hierarchy that Pauline pointed out: the 'delegates' and 'minions', which caused hilarious fun with everybody except the 'delegates'. You could tell who the 'delegates' were, because they didn't laugh. It was good that she pointed out the hierarchy that everyone tried to pretend wasn't there, and she did it in this hilariously funny way. I mean, visitors were lower than 'minions' [. . .]. I was a 'minion'.
>
> (Jenny Heron, 30, camper)

'Delegates' were so called because they were the women who tended to do the 'speaks', and to travel abroad as Greenham women. They were the women whose opinions were particularly valued within the camp:

> When a decision had to be made, everyone had their say. But it was never really talked about that you might just give a one word answer and the person next to you might go on for half an hour. Everyone took what the group of 'delegates' said very seriously.
>
> (Sarah Benham, 17, stayer)

To some extent it was inevitable that such hierarchies should develop; the length of time a woman had been at the camp *did* matter, not least because newcomers had much to learn about how the community worked and about its ethos. Friendship groups grew up amongst women of the same 'cohort', on the basis of the shared experience of being at the camp, and these were not always open to newcomers. It was also the case, as I will argue in Chapter 8, that being at Greenham facilitated women's self-confidence, and so the longer a woman had been there, the more powerful she was likely to appear. However, as Jenny Heron recognized in retrospect, the power and strength of the 'delegates' also rested in attribution from the 'minions':

> I didn't feel I fitted in with the big shots [. . .]. They were all much more everything than me. They were funnier, they were more attractive, they were more experienced, they had more to say [. . .]. But I haven't put women on a pedestal since then.
>
> (Jenny Heron, 30, camper)

The ethos of Greenham meant that there was a high degree of sensitivity to inequalities of power, and conflict and tension therefore arose in situations where hierarchy and inequality were slight in comparison with that in conventional political organizations and living arrangements. There was much discussion about these issues, and many meetings were devoted to collective analysis of the problems, particularly as they related to class. This commitment to reflexivity and discussion helped prevent the entrenchment of disputes, and the constant through-flow of the population of the camp served to ease tensions. Above all, though, the shared belief in the importance of Greenham's anarchist–feminist principles and the unifying factor of opposition to the missiles acted to bind together the camp, notwithstanding significant differences between women.

The King's Cross affair

The one significant dent made in the cohesion of Greenham did not occur until the camp was passed its peak of mobilization in 1987. Working in a Leninist entryist style, women from the King's Cross Women's Centre/Wages for Housework Campaign in London gradually took over Yellow Gate, by a dual-pronged process of sending their own women to Greenham and targeting women they perceived as powerful and convincing them that they should accept direction from Wilmette Brown, one of the leaders of the Wages for Housework Campaign. The way they did this was by mobilizing the discourse of anti-racism to divide the camp into 'racists' and 'anti-racists'.

There had long been a concern amongst women at Greenham about racism, and the analysis which developed over time involved making connections between racism, imperialism and militarism. Many women had, over the years, expressed concern that the women's peace movement was predominantly white, and indeed there had been many discussions and meetings at Greenham about the issue. The generally accepted view, in part derived from the writings of black feminists about the peace movement, was that most black women in Britain were occupied by issues of more immediate concern to them, such as racism and poverty, than the nuclear threat, and that taking non-violent direct action against the state involved more risk for black women. However, at Greenham, as in the wider women's movement, there was considerable white guilt about the absence of black women.

The King's Cross Women's Centre offered to solve this problem by proffering the leadership of a black woman, Wilmette Brown, who appeared to believe that Greenham was an important site of struggle, unlike many black feminists in Britain (compare Brown 1984 with Amos and Parmar 1984). If Greenham women accepted her leadership (delegated in her absence to two of the longstanding campers who had joined the King's Cross project), they were not racist; if however, they refused it, on whatever grounds, they were. The ways of working employed by the King's Cross women were in direct contrast to the Greenham ethos. They believed in the importance of leadership; participation in meetings was not encouraged, and they argued that only those living permanently at Greenham could speak about what should happen there (thereby excluding stayers and visitors – the wider Greenham network); video and tape-recorders and notebooks were used to record everything that was said in meetings; and meetings were structured around a closed agenda. Meetings were also often patrolled by a number of 'guards' with dogs and cameras whom many Greenham women found intimidating and physically threatening. Above all, the King's Cross women attempted to impose their brand of materialist feminism on Greenham, a project which was contrary to the theoretical openness and non-alliance which characterized the movement.[16]

Given the structure of Greenham it was impossible for the King's Cross women to be excluded or removed. Indeed many women for a long time held on to the belief that Greenham should be open to all, and were reluctant to criticize the King's Cross women because they firmly believed that they had to take seriously the issue of racism, particularly as expressed by a black woman. However, as the women who did not join the King's Cross group left Yellow Gate and moved to one of the four other camps that were open at the time, they began to spread the news about what had happened around the Greenham network and through the peace movement. This galvanized thousands of women into action, many of whom had previously lived at Greenham, and in the winter of 1987 there were large gatherings at all the other gates, and the problem was widely discussed. Effectively, the dozen women at Yellow Gate were isolated. They retained control over the water supply and refused women from the other gates access to the incoming mail, and hence to donations of money. But the other gates bypassed these problems by fetching water from elsewhere, and publicized Blue Gate as the new postal address for Greenham.

The King's Cross affair did not cause a split within Greenham – rather a small splinter. Greenham's fluidity and flexibility enabled it to survive as an autonomous movement committed to anti-hierarchical, open and participatory forms of organization. Ultimately this attempt to take over and destroy the camp served to illustrate many of the strengths of Greenham's internal mode of action. The internal action of Greenham was, whatever its flaws, a unique experiment in the creation of feminist community, in which practices of everyday life were challenged and reinvented.

6

The external mode of action

As important as they were in disrupting conventional ways of doing politics and traditional modes of living, the internal dynamics of Greenham are only half the story. It was Greenham's public face, its externally directed action, which constituted the more immediate and obvious challenge to the nuclear state and to patriarchal gender relations. This aspect of Greenham deserves more detailed treatment than I am able to give it here, and this chapter is necessarily something of an overview. In it I trace the broad contours of Greenham's external mode of action, highlighting how Greenham's ethos was put into practice.

The problem of 'strategy'

In reacting against LeBon's (1969) classic depiction of collective action as emotional, irrational, and crowd-like, which is also the way protest is usually represented in the media, social movement researchers have been keen to adopt a perspective which emphasizes the rational, deliberate, and strategic orientation of social movements.[1] Resource mobilization theory, in particular, utilizes rational choice theory to posit an image of movements as directed by a leadership of calculating strategists, weighing up the potential costs and benefits of a range of different actions with the aim of maximizing the latter and minimizing the former.[2] Even when the formal adoption of cost–benefit analysis is modified, critiqued, or even rejected, social movement research tends to be framed within this discourse of rational, strategic choice.[3] It is widely assumed that, operating within the constraints of their resources and the existing 'political opportunity structure' (Kitschelt, 1986), social movements construct strategies to pursue their aims.

However, action at Greenham, both internal and external, cannot be understood using the notion of 'strategy'; Greenham did not formulate strategies.[4] This is not to say that action was irrational, unconsidered and somehow instinctive or traditional (in the Weberian sense). On the contrary, it was conscious and chosen, but the concept of 'strategy', with its connotations of instrumental rationality, cost–benefit analysis and military-like planning, does not capture the complex nature of the processes by which Greenham's action was constructed.[5] Whilst it is (just) possible that a conscious, long-range plan of action could be formulated within a segmentary, polycephalous, reticulate movement without leaders or formal structures, the ethos of Greenham rejected such a mode of operating.

First, Greenham's anarchist emphasis on personal responsibility and on respect for diversity and individuality valued individual women acting on the basis of autonomous decisions above the following of a 'strategy'. This meant that many women (though not all) believed that it was better for a woman to act according to her own conscience, as long as the basic principle of non-violence was respected, than for her to submit herself to an edict, or even a collective decision, about the camp's strategy. Second, action at Greenham was not exclusively, or even primarily, directed by instrumental rationality. Affective and emotional impulses, often described by women as 'gut feelings' or 'intuition', were important considerations when actions were being contemplated. Actions were frequently even altered mid-way, and plans abandoned, if one woman's feelings about the situation changed. Third then, the reflexive orientation of Greenham, and the openness to change which characterized the movement, militated against the pursuit of strategies. Above all, Greenham's rejection of the idea that the ends justify the means and the stress placed on process, meant that the single-minded determination required to implement a strategy was out of the question.[6]

The notion of strategy implies the pursuit of a clearly defined objective or set of objectives, yet Greenham's 'objectives', if they can be called such, were never explicitly defined. Action was, as I suggested in the previous chapter, *implicitly* directed as two goals – that of opposing nuclear weapons, particularly Cruise and challenging patriarchy, and of maintaining and reproducing the camp. But individual women had a range of different reasons for being involved and many different political agenda, and both changed over time. The orientation of Greenham was not exclusively, or indeed primarily, instrumental, as would be suggested by the use of the concept of strategy. Indeed, the commonly posed dichotomy between instrumental and expressive orientations to action was challenged at Greenham, as the project of women's self-actualization and empowerment was considered an essential aspect of the struggle against nuclear weapons; and this 'instrumental' goal was rooted in 'expressive' motivations and demanded emotionally charged forms of protest.[7]

In addition to the problem that it suggests the existence of explicit objectives, the concept of 'strategy' invokes the idea of a clearly formulated plan of how to proceed, which also did not exist in the case of Greenham. During the life of the camp, the ways in which the goals of action were pursued changed, and never were they pursued 'strategically'. The initial march to Greenham sought to inform the public about the nuclear issue, and demanded a televised public debate about Cruise and nuclear weapons with the Defence Secretary.

Underlying this was the idea that raising public consciousness about the issue would exert pressure on the government to abandon Cruise. Whilst this educational orientation never entirely disappeared, the camp increasingly chose to engage in confrontation with the state.[8] Some of the confrontational actions were intended to obstruct the process of deployment, others to undermine government claims about the security of the base. There were actions which sought to challenge the consciences of those working in the base, others to ridicule them and the policies they were enacting. All actions expressed dissent to the process of nuclear rearmament. However, any attempt to identify the objective behind actions at Greenham often serves to impose an *ex post facto* intentionality on actions which may have been carried out as much to lift the spirits and strengthen the affective bonds between the women involved as to pursue even these loosely-defined routes to change.

Greenham's repertoire of action

Although the concept of strategy is inapplicable to Greenham, Charles Tilly's (1978, 1979) work on 'repertoires of collective action' is useful in understanding how particular forms of action were chosen.[9] The notion stresses that decisions about what actions to employ are historically located. At any given time and place there is a limited array of actions from which actors select, whether with cool deliberation or rashly and without premeditation. This repertoire of action is constructed from the prior experience and knowledge of the movement's participants, according to the ethos of the movement and its mode of internal organization, and is constrained by the patterns of repression and control exercised by the forces which the movement opposes (Tilly 1979:134).[10] Any movement can be located on a continuum according to the degree of flexibility or rigidity of its repertoire. Whilst '[t]he repertoire is the repertoire of jazz or commedia dell'arte rather than of grand opera or Shakespearean drama' (Tilly 1979:131), some performers are more inclined to improvise than others.

Greenham's repertoire of externally-focused action was at the jazz end of the spectrum; it was extremely flexible and open to innovation, and expanded over time. Many of the actions in which women engaged drew from the repertoire of the peace movements of the 1950s and 1960s, and the anti-nuclear power movement of the 1970s, as well as from the far longer history of popular protest in Britain.[11] However, some of these actions, which were commonly used early in the camp's history, fell out of favour or were deliberately abandoned, and new actions were devised, often in response to changed circumstances. Other forms of action continued to be used throughout the life of Greenham. All of the actions, whether old or new, were stamped with the distinctive ethos of Greenham, and often with a carnivalesque exuberance and emotionality.

Mapping the development of the repertoire is a difficult exercise, and the dangers of false universalism and historical inaccuracy lurk, given the impossibility of constructing a detailed history of all the thousands of actions undertaken at

Greenham. None the less, I have identified, in the most general terms, a number of ways in which the forms of action performed at Greenham shifted over time.

In general, there was a shift from actions located outside the base to actions which breached the boundaries and entered the base; from demonstration-type actions to direct, confrontational actions; from legal to illegal actions; from the use of women's bodies as tools of protest to the use of mechanical tools (e.g. bolt-cutters). Whilst all of Greenham's actions were symbolic (of women's refusal of Cruise), there was an increasing tendency for actions to have a direct impact as well as a symbolic one, that is, for them to involve physical interventions in the work of the base or sabotage and/or damage. The other major change was in the planning and organization of actions. As certain forms of action became established in Greenham's repertoire, and as the individual women doing the action became accustomed to the experience of breaking the law, being arrested, and working together, there tended to be less preparation for actions. Actions became more spontaneous and, paradoxically, also more routinized. Rather than being considered in a meeting at which women expressed their doubts and fears and developed a consensus agreement about how the action was to proceed, the decision to do an action would increasingly be made shortly before it was actually performed, and without much discussion of what was intended. Thus, actions occurring in this way would often take on a familiar course and end up much like others in which the women involved had taken part.

This later tendency to routinization notwithstanding, the range of different actions undertaken was enormous. In order to impose a framework for the discussion of these actions and the responses to them, I have divided them into seven categories, each of which groups together a variety of actions and a considerable number of significant 'events' in the history of the camp:

1 Gatherings and demonstrations.
2 Blockades.
3 Incursions.
4 Courtroom actions.
5 Monitoring.
6 Roving: 'carrying Greenham home'.
7 Being there: the politics of place and presence.

These seven categories do not represent types of action which succeeded each other chronologically, as some continued throughout; however, I do indicate how the emphasis shifted between categories of action over time.

Greenham actions

Gatherings and demonstrations

Gatherings and demonstrations were ostensibly the most traditional form of action to take place at Greenham, drawing on a long history of social movements assembling at the site of their grievance in order to draw attention to it. However, this form of action at Greenham was significantly different from the sort of demonstrations which were commonplace in radical politics in Britain in the 1970s and 1980s. For instance, gatherings and demonstrations at Greenham (with the exception of that at the end of the walk from Cardiff after which the camp was established) did not constitute the end-point of marches, but were protest events in their own right. Nor was there the usual platform and procession of well known figures to speak to the assembled crowds; rather the women taking part created their own demonstration, by singing, dancing, keening, and chanting. There were no stewards or organizers to direct the proceedings or to police the event for the authorities. Indeed, gatherings at Greenham were initiated rather than organized. The idea would usually originate from the camp, and would be spread through the Greenham network by chain letter and word of mouth. Local groups would then hire coaches and publicize the event in their area in order to bring women to Greenham. Rather than placards and the banners of the organizations which they represented, women would bring musical instruments, candles, torches, and sometimes symbols of personal significance, such as paintings and photographs (at the 'Embrace the Base' demonstration, the maternalist high-point of Greenham, these were often of their children). Gatherings at Greenham were expressive and emotional, involving the harnessing of women's creativity to draw sharp contrasts with the world behind the fence.

The first mass demonstration at Greenham, 'Embrace the Base' on 12 December 1982, was an important moment in the history of the camp.[12] It was the occasion which first drew large-scale media attention to Greenham, and was the entry-point for hundreds of women who later went to live at the camp and thousands who became regular stayers or visitors. The idea for enough women to assemble at Greenham to encircle the entire perimeter of the base arose several months earlier during a conversation about what actions women would most like to do (Harford and Hopkins 1984:61). Initially cautious that the ten thousand or more women needed might not come, no figure was quoted in the leaflets which invited women to Greenham, and everyone was encouraged to bring scarves to hold between them, in case there were not enough women to surround the base holding hands. In fact over 35,000 women gathered at Greenham that day, establishing a distinctive Greenham protest style and galvanizing the movement into action.

The 'Embrace the Base' demonstration was a liminal experience (Rothenbuhler 1988) in the lives of the women who constituted it.[13] Outside the structures and routines not just of daily life, but also of 'normal' protest and political action, it was a moment of dedifferentiation, when individuals gathering together experienced an almost 'sacred' sense of solidarity and collective strength. Tiryakian suggests that this process is typical of revolutionary movements:

> The process of dedifferentiation at the societal level involves a transformation of consciousness, one in which the relatively distinct individual

consciousness of everyday life becomes sentient with others in a common situation and common enterprise; this transformation is characterised by a high level of energy, for the individual and for the aggregate.

(Tiryakian, 1988:45)[14]

This sense of collective strength and temporary dedifferentiation had, at Greenham, a particular gendered significance. Unlike men, whose sporting events occupy large areas of towns and cities every weekend, women rarely gather together in any number, taking up public space *en masse*. Seeing, for the first time, huge crowds of other women, was an exhilarating experience:

> You never saw so many women in such a big group before. I remember when we turned up that weekend, and we started looking out of windows when we knew we were nearly there and we started seeing coach loads of women, more and more. It was incredible. So many [. . .].
>
> (Ann Armstrong, 44, stayer)

For all of the women interviewed who had been at the 'Embrace the Base' gathering, it was a moment of 'creative effervescence' (Durkheim 1961:475).

> I was elated, absolutely elated, I really was. It was just very thrilling. I was happy being on my own because it was so crowded, so many women. I enjoyed this feeling of keeping on walking and being in this atmosphere, and feeling, where have I been all this time?
>
> (Carola Addington, 29, camper)

> One of the evenings suddenly there was a circle dance, only it wasn't formal. Somehow we just danced, and it was so exciting. There were all these women, and it was like a snake dance. It was all very spontaneous, and it was so exciting when I looked around. There were women of all ages in that dance, and all having such a good time. Everyone looked so pleased to be there and doing that. It was really magical.
>
> (Carmel Cadden, 30, camper)

> I spent the day plodding around the perimeter, being amazed at how big it all was. And I just remember the candles in the evening, when the candles started lighting up all around, just being very, very moved by it, the symbolism of the power of individual women gathered together. Whatever was in there [the base], it could be stopped.
>
> (Sian Edwards, 33, visitor)

Over the years many more gatherings and demonstrations were held at Greenham. The second weekend in December became established as an annual mass protest, drawing over 50,000 women in 1983 and continuing to bring women to Greenham until after the missiles were finally removed. The December demonstrations were the occasions on which women who supported the camp but for whom nuclear weapons were not a personal or political priority could register their objections to nuclear militarism and draw strength from the largest women's gatherings to take place in Britain. Each year's event was given a slightly different theme. 1983's theme was to symbolically reflect the base back on itself using mirrors. In 1985 it was 'widening the web', to direct attention to the connections between nuclear militarism and other struggles and to 'celebrate our differences'. In 1986, it was 'reclaiming our lives', focusing on all forms of violence. By 1987 the theme was 'reweaving the web' and 'celebrating the birth of a post-nuclear age'.

Other gatherings tended to be smaller (thousands rather than tens of thousands) and to involve those who were more centrally part of the Greenham network. There was, for instance, the Dragon Festival on the summer equinox in 1983, at which 2000 women sewed together a four-mile long patchwork dragon, made from thousands of pieces of cloth sent by women from all around the world, and then performed a play about men's ownership of women.[15] New Year's Day in 1984 was celebrated by a thousand women weaving a giant web from wool on the clearing at Green Gate to which helium filled balloons were attached, to carry the web over the fence and into the base. In May 1984, regular monthly gatherings on Saturdays were initiated, 'Common Women's Days', at which women were encouraged to 'make your own contribution, from simply being here, planting, picnicking, singing, sharing experiences, to non-violent direct actions'.[16]

The organization of demonstrations and gatherings at Greenham was, at times, an arena of conflict within the camp and the wider network. For instance, dispute erupted later in 1984 when a call was issued by women from Yellow Gate for 10 million women to gather at Greenham between 20 and 30 September (which was the period when major NATO exercises were being conducted in West Germany). The initiative was extremely controversial within the camp, and was taken without consensus having been reached. The women whose idea it was believed that a 'miracle' could be wrought if all the women in Britain opposed to Cruise missiles (according to the opinion polls, over 10 million) came to Greenham; not just could the arms race be halted but the world could be fundamentally changed. Others argued that specifying a target number was a mistake and left Greenham open to ridicule if the target was not met, as they believed it would not. Another group, particularly working class women from Blue Gate, objected to the hierarchical and centralist idea that women should be called to Greenham, suggesting that this was not feasible for many women. Greenham and Cruise missiles were not a priority for poor women who had more immediate material concerns, and the demand for women to leave their work on rape crisis lines and for women's refuges to come to Greenham would cause divisions within the women's movement. Instead, they argued, the Ten Days action should consist of women taking action in their own neighbourhoods. Another group of women, influenced by the Wages for Housework Campaign at the King's Cross Women's Centre, envisaged the Ten Days as a women's strike, and issued leaflets calling on women to withdraw their labour and to 'make their work visible'[17]. A further compromise position invited women to come to Greenham during the Ten Days, or, for those unable or unwilling to do so, to 'act about what is closest to you, wherever you are'.[18]

The debate about the Ten Days action crystallized many of the conflicts which already existed within Greenham – about class, about hierarchy both within the camp and between the camp and Greenham women in the wider network, about decision-making processes, and about whether Greenham should be the central focus for women's peace campaigning or just one of many different local actions. The fact that the action went ahead (though not attracting 10 million women!) without consensus having been reached, and without even a clearly agreed location, let alone an agreed theme, illustrates well my earlier argument about the inapplicability of the concept of strategy to understandings of Greenham's external mode of action. It also demonstrates how Greenham's ethos of personal responsibility, which encouraged women to take initiatives and act according to their own beliefs, could collide with an emphasis on collectivity and process. In this case, as usually happened at Greenham, the former principle overrode the latter, with the result that a small number of the women who had objected to the action left the camp. However, also discernible in the debate which arose over the Ten Days action was one of the strengths of Greenham's structure. It was possible for the diversity of political priorities and orientations of the women involved to find expression. Even though the positions taken by the various groups of women were contradictory and the leaflets they issued called for completely different forms of action, Greenham as a collective identity and a movement was supple enough to accommodate them all.

Blockades

The blockade was the first form of non-violent direct action to be undertaken at Greenham, and was a regular part of the repertoire of action for the first few years. Mass sit-downs had been a feature of the radical wing of the British peace movement in the 1950s and 1960s (Randle 1987), of the anti-Vietnam War campaigns of the late 1960s and early 1970s, and of the anti-nuclear power movements across Europe in the 1970s. Such actions, whilst causing some obstruction to military bases, city centres, or nuclear power stations, were primarily symbolic in importance and effect; they tended to be brief, and to be intended as 'a kind of propaganda by the deed' (Randle 1987:144).

At Greenham both the symbolic power and the direct impact of 'blockades' (rather than 'sit-downs') was greater than in previous movements. Women were choosing to place their bodies in roads in front of a nuclear base, to make their bodies limp, to be thrown in ditches by policemen, loomed over by horses, and driven at by riot vans. Within a cultural context which constructs and prefers women's bodies to be fragile, in need of male protection, and extant for the use of men, such action transgressed dominant notions of women's corporeality. In the course of blockading, women's bodies were refigured, individually and *en masse*, as powerful, disruptive, and autonomous.[19]

Moreover, blockades at Greenham had an immediately obstructive impact on the operations of the base. There were two sorts of blockades: mass blockades, 'planned' in advance, for which women were invited to come to the camp to participate, and spontaneous blockades, which arose in direct response to unforeseen events in the base or at the camp. Mass blockades, such as the first major action at Greenham in March 1982, the 'Close the Base' blockade the day after 'Embrace the Base', and the week-long July blockades in 1983, involved several thousand women and caused serious disruption to the everyday work of the base and to the construction of the Cruise missile silos. In the latter two, every gate and gap around the base was blockaded and few of the dozens of bus loads of workers who normally entered the base were able to do so. The smaller scale, more spontaneous blockades were often even more effective because the lack of warning for the authorities meant that they tended not to have sufficient police immediately available to move women from in front of the gates. Spontaneous blockades were often provoked by unexpected visits of senior politicians or military personnel to the base, or by the arrival of particularly significant military equipment. Women would also sometimes blockade bailiffs carrying out evictions and police vans attempting to drive away women who had been arrested.

Taking part in blockades was reported by many of the women interviewed as an empowering and exhilarating experience. For instance, of the 'Close the Base' blockade in December 1982:

> It was a real buzz. It was a real adrenalin buzz, being there, doing something like that with such a big group of women. There was lots of music going on, food being brought round, women looking after each other. It was an incredible atmosphere, and whatever they did to you, you'd sort of bounce back out of the ditch and carry on. It was great.
>
> (Kim Smith, 25, camper)

However, after the police's initial confusion about how to deal with blockades in 1982, during which time they sometimes just waited for the action to finish, and as the date for the deployment of Cruise approached, the police became more violent in their handling of women and developed new techniques for policing blockades.[20] Although hundreds of women were arrested for obstruction during blockades, it was impossible, even with processing stations set up at Newbury racecourse, to arrest everyone. Thus the repetitious performance was established of policemen picking a woman up under the arms, dragging her away from the mass of bodies, and dropping her at the side of the road, whereupon, having taken a brief break, she would return to the blockade. Individual policemen differed in the degree of force they used, but most women would sustain bruises and scratches, and often had their shirts pulled off them. A smaller number of women were badly hurt, suffering broken limbs, concussion, torn ears, and severe friction burns as their bare skin was scraped along the surface of the road. Certain women were targeted for rough treatment, particularly women from the camp and thought to be leaders, big, powerful-looking women, women who were obvious lesbians and black women. The July blockades in 1983 saw the police practising techniques which were later employed during the miners' strike. They organized into wedge formations, marched along the road towards the blockades, rhythmically slapping their thighs, and charged at the women lying in the road, while policemen on horses also rode at them.[21]

Whilst many women continued to believe in the power of blockades as a form of protest, others began to question the wisdom and utility of actions which were resulting in more and more injuries for the women involved. The principle of non-violence meant that women did not lash out physically if hurt by policemen during blockades. But some women suggested that deliberately entering a situation in which women would be on the receiving end of men's violence was a form of masochism, of women martyring themselves and offering up their bodies for a greater cause. So it was that increasingly women at camp began to turn their attention to other ways of taking action against the base. One result of this was a 'blockading' action in April 1983 which did not involve women placing their bodies in the line of policemen's boots. The 'Citadel locks' action involved simultaneously locking each of the gates around the base with a solid reinforced metal U-lock; so impenetrable are these locks that policemen trying to remove the lock from the Main Gate using five-foot long boltcutters actually pulled the gate off its hinges.[22] Another consequence was a move towards actions inside the base rather than on the perimeter.

Incursions

Women first entered the base in August 1982 to occupy the MOD sentry box. After this, which took the police completely by surprise, the guarding of the gate was stepped up, and actions remained largely focused outside the base until the silos action on 1 January 1983. It was the 'silos action', in which women climbed over the fence at dawn and danced on the (as yet empty) missile silos, which established the project of invading the base to demonstrate its insecurity as the most frequently undertaken form of action at Greenham.[23] During the first half of 1983 women entered the base on several occasions, playing a game they called 'snakes and ladders' – sometimes over the fence using ladders, at other times, unbolting sections of fence, to 'snake through'. On 1 April 1983, partly in response to the earnestness of CND – which was organizing a human chain from Burghfield to the Atomic Weapons Research Establishment at Aldermaston and calling pro-testors to Greenham against the wishes of many of the women at the camp – two hundred women climbed into the base dressed as furry animals, with a court jester in accompaniment, to have a 'Teddy Bears' Picnic'. The women involved in the silos action were charged with the civil offence of 'breach of the peace', which led to a high-profile court case, but other women entering the base in early 1983 were bussed out without charge; they were an embarrassment to the government and had not technically committed any crime.

During the planning of the silos action, there had been much discussion about the means by which women should enter the base. Some women suggested cutting the fence with boltcutters, so that everyone could just walk in, but consensus could not be reached about whether or not fence-cutting was a violent act which contravened Greenham's ethos of non-violence. By July of that year, however, many more injuries from blockading later, and incursions into the base an established form of action at Greenham, there was a group of women who were committed to cutting the fence, even though not everyone agreed with it. They argued that damage to property did not constitute violence, that damaging the fence around a nuclear base was a legitimate and transformative action, and that age and disability meant that not everyone could climb over the fence, whereas more women would be able to walk through.[24] Once again, the principle of personal responsibility overrode that of collectivity, and a group of women cut the fence to enter the base. However, this action served to move on the debate about non-violence, and almost everyone involved with Greenham came to accept that cutting the fence could be an important action in the repertoire of non-violent struggle. Thereafter, cutting the fence became both the usual way that women entered the base, and was seen as an action in itself, which demonstrated opposition to the base and caused huge expenditure and disruption to the military.

On 29 October 1983, just before Cruise was to arrive at Greenham, a mass fence-cutting action was held, organized secretly by word of mouth. Thousands of women, many dressed as witches, stood on each other's shoulders to cut down over four miles of fence, and 187 women were arrested for criminal damage. This action took the soldiers and police completely by surprise, and many women were badly beaten with sticks and truncheons, receiving broken fingers and arms, and dislocated shoulders, as the men struggled to cope with this huge act of criminal damage. Shortly afterwards, in order to deal with the escalating number of incursions and breaches of base security, significantly increased numbers of British soldiers were posted at Greenham to guard the perimeter, leaving the US military to protect the inner sanctum of the missile silos. Soldiers were stationed every few hundred yards around the base, searchlights were installed, watch towers built and extra fences and rolls of razor wire placed inside the fence. In November 1983, when Cruise arrived, the Secretary of State for Defence, Michael Heseltine, announced that women entering the base could be shot, and that any soldier who fired shots in the base in order 'to protect lives or property' would be immune from prosecution.

None of this prevented women breaking into the base, indeed, incursions reached an all time peak in 1984 and 1985, and continued until the camp ended in 1994. For a considerable period there were nightly incursions into the base by groups of women. Once inside women did a wide range of actions. These ranged from small acts of defiant criminal damage, such as the painting of 'Greenham Women are Everywhere' on base buildings, to the £2.5 million damage done to the titanium coating of a Blackbird spy plane by women who painted peace and women's symbols on it.[25] On other occasions women engaged in acts of sabotage of lighting systems and generators, or climbed into army vehicles and drove around the base. Some women saw their incursions as opportunities to test the security of the base, and three women occupied the air traffic control tower, and left taking papers which were marked 'top secret' with them. Another group of women actually camped inside the base for two weeks without being found, and many hundreds were only apprehended when they gave themselves up to police or soldiers. For many women, the ultimate aim of entering the base was to reach the missile silos, as this would represent the most serious violation of security; several women actually got through the last fence and into the high security area around the silos before being arrested, and dozens of others entered military buildings, wandering around freely for considerable lengths of time, and even listening in on briefings being given to US servicemen about the missile convoy.

To begin with women were charged with criminal damage for cutting the fence, and thousands of cases were processed by Newbury magistrates court over the years. In almost all cases the amount of criminal damage with which women were charged was less than that allowing trial by jury in the crown court ('criminal damage not exceeding £200'). As the amounts seemed to be completely random, and to bear no relation to how much damage an individual woman had actually done, it appeared to be the case that the Department of Public Prosecutions was deliberately choosing to keep cases within the summary system, and to remove the possibility of acquittal by a sympathetic jury.[26] Later, with Newbury magistrates' court clogged by women defending themselves in lengthy trials which consumed considerable police, military, and court time, a new policy of non-charging was adopted. Increasingly women were ejected from the base without charge (usually deliberately at the gate furthest from that at which they lived).

Then, in 1985 the Defence Secretary, Michael Heseltine, instituted new by-laws to deal with the problem of women's incursions into the base. The by-laws (RAF Greenham Common By-Laws 1985, SI 1985 No. 485) were made under the Military Lands Act 1892, and made it an offence of trespass for anyone without authority to 'enter, pass through or over or remain in or over' the parts of Greenham Common occupied by the base. Thereafter thousands of women were charged with trespass for entering the base, and charges of criminal damage, which were much harder to prove, became less frequent. At this point, two women, Georgina Ashworth and Jean Hutchinson challenged the legality of the by-laws, taking the case as far as the House of Lords. They were eventually declared *ultra vires*, and all convictions under the by-laws were therefore invalid. Only a fraction of the women convicted have applied to have their convictions quashed and for financial redress.[27]

Courtroom actions

Engagement with the legal system was seen by many Greenham women not just as the unavoidable outcome of taking non-violent direct action against the base, but as a form of political action in itself.[28] Over the years, thousands of women were arrested, charged, and convicted in Newbury magistrates' court for a variety of offences, primarily, 'criminal damage' (for cutting the fence and painting symbols and slogans), 'obstructing the highway' or 'obstructing a police officer in the course of his duty' (for blockading), and 'trespass' (for incursions). There were also charges of 'breach of the peace' in the first two years, and of 'taking and driving away', when women drove around the base in a military bus.

Greenham women transformed the courtrooms in Newbury by the simple act of refusing to play the parts assigned to them in the proceedings; they would be neither victims nor supplicants, and turned the trial process on its head by accusing the state of crime.[29] The court became the site of political theatre. Instead of sitting nervously on the edge of their seats in the corridors, dressed in their smartest suits, women sprawled in huge numbers, often on the floor, unpeeling layers of jumpers in the centrally heated building and singing and talking loudly as they waited. Once inside the courtroom, those on trial would refuse to stand when the magistrates entered the room and most would refuse to swear on the Bible (except the few Christians), often offering to swear on the goddess instead. The public gallery would usually be packed with other women, who would sometimes intervene in the proceedings by humming loudly when policemen were lying or by singing when women were convicted. This sometimes resulted in women, both defendants and supporters in the gallery, being sent to prison for 'contempt of court'.

A wide range of tactics were employed in court. In the early trials, and at crown court, women were generally represented by feminist barristers and solicitors who were sympathetic to Greenham, and who worked with the women to construct cases which would allow the maximum opportunity to raise the issues at stake. At the silos trial, for instance, a series of women expert witnesses was called to testify about nuclear proliferation, the effects of radiation, and the connections between uranium mining for nuclear weaponry and the oppression of black people in Namibia.[30] Later on, however, the vast majority of women defended themselves. This was partly because legal aid applications began to be regularly refused, but more importantly women discovered that there was more opportunity for them to explain their actions and to seize control of the proceedings if no lawyer was present. Bound by their professional codes of conduct and knowledge of court procedure, it was very difficult for the lawyers to let women have the floor in court to the extent that most wanted.[31]

On many occasions, particularly early in Greenham's history, women pleaded not guilty to the offences with which they had been charged and argued that they had acted to prevent the commission of greater crimes, often citing international law on genocide in their defence. Some women, on the other hand, pleaded guilty, if they had done that with which they were charged, and then explained the motivation for their actions. Others vigorously defended themselves, cross-examining witnesses and often uncovering contradiction and holes in the prosecution case. Mostly women did this when they had been charged for an offence they had not committed, or when police were lying, confused, or incorrect in their account of the incident, which was frequently the case. Some, of a more anarchic bent, chose to do this just to use up court time and to cause disruption.

When women were found guilty, which the vast majority were, they took the opportunity to explain their actions. Some statements were cool, rational, and descriptive, posing the case against Cruise and for disarmament, but others were intensely personal, sometimes involving the recounting of dreams, the reading of poems or singing songs. Many women drew explicit links between patriarchy and militarism, and made passionate speeches about male domination and the threat of nuclear war. Frequently women ended by declaring their contempt of the court and their refusal of its authority over them.

Over time, trials became routinized; the court officials largely gave up trying to make women stand-up or shut-up, magistrates appeared to have decided verdicts before cases were heard, and women tended to progress from investing court appearances with great political and personal significance to treating them as everyday occurrences, involving a trip into town for the morning and lunch in the Court Cafe afterwards. As women clocked up lengthy criminal records, and many went to prison repeatedly, some began to alter their approach to the criminal justice system.

There was a gradual shift away from seeing the courtroom as an arena in which to contest militarism, and jamming the courts and the prisons as a form of protest which would bring about the collapse of the system. Thousands of extra police had been drafted in to deal with the mass blockades and fence-cutting of 1982–4, and emergency holding centres had been set up at Newbury racecourse and in police stations around the county so that thousands of women could be processed. Newbury magistrates' court had a huge backlog of cases in 1983 and 1984, and stipendiary magistrates were employed to clear it. Hundreds of women had been to prison, often causing severe overcrowding. The system groaned, but was able to cope. As a consequence many women began to give false names when arrested (there were dozens of 'Bridget Evans' living at Greenham), and decided not to attend court, explaining this as a way of avoiding victimization by the legal system.[32] One result of this was that the police clamped down on bail, often refusing it to those they suspected would not turn up in court, or insisting that women gave an address other than Greenham so that they could be traced more easily.

There was some controversy about the tactic of non-appearance within the camp. The argument was expressed that such action constituted a refusal to take responsibility for the consequences of one's actions, and that each woman should be prepared to see her protest through to prison. Those who took this position tended also to argue that women should never pay fines, as this was a contribution to the state and a tacit admission of guilt. The riposte to this mobilized Greenham's principle of respect of diversity and individuality, suggesting that the material conditions of some women's lives, having children for instance, meant that they could not go to prison, or that prison was an easier option for middle class women than working class women, for whom the stigma was greater. Generally, however, it was the notion that women should act according to their own consciences and feelings, and that their choices should be respected, which guided discussions about the legal process.

Monitoring

The arrival of Cruise on 14 November 1983 was hailed by the government and the press as defeat for the peace movement as a whole, and for Greenham in particular. Many women experienced the day the first missiles were flown in as one of grief and deep fear for the future. However, actions immediately took place at Greenham – over a thousand women blockaded the base the next day, and over 50,000 gathered to demonstrate and pull down the fence in December. With Cruise came a new form of action for Greenham – the monitoring of activities within the base and of the Cruise missile convoys when they were taken out on exercise.

On 9 March 1984 the first convoy was brought out of the base in the middle of the night. Dozens of police surrounded the women at Blue Gate, pinning them up against the fence and throwing to the ground any woman who tried to get away. This first exercise was experienced by the women at Blue Gate as a terrifying indicator of the liaison between the police and the military, and the sight of Cruise missile launchers driving out of the base made real in a new way the preparation for nuclear war. Over time, ways of protesting against the convoy were developed. As soon as they were able, women would get to a pay phone and set the telephone tree in action. This was an elaborate system by which one initial phone call from a Greenham woman activated a large network of individuals around southern England, who would get out of bed to track the convoy. This network of activists, 'Cruisewatch', involved both men and women, and worked closely with some women from the camp. Other women preferred to track the convoy in women-only groups, and regarded Cruisewatch as 'action-men' peace campaigners who operated rather too much like the military.

Convoys of launchers and support vehicles left the base almost monthly from March 1984 until after the signing of the INF treaty. Women accepted that they could not prevent the convoys leaving the base on exercise; the violent policing of the first excursions made this clear. However, every convoy was followed by Greenham women and by Cruisewatch, usually to the army ranges on Salisbury Plain. Their presence at the site of the exercises often provoked extreme violence from the police, and women were, on a number of occasions, held in pits surrounded by barbed wire for hours at a time.[33] Along the convoy's route, small groups of protesters would gather to hold up banners, throw paint, and blockade the convoy with their vehicles. Once the convoy was halted women would climb aboard the vehicles and sabotage fuel tanks by filling them with sand and sugar, or by cutting the fuel pipes. This disruption and monitoring of the convoys was intended to demonstrate the falsity of NATO claims that Cruise would 'melt into the countryside', untraceable by the Soviets and invulnerable to attack. If Cruise could be followed by a few dozen peace activists with nothing more than citizen band radios and a handful of cars and vans, the Soviets could surely track it too. Moreover, the tracking of the convoys served the educational purpose of informing the public of the continued presence of nuclear weapons in Britain, and developed into a major problem for the military. In 1985, General

Charles Donnelly, Jr., head of the United States Air Force in Europe, admitted that manoeuvres of Cruise missiles from Greenham were limited to one five-day period per month 'because of the expense of providing civilian police to protect the systems from protesters' (*Aviation Week and Space Technology*, 5 August, 1985: 47).

In addition to keeping tabs on all excursions from Greenham, some women at the camp made it their project to watch closely the military activities within the base. The arrival of new equipment, particularly further flights of Cruise missiles, was noted and publicized, as women became familiar with the purposes of different aircraft. The presence of the camp also meant that the training in the conduct of nuclear, chemical, and biological warfare taking place at Greenham could not be kept secret. 'Red alert' exercises, for instance, involved the activation of nuclear warning sirens and the bussing into the base of all American personnel, including wives and children, in order to house them in concrete bunkers. The implications of their disappearance into shelters, whilst the British soldiers, police and civilians, whom the United States Air Force was supposed to be protecting, remained outside were pointed out by Greenham women and information was distributed to the press and through peace movement networks. Later, after the INF treaty, women at Greenham began to campaign for citizen verification of nuclear disarmament in order to open up the military process to democratic accountability.

Roving: 'carrying Greenham home'[34]

'Greenham women are everywhere' was a slogan coined early in the life of the camp, to suggest that Greenham actions took place beyond that one corner of Berkshire, and were not confined to women who lived at Greenham. Whilst there was, at various times, considerable tension about the label 'Greenham woman' and over the centrifugal pull of the camp, women's peace actions inspired by Greenham, and conducted by women who identified as 'Greenham women', took place all over Britain. Some of these were the actions of campers, 'roving troublemakers', but most were those of stayers and visitors, women whose primary commitment was to working in their home communities. It was particularly in taking action beyond Greenham that the project was pursued of 'making connections' between nuclear weapons, women's oppression, and other forms of injustice. Roving actions can be divided into two main groups: those that related directly to Greenham, but which took place away from the camp; and women's peace actions in the style of Greenham, but not concerned primarily with Greenham.

The first group of actions was directed mainly at raising public awareness about Greenham or at taking the protest about Cruise to other locations. Examples of such actions were the occupation of the lobby of the House of Commons in January 1983 to demand that the issue of Cruise be debated, and the dumping of a van load of Greenham fence outside the Ministry of Defence to highlight the amount of damage women were doing to the fence which was not being reported in the press and for which women were not being charged. To protest against Cruise and publicize Greenham, local women's peace groups throughout Britain held demonstrations in town squares, set up peace camps on roundabouts and engaged in dramatic street theatre, particularly on 24 May each year, International Women's Day for Disarmament. Blockades were held in London and other cities to protest against and publicize the exercising of Cruise missile convoys, and in 1985 there was a walk to 'reclaim Salisbury plain' which passed over the firing range and the area in which convoys were exercised, visiting *en route* ancient religious sites, such as Avebury and Stonehenge.

Perhaps the most ambitious action in this category was the court case brought in the New York Supreme Court by 13 Greenham women, their 17 children, a larger group called Greenham Women against Cruise and two US congressmen against Ronald Reagan, Defense Secretary Caspar Weinberger, and US military chiefs of staff. The aim of this case was to get an injunction against the deployment of Cruise at Greenham, using international law and the US Constitution to argue that deployment was illegal.[35] The case caused considerable dissension within the camp. Many women argued that the huge amount of money being thus spent should be directed at the basic needs of the camp. Others objected to working so closely with men and with lawyers in a manner which they believed deradicalized and incorporated Greenham into the system. None the less, the case attracted widespread support from the wider Greenham network and from the mixed peace movement, and for twenty four hours on 9 November 1983 camps were set up at all 102 (known) US bases in Britain in support of the case.

The second group of actions was inspired by the distinctive ethos and style of protest of Greenham but went beyond the issue of Cruise, often aiming to draw attention to the connections between nuclear militarism and other issues. For instance, on the occasion of President Reagan's visit to London (7 June 1982), women from the camp and from the wider Greenham network performed a symbolic die-in outside the Stock Exchange to highlight the huge profits made by the international arms trade. In February 1983 women camped outside Holloway Prison to protest about the treatment of women prisoners, and six women were arrested for climbing *into* the prison. In March 1984, women demonstrated outside a missile systems sales conference in London, throwing red paint at the building in which it was held. Making links between militarism, the exploitation of animals in research and women's oppression there was also a women's camp at Porton Down, (the chemical and biological weapons research establishment).[36] To publicize the use of uranium mined in Namibia in the production of warheads for Trident nuclear submarines, a women's action was held at the British Nuclear Fuels plant, Springfields. During the 1984–5 miners' strike, Greenham women, working with Women against Pit Closure groups also organized a series of women's walks from mining villages in South Wales to Hinckley Point nuclear power station, to demonstrate the relationship between the closing of coal mines, the expansion of nuclear power, and the manufacture of nuclear weapons. The other major form of action in this category was the establishment of women's peace camps at other

nuclear bases. Inspired by Greenham, there were, at different times, camps at
military installations at Menwith Hill, Waddington, Morwemstow, Rosyth,
Capenhurst, Fylingdales, and Brawdy, amongst others, and blockades, fence-
cutting and incursions took place at these and other bases.[37]

The other facet of Greenham's roving public face took the form of speaking
about the camp at meetings, conferences, and demonstrations. Over the years
Greenham women were invited to thousands of such events, ranging from CND
and other peace groups, student unions and Labour Party branches, to the
Women's Institute, Housewives' Register and Townswomen's Guild. Greenham
women were also asked to take part in delegations to Nicaragua, to give lectures at
peace conferences all over Europe and the US, and to speak at miners' rallies and
galas during the strike. Without ever appointing spokeswomen, most of these
requests for speakers were met. To a large extent the women who did 'speaks' were
self-selected; a list of requests was read out after the weekly money meeting and
volunteers called for. Many groups asked for particular named women, usually one
of the four or five women whom the media had designated as Greenham's leaders,
and were often disappointed to find an unknown woman arrive to speak to them.
Most women found themselves fielding questions about Greenham's women-only
policy, and meetings often divided between those who thought the camp a diver-
sion from the real business of opposing nuclear weapons, a 'lesbian separatist plot'
and a 'bourgeois deviation', and those who constructed the camp as the apotheosis
of heroic martyrdom in the cause of peace. 'Doing speaks', as Greenham women
referred to it, was a tiring form of action, but one which many women believed to
be very important. Not only did it inform the peace movement about what was
happening at Greenham and raise money for the camp, it also encouraged the use
of non-violent direct action by others, initiated discussions about feminism,
patriarchy and women's autonomy in mixed groups, and provided a link to Greenham for women who might otherwise have felt the camp too remote an ideal for
them to join.

Being there: the politics of place and presence

The most important externally-focused action of Greenham was simply its very
existence. The camp's visible public presence outside the base, maintained continuously for twelve and a half years, constituted its most powerful statement of
resistance to nuclear weapons. From September 1981 onwards, throughout the
preparations for the installation of Cruise, the building of the missile silos and the
infrastructure within the base, at the time of the arrival of the missiles, and during
the years in which they were kept operational and ready for use, there was a
permanent protest at the heart of nuclear militarism in Britain. It was this presence, at this place, more than any mass demonstration organized by CND in
London, which focused attention on the issue of nuclear disarmament. The fact
that there were women prepared to engage in full-time protest, outside the fabric
of twentieth century domestic comfort, captured headlines (in the early years) and

the imaginations of hundreds of thousands around the world. The word 'Greenham' came to be understood not as the common near Newbury, nor even as the USAF base for Cruise, but as the women's peace camp.

The location of the camp directly outside the site of US nuclear weapons made concrete the physical presence of the weapons in the Berkshire countryside and of the US military which controlled them. It challenged the abstractions which usually surround discussions of military policy, by directing the public's gaze at the actuality of nuclear militarism, at one concrete example of the Cold War. The juxtaposition of the colourful, domestic, ramshackle camp and the decorations of women's symbols, doves, and handwritten messages hung on the fence with the rolls of razor wire, watch towers, searchlights, and soldiers in fatigues was highlighted in countless newspapers articles and represented in photographs, postcards, and television footage[38]. As a tangible focus for the expression of opposition to Cruise, the camp became a place of homage, visited by hundreds of thousands of people over the years. Between 1981 and 1985, every weekend brought at least a few dozen visitors, often hundreds. Although many such visits were perhaps attempts to vicariously experience Greenham, involving the consumption of the spectacle of the camp, those that visited left having at least seen a nuclear missile base. The importance of this should not be underestimated. The whole conduct of nuclear militarism from its very beginnings has been rooted in the highest levels of secrecy, as I argued in Chapter 2. Greenham attacked that secrecy, by bringing public and media attention to one of the sites of the world's most advanced first strike nuclear weapons. Unlike other nuclear bases around the world, which tend to enforce strict policies against the taking of photographs and to display prominent notices warning away anyone who gets too close the USAF base at Greenham Common could not remain anonymous.[39]

Above and beyond the daily work involved in the reproduction of life at the camp, maintaining the physical presence soon became a struggle in itself; being there turned from being an implicit challenge to the state into an explicit act of defiance. During the first weeks of the camp, when neither the women nor the military or the police knew that the camp was there to stay, relations were reasonably cordial, and men from the base even assisted in the attaching of a standpipe to the water supply (Harford and Hopkins 1984:18). This changed in December 1981 when construction workers were prevented from laying sewage pipes which were intended to run through the middle of the camp. The women refused to move the caravan and tipi which stood in the way, and they then sat down in front of the diggers (Harford and Hopkins 1984:27). This spontaneous act of resistance constituted Greenham's first blockade, and made it apparent for the first time that the existence of the camp was going to hamper preparation for Cruise. At this point, confrontation with the state became inevitable.

The presence of the camp, however, was more than a thorn in the side of the project of nuclear militarism. As a women–only community (from February 1982) occupying public space, and open to any woman who wished to join, Greenham enacted a constant challenge to patriarchal social relations. The symbolic statement made by its existence and persistence was that women can live without men, not just for short periods of time, out of necessity, but for years, in a functioning community, through choice. At Greenham, women appeared not to need men for any of the things that traditional patriarchal discourse holds them to be essential. Men were not needed to provide a roof over women's heads, to build shelters, or pitch tents. They were not needed to do the heavy or the skilled manual labour: to chop wood or mend cars. Their wages were not needed to provide the material comforts of late twentieth century Western societies and the household technologies which women want. They were not needed to protect or defend or represent women. They were not needed to act for women in the public sphere, to do politics on their behalf. But, above all, their approval and their company were not wanted. Greenham challenged the notion of men and women's complementarity, and gave the world an image of women who were independent and autonomous.

Women living outdoors, all year round, without the conveniences of gas, electricity, and running water, in a culture which still constructs woman as 'her indoors', raised questions about femininity. Like the 'rational dress reformers' of first-wave feminism (Banks 1986), and women punks in the late 1970s, Greenham women rejected the fashions of femininity, wearing big boots before DMs were fashionable and scruffy clothes before 'grunge'. They dressed for warmth and practicality, and created their own aesthetic of short hair, often shaved at the sides, colourful knottings and jewellery.

Moreover, just by being there, as a place that was full of lesbians, Greenham cut through the public silence which still existed about lesbianism, notwithstanding the gay liberation movement or the involvement of lesbians in the women's liberation movement. In the early days, sexuality was a line of fracture within Greenham, as some of the women who had been involved at the beginning believed that the predominance of lesbians at the camp should be played down, or even denied, and the presence of mothers and housewives – 'ordinary women' – should be emphasized. There were a number of rows about 'public displays of affection' within the camp, especially when journalists or visitors were present, and a case was made for the importance of impression management and the need not to detract from the 'real issue' of Cruise missiles. Lesbians at the camp, particularly those who had come to Greenham already lesbian feminists, argued back not only that lesbians had a right to exist and to take part in Greenham, but also that the politics of Greenham should recognize heterosexuality as oppressive of women. Over time, anti-lesbian views were increasingly rarely expressed as the women concerned either left Greenham in disgust or, more frequently, changed their minds (see Chapter 8).

Thus, not long after the camp became women-only, it had become a place where women were openly and unashamedly lesbians, and where affection and love between women were not concealed. Many women carried their visibility as lesbians into Newbury, and would allow themselves to behave in public as heterosexual couples do:

We were young raving dykes and we were holding hands and kissing in the bus stops. We'd found our lesbianism and we'd found a place where we could be lesbians.

(Linda, 22, camper)

More than this, some women saw performing lesbianism with a blatant theatricality as an important action against patriarchy. So, whilst everyday relationships and affairs between women at Greenham proceeded without being covered up for the benefit of public gaze, some women deliberately demonstrated their sexuality to the world:

[W]e used to take a lot of delight in going into Newbury and ordering beans on toast and then sitting there and [. . .] flaunting our lesbianism at people [. . .]. You'd all deliberately go and sit with your arms around each other drinking tea, but sort of acting amazed that anybody was staring at you.

(Bridget Evans, 23, camper)

Thus women at Greenham, by being lesbians openly and in large numbers, whether with added production values or not, enacted a politics of presence which made lesbianism exist beyond the privacy of personal relationships, and propelled the word into the tabloid newspapers and mainstream discourse.

In sum, the range of actions employed at Greenham was extensive. Some drew on traditional modes of protest, reworking them with a new passion and emotionality. Others were fashioned to meet the specific circumstances that prevailed there, changing as conditions changed. In their anarchy and unpredictability they posed, at times, serious problems for the military, and in their constancy over the years, they waged a campaign of attrition against the defences of the nuclear state. At a symbolic level, they disrupted dominant constructions of femininity and contributed to the creation of new meanings about gender. As such, the external face of Greenham called forth a plethora of responses from the institutions and actors it challenged.

Boys against girls, girls against boys:
the dynamics of Greenham's challenge

The externally directed actions of a social movement are created not just according to the movement's internal ethos and its discursive framing of the issues at stake, but also in a continual process of interaction with the forces it opposes. In comparison to the sociological attention given to analysing the origins, contexts, and mobilization processes of social movements, much less has been written about responses to social movements, and their influence on the direction and course taken by movements.[1]

The discussion in Chapter 6 has already examined the way in which the use of the criminal law by the state opened a new arena of action for Greenham women, and I have indicated how the changing policing of Greenham led to the adoption of new forms of action. In this chapter I seek to further the analysis of the dynamics of Greenham's challenge. This is done by examining the various responses called forth by the existence of the camp itself (the seventh form of action considered in Chapter 6) and how the movement grappled with them. I focus particularly on the ways in which the state attempted to deal with Greenham, both officially and unofficially, and the popular backlash against Greenham in the locality. The one area which is passed over is that of media reporting of Greenham, as this has been well covered by others.[2]

The response of the state

Recent feminist analyses of the state, from both Gramscian (e.g. Sassoon, 1987) and poststructuralist (e.g. Pringle and Watson 1992) perspectives, have argued that the state cannot be adequately understood as straightforwardly and monolithically patriarchal, as the 'instrument' of men's power, as some earlier feminists have suggested.[3] Rather, they propose that the state is the locus, and product, of struggles over meaning and resources, and an arena through which gender is constituted. I have considerable sympathy with such work, which demands that 'the state' is historicized and studied in its complexities and particularities rather than presumed to be a constant and unitary actor operating in the interest of men. In particular, it is important in shifting the terms of feminist consideration of the state away from unitary notions of 'men's interests' and 'women's interests', as in the realm of military policy it would be hard to argue that nuclear militarism serves the interests of men (beyond that small group of men who have profited from it and controlled it). Such an approach would also focus attention on the ways in which gender is constructed and contested within specific areas of state action, such as the military, which as Enloe (1983, 1989) has shown, has historically been an arena within which hegemonic notions of masculinity have been produced and the meaning of femininity both produced and challenged.

However, application of this approach to the theorization of the state to the sphere of military and foreign policy could overstate the extent to which conflict and contention is allowed to exist. As I argued in Chapter 2, this arena of state action is conducted in a singularly secretive manner, to a large extent beyond both the public's gaze and political debate. In state dealings with Greenham there was little sign of internal tension and struggle. Decisions had been made, at a trans-national level, to deploy Cruise missiles at Greenham, and the various arms of the British state were required to facilitate this. The actions of these institutions – the Ministry of Defence, the Department of Transport, the Home Office, Thames Valley Police, Berkshire County Council and Newbury District Council – were directed towards the implementation of this policy.

Within the framework of a liberal democracy, and bound by the need to retain public support, the state pursued NATO nuclear policy by using the law, primarily civil, to challenge Greenham's existence. In so doing the state acted in a gender-neutral manner, without reference to the fact that the protest was conducted by women. As women are *formally* equal citizens, laws were not available which would enable female protesters to be treated differently from male protesters.[4] However, in its actions, the state was effectively reinvoking the patriarchal 'fraternal social contract' (Pateman 1989), the founding discourse of the modern state. According to the fraternal contract, only men are political actors, and the public world of politics is a masculine one (Pringle and Watson 1992:57). The state's response to Greenham, which was primarily to attempt to eradicate its existence as an ongoing protest, can be seen as an attempt to rebuff claims to a political voice and to political participation, in unconventional ways, by women. The gender of state actors is, therefore, significant. Women protesters were, overwhelmingly, arrested by police*men*, sentenced by *male* magistrates, and acted against by local authorities, government departments, and civil courts run by *men*.[5] In doing this work, these men were not, for the most part, explicitly and consciously acting as patriarchs, to uphold male interests; but the effect of their actions constituted an attempt to do so, as it sought to obliterate this particular intervention by women into military policy.

Moreover, the response of the state to Greenham was not limited to the formal measures taken legally and publicly to oust the camp. State employees, particularly the police and soldiers, also engaged in 'unofficial' action against Greenham. It could be argued that their actions were taken as individual men, as private citizens, and as such should be analysed together with the response of the local community. But such a position is untenable; these state employees took their 'unofficial' action during the course of their work for the state, wearing uniform and under the command of senior officers. Few of the complaints made against them using official channels were ever successful. It is, therefore, necessary to examine both the official and the unofficial state response to the existence of the camp.

The official state response

At the point at which it became apparent that the presence of the camp was going to obstruct work at the base, the matter was taken up by the Recreation and Amenities Committee of Newbury District Council (NDC). This committee had responsibility for those parts of Greenham Common which had not been requisitioned by the Ministry of Defence for use by the RAF during the Second World War and which had subsequently been handed to the USAF in 1950.[6] The result of this was a formal letter from Newbury District Council (dated 20 January 1982) requesting the removal of the camp within 14 days, and threatening court proceedings to secure eviction if the camp did not disband.[7] The letter written to Newbury District Councillors in reply pointed out that the law was not neutral and independent and that there been have times in the past when laws have had to be broken; if there was a law which allowed the council to destroy the camp, it was an unjust law, and the councillors were enjoined to ignore it.

The first eviction took place on 27 May 1982. Bailiffs, backed by 100 policemen and with subcontracted bulldozers, arrived to remove the camp. However, the women there refused to leave; two climbed up into the tree house and were pulled down by bailiffs and policemen. Other women started weaving webs around the bulldozers and lying down in front of them, and one woman climbed into the cab to prevent damage to a tree (Harford and Hopkins 1984:46–53). The bailiffs and police used considerable force to move women out of the way of the bulldozers in order to pull down the camp shelters, and a number of women sustained minor injuries and bruises; many were also the target of verbal sexual harassment. In all, five women were arrested for breaching the peace, and the next day, refusing to agree to be bound over to 'keep the peace' (except under their own definition of 'keeping the peace'), four were sent to prison for a week. Meanwhile, the women who had been living at Greenham did not leave after the eviction, but moved onto a piece of land owned by the Department of Transport right next to the common land from which they had been evicted. Moreover, the publicity following the first imprisonments meant that the actions of the local state and the police had the unintended consequence of drawing more women and more support to the camp.

By now it was clear that the government was determined to get rid of the camp and, later in May 1982, the Department of Transport obtained a High Court order to remove it from the land it controlled. When the second eviction eventually occurred, on 29 September 1982, all the camp's caravans were taken away and lorry loads of boulders were dumped on the DoT land in order to prevent women from moving back there. However, the women had managed to salvage tents, bedding, and cooking gear, and set up camp later that day back on the common land where they had been before the first eviction.

Many women had now been living at Greenham for several months, some almost the entire year of its existence, and considered the camp home. Twenty one women therefore decided to register to vote with the camp as their permanent address. It was then that the opposition of local residents to the camp began to appear. An objection was lodged to the entry of the women's names in the electoral register on the grounds, first, that they were not British subjects and second, that they did not have a residential qualification. At the hearing at Newbury District Council Offices on 22 December 1982, however, the objection was overruled as women produced passports and argued, using a dictionary definition of 'home', that 'home' was an affective concept and did not necessarily require a 'house'.[8] The fact that Greenham was accepted as a residential address by the Department of Health and Social Security, the Post Office, and Thames Water was also adduced in evidence.

Whilst this victory indicated that liberal democratic principles could be mobilized to protect the right to live at Greenham, other arms of the state continued to act, increasingly in concert, against the camp. For instance, within a few weeks of the electoral register ruling, a small group of councillors on a special working party met in private to revoke the common land by-laws which related to Greenham Common, thereby taking for Newbury District Council the rights of private landlords. This enabled NDC to issue a High Court writ against the 21 women listed on the electoral register, who were seen as the leaders of the protest. The writ was the most draconian use of the law to be attempted against Greenham women, and with the feminist solicitor, Jane Hickman, they fought it at the High Court on 9 March 1983. The first charge was 'conspiracy to trespass', for which an injunction was granted by the Court. This required the named women to vacate Greenham Common and 'be perpetually restrained thereafter' from setting foot on Greenham or Crookham commons, and from conspiring with anyone else to trespass on the commons. The penalty for so doing would be up to two years' imprisonment. The second charge of 'conspiracy to incite others to trespass' which was successfully challenged, would have allowed the imprisonment for up to two years of any of the named women for no more than mentioning Greenham in public.

Being banned for life from Greenham Common did not prevent those women from returning to Main Gate. They moved the camp off common land, back onto the narrow strip of Department of Transport land from which it had been evicted in September 1982. It was, however, impossible to live at Greenham and not violate the injunction, because the DoT plot of land was so small.

Rowan Gwedhen, one of the women named in the injunction, described its impact:

> I remember being quite terrified, going back. 'Cos you know what bastards they are, and you didn't know if you were going to get out of the car and a policeman was going to say, right, you're nicked [. . .]. There was quite a bit of wondering about whether policemen were going to jump out of the bushes when you went to the shit-pit.
>
> (Rowan Gwedhen, 24, camper)

The injunctions were never invoked, although there was every opportunity to arrest women in the act of defying them. Why they were not put into effect can only be surmised. Perhaps they were only ever intended to intimidate and threaten, it being anticipated that the women would obey them for fear of two years in prison. Or perhaps the huge publicity which had surrounded the imprisonment of six anti-nuclear activists, for up to 18 months, under the Official Secrets Act in 1962 warned the state against taking this action against a group which had, at this time, huge support and intense media interest.[9] Since the 'Embrace the Base' – 'Close the Base' actions in December 1982 and the silos action of 1 January 1983, media coverage had been heavy and it was clear that Greenham could mobilize not just the 35,000 women who had come to Greenham but also large parts of the increasingly vociferous mixed peace movement.

Later in March, NDC secured another eviction order for the common land, and carried out the third eviction. This time bailiffs impounded eight vehicles from the camp, which would not be returned unless £3000, the cost of the eviction, was paid to the council. Women blockaded the bailiffs as they seized the cars, and were violently handled out of the way. Again, the unintended consequence of the eviction was to swell the numbers of women at the camp, and to increase the financial and other support being sent. From then until the beginning of 1984, there were no more evictions; the peace movement was at its height, the camp growing every week, and NDC backed away from confrontation for a while.

In November 1983, the month when the first missiles were flown into the base and which saw thousands of arrests of peace campaigners both at Greenham and in London, preparations were made for what was hoped would be the final push against the camp. New by-laws were enacted which forbade the erection of tents or other structures and the lighting of fires on the common, and gave NDC the power to remove such structures and extinguish fires. However, the Council shelved plans to enact them in November because of the large number of women at Greenham.

From November, the policing of the camp was stepped up; for five months there was a twenty-four hour a day civilian police presence close to each gate. Each day policemen would walk around each of the camps counting the numbers of women there (and women would run around them attempting to confuse them, or count loudly from a different starting point, making them lose count). The number plates of all cars at or visiting the camp were noted. Warrants were obtained to search tents and benders for boltcutters before major gatherings at the base, and on

11 December 100 pairs were confiscated. As the April 1984 *Green and Common Newsletter* described it:

> The police put out our fires to prevent us cooking and keeping warm at night, try to prevent us putting up tents and structures, stand at our fireplaces to harass and intimidate, follow women into the bushes when they go the toilet, prevent us parking our vehicles and intimidate visitors by saying they cannot park their cars along the road. This outrageous behaviour by the authorities is meant to force us to end our campaign and leave Greenham Common.
>
> (Jane)

In January 1984 the new stipendiary magistrate, who had been posted to Newbury to deal with the huge backlog of cases from the autumn, started to refuse to accept Greenham as a legitimate address. Dozens of women who had given Greenham as their address were refused time to pay fines, as the magistrate considered they were of no fixed abode, and they were sent immediately to prison.[10]

Later that month NDC appointed two full-time bailiffs solely to enforce the new by-laws, and a number of evictions of Blue, Indigo, Violet, and Red Gates were carried out. The bailiffs and police also began appearing at all times of the day and night to extinguish camp fires at all the gates, filling the fire pits with water or foam and making the re-lighting of the fires extremely difficult. At the end of February, Berkshire County Council appointed NDC as its agent, so that they could act together against the camps which were sited on roadside land controlled by the county council. Then, in the clearest evidence that the local and central state were working together, the Department of Transport joined the informal consortium, and requested that Berkshire act for it in securing the eviction of Yellow Gate from the land in its control.

Thus in March 1984, Newbury District Council, Berkshire County Council, the Department of Transport, and the police began to work together systematically. In the week beginning 5 March, the camps on the north side, whether by now on common land or roadside land, were evicted regularly, sometimes several times a day. The first few of these evictions were relatively gentle affairs, with women given time to take down tents and pack up communal property. However, by Wednesday of that week, anything not carried away within minutes of the bailiffs' arrival would be thrown into the refuse lorry (the 'muncher'); dozens of women lost all of their personal possessions, together with food, cooking pots, and firewood. The bailiffs became increasingly violent and struggled to snatch things out of women's hands, often hitting women in the face and pushing them roughly to the ground. Invariably the police stood by whilst this happened, though they sometimes stepped in to arrest women. During the early hours of 9 March it became apparent why this concerted effort to evict the northside gates had been made; Cruise missile launchers were brought out of the base on exercise for the first time.

Shortly after this, the Department of Transport announced its plans to permanently evict the camp at Yellow Gate; the access road to the base was to be widened, removing the land on which women were camped, and the women were given until 2 April to leave. The DoT was granted a possession order over the land it controlled and there was a blaze of publicity about the threatened eviction. Hundreds of women from around Britain came to the camp for 2 April, and NDC was forced to postpone the eviction at Yellow, though it went ahead at Green and Orange. When it eventually happened, two days after the deadline, 400 police and 24 bailiffs were used and a two mile stretch of the A339 was closed to traffic, the reason given on local radio being an overturned lorry. Thirty women were arrested during the course of the eviction, and fences were erected around the DoT land. Whilst Yellow Gate women re-established their camp on common land, the bailiffs moved on to the other gates. Newspaper headlines declared that Greenham was over: 'Peace Camp Cleared Out' (The *London Evening Standard*, 4 April 1984); 'Flaming Goodbye to Greenham' (The *Sun*, 5 April 1984); 'Dawn Raid by Bailiffs Ousts Camp' (*Newbury Weekly News*, 5 April 1984); 'Goodbye and Good Riddance!' (*Daily Express*, 5 April 1984). None of those papers reported that there were more women at Greenham after the evictions of 4 April than before, and all but the *Newbury Weekly News* allowed the camp to drop from their pages.

From April 1984 onwards, evictions of all the gates except Yellow were a regular part of life at Greenham. Their frequency was exhausting and served to wear down the spirits of women living at the camp. Over the months, the bailiffs became more aggressive and increasingly violent, and women were often injured trying to save things from being thrown into the muncher. The uncertainty about when the bailiffs would come meant that it was difficult to do anything but wait for them; for more than one or two women to go into Newbury to shop, wash or sign on, was a risk, and vehicles always had to be available, with a driver, to load with possessions. However, women devised ways of coping with the evictions, ranging from humour, and teasing and hexing the bailiffs, to treating it as a refuse collection service. Possessions were pared down to an absolute minimum, with most sleeping in Gore-Tex survival bags rather than tents or benders, and systems were developed for packing up quickly. For instance, kitchen equipment was kept in prams and trolleys so that it could be wheeled away from bailiffs. The numerous attempts of Newbury District Council to eradicate, or at least displace, Blue Gate by erecting fences around the triangle of land it occupied were foiled by women taking axes to them and using them for firewood. In all, evictions became something of a routine 'cat and mouse' game, a regular form of harassment, and although they may have shortened the length of time individual women were able to live at Greenham, they never achieved the goal of eradicating the camp.

The 'unofficial' state response

In taking the above actions the state was ostensibly merely utilizing the law to remove a hindrance to the conduct of military policy and a nuisance to the local community. This project was also pursued in the 'unofficial' actions of state employees, often in ways that contravened the rights of the women concerned and that circumvented or broke the law.

British soldiers were first brought to Greenham to guard the base from the inside during the July blockades in 1983, and a number of different regiments were stationed there for short tours, in rotation. Some regiments engaged in more harassment of the women than others, with the worst coming from the Paratroopers who were at Greenham at the time that the missiles were installed. Levels of harassment also varied according to the officers in charge; some officers clearly encouraged their men to make life hard for the women, whereas others did not. For instance, there were a number of periods when officers commanded their men to blow horns or bang oil drums every quarter of an hour throughout the night, to prevent women sleeping. Others did drill calls as soon as it was light, and brought brass instrument players to the fence to play into the middle of the night. This sort of low-level harassment served to deprive women of sleep, and was experienced as extremely stressful.

At those camps which were very close to the fence, soldiers often engaged in prolonged bouts of verbal sexual harassment. All of the Violet Gate women interviewed recalled one particular group of soldiers who kept up a barrage of grotesquely explicit verbal sexual abuse for several days. Penny Gulliver from Blue Gate described the more everyday insults:

> The soldiers would be shouting, 'we're going to come in and rape you in your tents tonight', or 'I wouldn't fuck you if you were the last bit of meat in the world'. It ranged from one to the other, but all sexual.
>
> (Penny Gulliver, 22, camper)

On other occasions, and more immediately dangerous, verbal abuse was combined with physical assault.

> At Orange Gate one night there was a maniac sergeant in charge of the men who was just exciting the men, all the time, and using filthy language, and calling us everything. And they started throwing clods onto the bender and suddenly they got hold of a big spike, part of the fence, and just rammed it through the side of the bender. I suddenly felt this thing hitting my arm. And I just went out and screamed at them. And they were shouting, 'lesbian slags, fuck them whatever way you can'.
>
> (Sian Edwards, 33, visitor)

The techniques employed by soldiers included throwing skinned rabbits and buckets of cold water over the fence at women sitting around the fire, throwing rocks and stones at women, both during the day and at the tents and benders at night, and heating metal rods in their braziers and then poking them into tents and benders.

The fact that not every regiment of troops engaged in this sort of behaviour suggests that there was no consistent policy of harassment directed from the Ministry of Defence. However, many officers encouraged it, and many more tacitly supported it. None of the complaints made by women to the Commanding Officer of the base was reported to have resulted in disciplinary action, nor indeed were any of the complainants informed that their complaints had even been upheld.

Many women found living in close proximity to soldiers engaged on informal campaigns of harassment distressing and, at times, frightening. As Penni Bestic explained, it was this, rather than the officially sanctioned threat of being shot inside the base, that constituted the immediate danger to women at Greenham:

> I never thought that anyone was in danger from being shot. I think where women *were* in danger was being harassed by soldiers. I remember one night when we had the benders up against the fence, there were some squaddies who were lobbing lumps of concrete onto the benders, and Mary got hit. And metal stakes that they were shoving through. But that was their extra-curricular activity.
>
> (Penni Bestic, 31, camper)

Whilst these activities were not officially stated as military or government policy, they were empirically observable to the women affected, who had to hand theoretical tools, such as the concept of sexual harassment developed by second-wave feminists, with which to understand them. Developing an analysis of why soldiers acted in this way, and reading about military training (for example in Brownmiller 1976) enabled many women to cope. Women also moved tents and benders further away from the fence. Some decided to attempt to reason and converse with the soldiers, to demonstrate shared humanity. Women at Violet Gate for instance, after the period of severe verbal harassment, developed cordial, and even friendly, relations with certain groups of soldiers. For some this was purely to make life more bearable up against the fence, whilst for others it was a deliberate attempt to initiate change and to incite disaffection in the ranks (the telephone number of 'At Ease', a counselling service for military personnel wanting to leave, was always kept to hand). The rapprochement reached the extent of soldiers giving women mugs of tea after evictions, bringing out shovels of burning coals to help them re-light the fire after the police had extinguished it, and even, on a number of occasions, cutting holes in the fence to let women into the base and giving them keys to the padlocks on the gate. Far more women, however, chose to ignore the soldiers completely.

What was considerably more difficult for women to deal with, and in many respects far more successful at attacking the presence of the camp, was the electro-magnetic radiation which emanated from the base.[11] Women at Green Gate first became aware of a pattern of ill health among the group in the second half of 1984, at about the time when the mass presence of soldiers inside the perimeter was reduced and replaced with electronic security systems. The physical symptoms included nose bleeds, dizziness, severe headaches, earache, swelling of the tongue, nausea, chest pains, palpitations, loss of hair, change in menstrual cycles, post-menopausal bleeding and persistent rashes, and mental symptoms such as impaired co-ordination and short term memory, disorientation, depression, sleep disturbances, and unreasonable panic.[12] These symptoms affected campers most strongly, but were also reported by stayers and visitors. The symptoms seemed to come and go, becoming particularly acute just before the convoy would be brought out on exercise, and were experienced by women at different gates at the same time, even when they were not in contact with each other. Once food and water poisoning had been discounted as a cause, the idea arose that the camp was being 'zapped'. A number of women began researching into electronic weaponry and electromagnetic radiation, and invited experts to measure emissions from the base. They found that there was a 'marked increase' in the background signal level at times when women were experiencing ill effects, and low signal levels 'rose sharply' when women created a disturbance by the fence (*Electronics Today*, December 1985). At certain places around the base, particularly close to the camps, low-level radiation was 100 times above normal levels, and Rosalie Bertell, who has researched biological effects of non-ionizing radiation, identified the symptoms as consistent with low-level radiation (Besley 1986).

The Ministry of Defence denied that any form of electronic signal was being used against the camp. However, there is considerable evidence to suggest that electronic weaponry, in the form of ultrasound, was used by the US military during the Vietnam War, and that the US police have tested infrasound generators as riot-control weapons (*Electronics Today*, December 1985). Moreover, the US embassy in Moscow was the target of low-level microwave radiation in the 1950s, 1960s and 1970s, and there has been a high incidence of cancer and disorders of the blood and nervous systems in those who worked in the embassy during this period (*Electronics Today*, December 1985). In this latter case, as at Greenham, it was never possible to prove whether the microwave radiation was the incidental product of radar and other surveillance equipment, or whether it was deliberately targeted as a 'non-lethal' weapon, which could be used without provoking political reaction, to induce illness and disorientation.

Whatever its purpose, 'zapping' took its toll on Greenham. Whilst not all women were affected by it, most were inclined to believe in its existence, particularly as information was gathered about electronic weapons and the medical effects of exposure to radar. Women who were badly affected had to leave the camp, either permanently or when the symptoms flared. Others stayed on, but were often below par in actions and irritable with those around them. A few women doubted the existence of 'zapping', and suggested that living at Greenham was making some women paranoid. This may have been the case, as twenty-four hours a day confrontation with the nuclear state would take its toll. However, as the old adage says, 'just because you're paranoid, doesn't mean they're not out to get you'.

Above and beyond this, there were a number of forms of unofficial harassment and surveillance directed at Greenham as a movement and at individual women, which were almost certainly co-ordinated by MI5.[13] A number of women reported being subject to violence and surveillance by unidentifiable sources whilst away from Greenham. Simone Wilkinson, who stood as a parliamentary candidate in the 1983 general election against Margaret Thatcher, was closely followed for miles as she drove back from a meeting one night during the campaign. When the car pursuing her attempted to force her off the road, she took refuge in a hotel at Heathrow Airport. Around the same time, she and a group of other women were also badly beaten up by a group of men who appeared to have been following them on the London Underground. Other women reported being followed on the tube and as they travelled around London. The public telephones closest to the camp were invariably out of order when the Cruise missile convoy was brought out on exercise, as were the telephones of many women on the telephone tree and those at the London Greenham office. These telephones also appeared to be tapped, evidenced by frequent 'clicks' on the line, the sound of tapes in the background, and the fact that police were assembled to arrest a group of women at Luton Airport who had booked tickets over the telephone from the London office. It was also widely suspected that mail to the camp was being intercepted.

The local response

Besides provoking an extensive, and expensive, response from the state, the presence of the camp also called forth a vitriolic and often violent reaction from amongst the local population. Newbury was a strongly Conservative area, one of the M4 corridor boom towns of the Thatcher years, and firmly embedded in the British military project.[14] The airbase at Greenham Common, with its large complement of dollar-rich US servicemen, contributed significantly to the area's prosperity, providing substantial income for local landlords, lucrative contracts for building contractors, and employment for hundreds of civilians.[15] Thus, in part, the anti-Greenham feeling amongst local residents was motivated by support for the nuclear policies of the US and British government and a fervent anti-communism, combined with material self-interest in the expansion of the base.[16]

There was also a strong element of what has come to be known as 'nimbyism' – the not-in-my-back-yard attitude of those who oppose something because it is close to them, but who would be completely uninterested in it if it were a hundred miles away. Some of the opposition to Greenham focused on the unsightliness of the camps, the inconvenience, blocked roads and traffic jams caused by large demonstrations, and the burden on the rates. A number of letter writers to the local press and local councillors at meetings linked the 'problem' of the camp with the long existing, though far smaller, 'problem' of gypsies who occupied parts of the common. What was particularly ironic about this sort of antagonism to the camp was that it was never expressed by the same individuals towards the base, which was far more unsightly, and indeed dangerous, than the women's peace camp. The prime exemplars of this nimbyism were the inhabitants of a house directly opposite Blue Gate. Mr and Mrs Scull were persistent critics of and campaigners against the camp, frequently giving media interviews about the squalor of the camp, and blaming it for their inability to sell their house. However, they never mentioned the fences and rolls of razor wire, the portakabins and missile silos, the intrusive lighting, or the constant noise of the generators from the base.

The third factor behind the response of the local population was the gender and sexuality of those at Greenham. Whilst a direct comparison with other peace camps is hard to make, not least because none was as large, as long-lived, or as politically important as Greenham, the local communities around Molesworth, Faslane, and Upper Heyford were never galvanized into action in a way comparable with that of Newbury. These mixed peace camps attracted some criticism of the 'nimby' variety, but the intensity of opposition to Greenham was far greater. Indeed one of the Faslane campers was elected onto the local council, whereas Jane Dennett, a Greenham woman who stood for a seat in Newbury received only 147 votes and considerable violence (Harford and Hopkins 1984:151).[17] The grass-roots opposition to Greenham had a clear gender politics, and was frequently strongly misogynist and anti-lesbian.

The 'public' face of the anti-Greenham campaign in the area was composed of two groups, Greenham Common Women Out, and RAGE, Ratepayers Against Greenham Encampments. The former organized a march against the camp in June 1983 which attracted over 300 participants, and a second one the next month. RAGE was founded early in 1984 by Anthony Meyer, who had been incensed that a Greenham woman invited to a local school to give a talk should have breast-fed her baby in front of children.[18] RAGE placed a series of advertisements in the *Newbury Weekly News*, each with a picture of a short-haired, women's-symbol-earring-wearing woman sitting astride a phallic-shaped Cruise missile. The first of these invited 'your help to send a Greenham Camper on a Cruise this Summer', and asked residents to sign the tear-off slip 'to express very strong opposition to the Greenham squatters' (*City Limits*, 2–8 March, 1984). A further advert appealed to members to help RAGE 'give an early send off to a Greenham wire-cutter' (*Newbury Weekly News*, 8 March, 1984).

RAGE's campaigning was directed primarily at national and local government, and at various public sector institutions. It petitioned Margaret Thatcher to evict the camp and lobbied the local MP, Michael McNair Wilson, who kept up a barrage of parliamentary questions about who was paying for the policing of Greenham. Its main focus, however, was NDC, which it blamed for failing to permanently evict the camp, and although a number of its leading figures were councillors, it threatened to sue the council. Another of the advertisements in the local press attacked 'officials and bureaucrats' for allowing the Greenham women 'privileged status'. Through a process of discursive reversal, the advert constructed Newbury 'ratepayers' as the victims of discrimination in favour of the peace women by the council (by allowing women to be registered to vote), the DHSS (by allowing women to claim benefits), Thames Water (by supplying the camp with water), the Post Office (by delivering post to the camp), and the courts (by accepting Greenham as a legitimate address).[19] The advert appealed to readers' sense of justice: 'Help us to Right these Wrongs' (*Newbury Weekly News*, 7 June 1984). In this RAGE employed the tool of discursive reversal which McNeil (1991) argues was much used by the New Right during the 1980s; ratepayers were one group amongst many (fathers, taxpayers, parents) who were seen as suffering discrimination, primarily at the hands of left wing public sector employees and women.[20] The reality of the situation at Greenham was that women had to struggle for each of the five 'rights' listed by RAGE, rights which are fundamental in an advanced industrialized and liberal democratic country, and in several cases had these rights withdrawn or interfered with at various times.[21]

RAGE aimed to project a public image of ordinary, concerned, and law-abiding citizens, wanting no more than a peaceful life. It claimed to have no antipathy towards the peace movement, and to be non-aligned on the nuclear issue; its only concern was to get rid of the camp (*Newbury Weekly News*, 31 May 1984). However, the treasurer of the group was also a member of the Freedom Association, a New Right organization which was engaged in a campaign against the peace movement. RAGE never held public meetings and would not send information about its activities to members of the local peace group, Newbury Against Cruise Missiles.[22] Moreover, RAGE was unable, or unwilling to control the behaviour of some of its members. Interviewed by *The Guardian*, John Learoyd, a local shopkeeper and founder member, described the Greenham women as 'traitors'; 'they take drugs, they are filthy dirty, they are sexual deviants' (*The Guardian*, 7 March 1984). Members of RAGE were also recognized by women at the camp as amongst those perpetrating vigilante attacks.

The representation of Greenham by its local opponents shared much with the themes identified by Alison Young (1990) in her work on the press reporting of Greenham. She suggests that the media painted five main portraits of the women: Greenham women as communists, Greenham women as unfit mothers and inadequate women, Greenham women as dirty, Greenham women as hysterics, and Greenham women as lesbians (A. Young 1990:45–88). Each of these themes was expressed in various ways by members of RAGE, as well as by others who did not publicly align themselves as such, in leaflets, and in letters to and interviews with the press. That these five themes occur in the pronouncements of local residents as well as in the media suggests not that local people plucked these ideas from the press, nor that the press was merely reflecting popular opinion. Rather it suggests that the ways in which Greenham women were spoken and written about are rooted in wider discourses about femininity and the appropriate behaviour of women, to which Greenham women posed a serious challenge.

Some of Young's themes are apparent in my discussion so far. For instance, John Learoyd's brief remark cited above strikes at least three of these chords. The objection, discussed earlier, to the women's application to register to vote from Greenham on the grounds that the women were foreign also became a common refrain in letters to the *Newbury Weekly News*, with the 'Britishness' of the women at the camp and their visitors frequently challenged.[23] And Anthony Meyer's motivating moment for founding RAGE was his horror at a Greenham woman's improper maternal behaviour.

The 'dirtiness' and 'squalor' of the camp and of the women themselves were regular complaints in the local press, and were also used as verbal harassment in Newbury, particularly from boys and young men, and as reasons for banning

Greenham women from shops, cafés, and pubs in the town. In a letter to the *Newbury Weekly News*, James D. Duffet commented, 'We are as disgusted and repelled by their presence as they are by the arrival of Cruise. At least Cruise is clean'.[24] In a more lurid exposition, Sheila Shedden, the chairman [*sic*] of the Newbury chapter of Women and Families for Defence and leader of Greenham Common Women Out, is quoted as saying at the anti-Greenham march which she organized in 1983: 'Speaking as a retired nurse, the place is ankle deep in human excrement, infested with rats . . . their behaviour is a threat to womanhood' (Jones 1987:187). As Young points out, women are traditionally 'agents of cleanliness, whether as maidservants, housewives or simply as women, made constantly conscious of their bodily effluence and the cultural coercion towards masking their "feminine odour" ' (A. Young 1990:60). Even in late twentieth century society, in which 'cleanliness', or rather, the consumption of personal and household cleaning products, is constructed as fundamental to health and happiness, men are culturally allowed far more freedom to be dirty, even smelly, than women. Men are also allowed to live, if without a woman, in a degree of mess and untidiness. For women to smell of woodsmoke, which was inevitable at Greenham, and to live outside, without cupboards full of cleaning products, without cupboards even in which to tidy away the clutter of everyday life, was to fundamentally disrupt hegemonic constructions of gender.[25]

The suggestion that Greenham women were hysterical and even mad, and incapable of rational discourse was also often made by local opponents. One example is a letter published in the *Newbury Weekly News* from Sheila Shedden, in which she explained why she had not tried talking to the women at the camp: 'it is not possible to have a discussion against the background of war cries and war dances' (*Newbury Weekly News*, 17 May 1984).

The final theme running through local opposition to the camp concerned the lesbianism of Greenham women. Linked to their unsuitable behaviour as mothers, and their penchant for dirt and squalor, the fact that they were 'sexual deviants' (cf. John Learoyd above) was often an open and explicit complaint. For instance, Councillor John White was explicit in his disapproval of the 'self-confessed lesbians, law-breakers and scroungers' of Greenham, whose 'openly lesbian sexual behaviour' was 'an outrage' (*Newbury Weekly News*, 19 April 1984). Another member of RAGE, Alex Hutcheon, described Greenham women as 'self-indulgent women flouting the law of the land, who do, in fact, run lesbian encampments and create an immoral situation' (quoted in Jones 1987:187). The Little Chef restaurant in Newbury, which banned Greenham women in March 1984, explained its decision partly in terms of their lesbian behaviour. Rocco Forte, chief executive of Trust House Forte, said their unacceptable behaviour had included:

> [. . .] pushing a number of tables together and sitting around them for three or four hours over a cup of coffee, making amorous advances to each other, [. . .] and stripping down in the toilets and carrying out their ablutions.
>
> (*The Guardian*, 14 March 1984)

None of the other pubs and cafés in Newbury which banned Greenham women (and there was only one pub and two cafés which did not) publicly explained their policies in this way, but many women were convinced that their lesbianism (real or not) was as important, if not more important, than their anti-nuclear politics. In addition almost all of the women interviewed, lesbian or heterosexual, recounted stories of anti-lesbian abuse from local men, both in Newbury and from men driving past:

> We got a lot of hassle along the north road. People shouting, but they'd always get a mouthful back. Like when somebody went past shouting 'lesbians', and this woman jumped up and down shouting, 'yes, it's lovely'.
>
> (Jenny Heron, 30, camper)

Far more often, however, lesbianism at Greenham was implied, an almost unspeakable undercurrent in the discourse of those who opposed Greenham. The woman depicted on the adverts placed by RAGE in the local press, for instance, was undoubtedly a lesbian; not the beatific, peaceful mother figure of some peace movement iconography, but a butch, burly dyke. Her positioning astride a nuclear powered phallus and the text encouraging readers to help send her off on it resonates with the commonly expressed sentiment that all lesbians need 'is a good fuck'. More subtly, a letter from Betty Warr to the *Newbury Weekly News* described the behaviour of Greenham women as 'hardly [. . .] the behaviour of normal decent women'. She went on:

> To conduct one's life, retaining dignity and respect in a law-abiding fashion with consideration for others, is surely a reasonable code of normal conduct. I resent strongly that my rates and taxes contribute to the continued squatting and law-breaking of these abnormal women. [. . .] Like many an average mother and housewife I find myself far too occupied to spend time debating.
>
> (*Newbury Weekly News*, 3 May 1984)

As in media reporting of Greenham, a focus on lesbianism did not arise amongst the local community until the camp had been established some time; lesbianism in the early 1980s was still, to a large extent, outside the boundaries of public discourse, silenced and invisiblized in a way that male homosexuality was not. The presence of men at the camp for the first six months, together with the prominence of the maternalist anti-militarism in the public face of Greenham militated against allegations of lesbianism for some time. However, as it became clear that Greenham was not a just a transient demonstration, that it could attract tens of thousands of participants, and that it was women-only as a matter of principle and politics, the 'L' word became more sayable. To point out the presence, indeed the predominance, of lesbians at Greenham was to cast the camp beyond normal society, and made any attack on it legitimate. These were not real women, deserving of male protection, but 'sexual deviants'.

Alongside the public opposition to Greenham of RAGE, Greenham Common Women Out, and the many individuals who wrote to the local press, there was a less respectable vigilante campaign against the camp.[26] This ranged from low-level harassment to life-endangering violence. At one end of the continuum were acts of harassment involving the property of Greenham women. Car tyres were regularly slashed and windscreens smashed; on several occasions paintstripper was poured over vehicles and 'NF' scratched into the paintwork. There were frequent thefts from tents and benders, and, more distressingly, cans of maggots and human excrement placed in sleeping bags and rucksacks. Car loads of young men would drive past the camps shouting abuse and throwing eggs, stones, firecrackers, and even acid, at women sitting by the fire. At Blue Gate, which experienced some of the worst harassment, there was a middle aged man who walked his dog every day through the middle of the camp, muttering under his breath and waving his stick before him, often hitting women who stood in his path or knocking over pots and pans. Flashers appeared at the camp from time to time (though they usually fled quickly when laughed at), and other men would drive dangerously close to women walking along roads by the camp, threatening to run them over. Amongst the most dangerous attacks, of which there were dozens during the life-time of the camp, were the slashing of tents with knives at night, physical assaults, such as one at Woad Gate in which two women were sprung upon, beaten unconscious and left seriously injured, several shootings in the direction of the camps by men with air rifles, and one sexual assault. There were also several spates of arson attacks, mainly at Yellow and Orange Gates. The arsonists invariably worked at night, and tended to use home-made petrol bombs thrown at benders and tents in which women were sleeping. At Orange Gate a number of serious fires which burnt considerable stretches of gorse were begun in this way.

Although a considerable number of women were injured over the years and most of the women interviewed reported having been seriously worried, from time to time, about vigilantes, the violence and threat of violence did not have the effect of driving women away from Greenham. Most of the more serious attacks and many of the thefts were reported to the police, but were met with almost complete indifference and inaction. On one occasion recounted by Pat Paris two MoD policemen witnessed a man hit a Blue Gate woman in the face but refused to arrest him. Even when the matter was reported at Newbury police station and a full description of the perpetrator and a photograph of him handed in, he was not prosecuted. Very quickly most women lost any faith in the police's interest in protecting them from violence and harassment, and tended not to bother reporting anything but the most serious incidents.

Instead of relying on male protection, women at Greenham developed ways of protecting themselves. One of these was the setting up of 'nightwatches', which involved having one or two women awake around the fire at all times. Nightwatches began at Blue Gate in the autumn of 1983, when attacks from vigilantes and soldiers were nightly occurrences, and spread to many of the other gates, combining the function of preventing attacks with that of monitoring manoeuvres in the base. Very soon there were groups of women from all over southern England who would come to Greenham regularly, sometimes every week, to do the nightwatch. They would usually arrive late, having driven down after work, would stay up all night, drinking tea, talking, and watching out for vigilantes. They would then leave first thing in the morning, often to do a full day's work. The nightwatches enabled women living at the camp to sleep more soundly, and were an important contribution to the continuation of the camp from women who were unable, or did not wish, to live full-time at Greenham.[27]

In addition to nightwatches, women used a number of other tools against the harassment and violence. At Orange Gate buckets of sand and water were kept ready in case of fires. At Blue Gate women started following the man with his dog on his daily progress through the camp, letting him know he was being watched, and asking him how he would feel if they walked through his living room, waving sticks at his ornaments and poking him as he sat in his armchair. Other women with a belief in the power of magic tried hexing the vigilantes, whilst others, as reported by Jenny Heron above, turned insults around and defused their power by agreeing with them. The two strongest weapons, however, were, first, women's solidarity with each other, which meant that women looked out for each other's safety, and would come immediately if any woman ever called for help; and second, the power of laughter and ridicule, which women turned against those who verbally abused them, and which raised the spirits at times of fear and anxiety.

Having examined the various forms of opposition which emerged to Greenham, I must propose a caveat to the title of this chapter: 'boys against girls, girls against boys'. The gender politics of Greenham's challenge and the response it produced *are* highly significant, particularly given the sexualized, misogynist, and anti-lesbian form taken by this response. However, as Walby points out, 'gender political forces cannot be read off from biological categories of men and women. Women do not always support feminist positions; men do not always take anti-feminist positions' (Walby 1988:229). Similarly, as I argued in the Introduction, there is no inevitable and biological impulse linking women with peace and men with militarism.

There were women prominent in campaigns against Greenham. At the local level, Sheila Shedden, was the chairman of Greenham Common Women Out, and her marches attracted many women. Mrs Scull, who lived opposite Blue Gate, gave regular interviews to the press extolling the virtues of Cruise and deploring the unsavoury habits of the Greenham women, and when the convoy exercises began she made a habit of greeting each excursion from her bedroom window with cheers of delight 'for our boys'. More significantly nationally were Lady Olga Maitland, the *Sunday Express* diarist, and Angela Rumbold, Conservative MP, who founded Women and Families for Defence. This group was launched in March 1983 to seize the discourse of maternalism for the pro-nuclear lobby, and achieved a high profile in the media. Lady Maitland's preferred interview site was in front of the fence at Greenham in fur coat, high heels, and make-up to draw attention to the differences between her organization, with its 'true' womanliness and family values, and the women at the camp. In addition, whilst not actively campaigning *against* Greenham and in favour of nuclear weapons, there was a small but vocal group of radical feminists who opposed the women's peace movement and organized a series of conferences to discuss the damage Greenham was doing to the women's liberation movement (Onlywomen Press 1983).

There were also men who supported Greenham. Much of CND and the mixed peace movement was, as I have argued earlier, ambivalent at best, and hostile, at worst, to the camp, primarily because of its women-only policy, and because it was thought to bring the cause into disrepute. However, there were small numbers of men who accepted that Greenham was closed to them, and offered material support none the less – regular deliveries of wood, donations of cars and vans and monetary donations. At a collective level, a gesture of support was even made by a state institution; Derbyshire County Council offered a week's unpaid leave to all of its 23,000 women staff so that they could attend the Ten Days action in September 1984.

This said, it remains the case that there was a concerted and co-ordinated response to Greenham from the state and from locals, which aimed to remove the public presence of the camp, and to thereby re-establish the pre-existing social order. Even in their ostensibly most gender neutral actions, which could and probably would have been taken against a mixed peace camp at Greenham, this response operated with patriarchal purpose, to crush women's most visible collective involvement in public politics since the suffrage movement. Ultimately, however, such efforts failed dismally. Greenham by-passed all attempts by the state, official and unofficial, to remove it, and the counter movements faded long before the camp. The strength of Greenham's collective identity and affective solidarity, and its fluid, flexible structure and openness to change enabled it to meet these challenges with defiance.

Transgressions and transformations:
experience, consciousness and identity at Greenham

The creation of new forms of consciousness and new identities is central to feminist struggles for social change. If women are effectively to challenge patriarchy, dominant modes of thinking and hegemonic gender identities must be transgressed and transformed. Feminist political action is forged through the construction of new consciousness and identities at the collective level. At the same time, new forms of consciousness and new identities, both individual and collective, are also the product and praxis of feminist political action. In other words, the challenging and reconstruction of consciousness and identity are both the medium and the outcome of feminist politics.

This chapter is concerned with these subjective and cognitive aspects of feminist political action. I begin by outlining my approach to theorizing consciousness and identity. I then go on to discuss the ways in which the women interviewed in the research experienced transgressions and transformations of their pre-existing forms of consciousness and identities through their involvement with Greenham. What this amounts to is the studying of the 'cognitive praxis' of Greenham: that is the collective intellectual activity and process of knowledge production which occurred there. As I have argued earlier, the cognitive praxis in which social movement activists engage serves to construct that movement, by turning groups of individuals into a collectivity with a shared identity and consciousness. It also produces new knowledge and sources of inspiration for the wider society. Thus this chapter is also concerned to explore what might be considered to be some of the lasting 'effects' of Greenham at the individual and societal level.

Theorizing experience, consciousness and identity

Despite Marxism's long-standing preoccupation with class consciousness, the question of how a 'class-in-itself' becomes a 'class-for-itself', orthodox Marxism and traditional left politics have generally failed to grapple seriously and successfully with the realm of subjectivity (Barrett 1991:110). As Barbara Marshall (1994:97) points out, Marxism's paradigmatic concentration on the processes by which domination is reproduced at the level of the social system has led to a lack of understanding of the importance of individual subjectivities in the reproduction of domination.

However, this issue has received considerably more attention, both in theory and political activism, since the 1960s. The black and civil rights movements in the United States, the students' movement and anti-war movements, and above all, the women's liberation movement and the lesbian and gay movements in the United States and Europe have all engaged, to a greater or lesser extent, with issues of consciousness and identity. Anthony Giddens (1991) has argued that the 'life politics' of these movements exemplify the impulse to self-actualization which characterizes a post-traditional era, in which a certain level of emancipation has been achieved. In late, or high modernity, he suggests, 'the self' becomes a reflexive project, in which individuals continuously create and re-create their biographical narratives, and hence their conceptions of themselves.[1] In a similar vein, Alberto Melucci (1989) argues that in contemporary societies in which mass education and universal citizenship rights exist, individuals increasingly possess resources of 'knowledge and action', which they employ to explore their self-identity. One of the ways many people choose to do this is through involvement in social movements. So significant is this tendency that many theorists of social movements highlight issues of identity, life-style, and personal autonomy as defining features of the 'new' social movements (e.g. Nedelmann 1984; Offe 1987; Scott 1990). However, despite this recognition at the level of theory of the centrality of these matters, there has been relatively little empirical sociological research which focuses on the experience of involvement and the transformations of consciousness and identity that occur within social movements.[2] This chapter is intended to contribute to the remedying of that situation.

The concepts of 'consciousness' and 'identity' as I use them here are two aspects of subjectivity. The notion of subjectivity has a broader sweep than is applicable here, as it usually encompasses both the conscious aspects of personal experience and the unconscious, and its effects, which are beyond the scope of this book. Chris Weedon usefully defines subjectivity as 'the conscious and unconscious thoughts and emotions of the individual, her sense of herself and her ways of understanding her relation to the world' (Weedon 1987:32).[3] For my purposes, 'consciousness' is an individual or a group's 'conscious thoughts' and 'ways of understanding her[/its] relation to the world'; identity is the somewhat narrower 'sense of self' or 'consciousness of self'. Nira Yuval-Davis explains identity thus: '[I]dentity constitutes the conscious "self"– the answer, or rather the answers, to the question "who am I?"' (Yuval-Davis 1994:409). Consciousness and identity are inextricably linked; the claiming of an oppositional identity, whether individual or collective, rests, at least partially, on the development of an oppositional consciousness.

However, none of the three concepts with which I am concerned – experience, consciousness, or identity – are entirely unproblematic, and all have been the focus of considerable debate within feminism. In order to specify further the way in which I am employing them, it is necessary briefly to explore these debates.

The linking concept – experience

The single most important issue of relevance to the usage of the concepts of consciousness and identity concerns the status of experience. Consciousness and identity are both tied to notions of experience, which has been understood in a number of different ways by feminists. One of the novel features of the women's liberation movement in the late 1960s and early 1970s was the importance it attached to women's experience. In contrast with traditional left-wing politics and Marxist theory, within which the specificities of women's lives were invisible, placing women's experience at the centre of the political and theoretical agenda was truly revolutionary. The typical way in which feminists conceptualized experience at this time was as providing the material for feminist consciousness and identity, through the process of consciousness-raising. This position is expressed by the Redstockings:

> We regard our personal experience, and our feelings about that experience, as *the basis for an analysis* [my italics] of our common situation. We cannot rely on existing ideologies as they are all products of male supremacist culture.
>
> (Redstockings 1970:535)

The italicized words are vital here, because they indicate that these early feminists of the women's liberation movement did not see experience as giving rise directly to analysis; rather experience was held to be that from which analysis was to be *built*. Unfortunately, the subtlety of this position on experience has not always been carried forward by feminists. The 'identity politics', which took off in the United States and in Britain in the 1980s, tended to see experience as the authentic truth, directly giving rise to an identity, which in turn leads directly to a politics. For instance, Barbara Smith states, 'As Black women we have an identity and therefore a politics which requires faith in the humanness of Blackness and femaleness' (cited in Fuss 1989:99, from Moraga 1983).[4] This particular causal link between experience, identity, and politics allows no real space for challenge or debate about politics or theory, because they are seen as given by the reality of women's lives. Experiential authority is exalted as the sole legitimate source of knowledge.

It is this problematic conceptualization of experience as authentic truth that has recently come under attack from feminist poststructuralists, whose arguments are exemplified by Joan Scott (1992, 1993b). Scott argues that there is, in fact, no direct, unmediated experience; experience is always discursively produced:

Experience is at once always an interpretation *and* is in need of interpretation. What counts as experience is neither self-evident nor straightforward;
it is always contested, always therefore political.

(Scott, 1992:37)

[W]e need to attend to the historical processes that, through discourse,
position subjects and produce their experiences. It is not individuals who
have experience, but subjects who are constituted through experience. Experience in this definition then becomes not the origin of our explanation,
not the authoritative (because seen or felt) evidence that grounds what is
known, but rather that which we seek to explain, that about which knowledge is produced. To think about experience in this way is to historicize it as
well as to historicize the identities it produces.

(Scott 1992:25–6)[5]

Scott suggests that the concept of experience has frequently been used by feminists in such a way as to essentialize identity and reify the subject. Her project, in
contrast, is to analyse the ways in which experience is constructed through
discourse.

This is a very important point, and directs our attention to the way in which
women's 'experience' of Greenham was framed by the discourses to which they
had access. However, it is also vital to recognize that actors do not just mobilize
pre-existing discourses to make sense of their experiences. If that were the case,
where did the discourses originate in the first place? Discourse is produced by
actors, and is at the same time productive of those actors; this, I would suggest, is a
basic implication of structuration theory, outlined in Chapter 1. Whilst emphasizing the importance of historicizing experience, and of seeing it as inevitably
socially constructed, Scott does not acknowledge that the discourses which construct experience as knowable may change. She does not allow that actors may
develop new discourses, which either reconstruct experience or make knowable
experience which had hitherto been unknowable. This possibility is, however,
recognized implicitly by another feminist poststructuralist, Chris Weedon (1987),
who writes that 'it is possible to transform the meaning of experience by bringing a
different set of assumptions to bear on it' (Weedon 1987:85).

Consciousness

Whilst 'consciousness' was an important concept within the women's liberation
movement, it appears recently to have dropped out of currency amongst feminists.
In the early days of the women's liberation movement the terrain of subjectivity
was identified as being at the heart of contestations between feminism/feminists
and patriarchy/patriarchal actors.[6] Women's 'internalized oppression', 'the ob-
stacles in women's own minds' (Jaggar 1988:149), were recognized as barriers to
change in gender relations. The feminist assertion that 'the personal is political'
underlined the importance that was accorded to the collective examination of

women's shared but privatized experiences, and to the personal change which feminists effect within their own lives. The practice of 'consciousness-raising', taking place within small, local consciousness-raising groups, aimed to contribute to the transformation of society through the articulation of women's anger and discontent with their lives under patriarchy, and the development thereby of feminist analysis. Indeed Catharine MacKinnon describes consciousness raising, which she does not see as being confined to consciousness-raising groups, as 'the major technique of analysis, structure of organization, method of practice, and theory of social change of the women's movement' (1981:29). According to Mac-Kinnon, within feminism '[t]he pursuit of consciousness becomes a form of political practice' (MacKinnon 1989:84).

The idea of the existence of 'raised' consciousness, the product of the feminist practice of consciousness-raising, is implicitly, and often explicitly, linked to the prior existence of false consciousness. Sandra Bartky, for example, puts it like this:

> Coming to have a feminist consciousness is the experience of coming to see things about oneself and one's society that were heretofore hidden. This experience, the acquiring of a 'raised' consciousness, in spite of its disturbing aspects, is an immeasurable advance over that false consciousness which it replaces. The scales fall from our eyes. We are no longer to struggle against unreal enemies.
>
> (Bartky 1990:21)

As Liz Stanley and Sue Wise (1993:121) point out, this model of consciousness owes much to Marxist theorizations, with their assumption that a more objective state of consciousness, which apprehends the 'real' conditions of social life, is attainable, in contrast to the mystificatory, pre-existing false consciousness.[7] Stanley and Wise reject this hierarchical model of consciousness, which rests on the proposition that there exists one true objective reality and one true objective way of understanding it. As I noted in Chapter 1, I have considerable sympathy with this position, which they later call 'fractured foundationalism' (Stanley and Wise 1990:41–2, 1993:9); whilst not denying the existence of material reality, material reality cannot be apprehended outside of discourse, in a once-and-for-all objective way. In other words, consciousness is never 'the truth', but rather one particular, historically located and discursively produced way of looking at and understanding the world. This way of conceptualizing consciousness allows us to find some forms of consciousness preferable, more adequate, better, but not to erect distinctions between true and false consciousness.

However, this is not the only criticism Stanley and Wise make of the way in which the concept of consciousness has been used within feminism. Equally important is their critique of the implication, for example in Bartky's work quoted above, that the achievement of a 'raised' feminist consciousness is an end state. They argue that consciousness should not be conceptualized as linear, evolving from false to feminist, but should rather be seen as 'a circle or spiral – there are no beginnings or ends, merely a continual flow' (1993:123). Consciousness is never static, and the consciousness of feminists continues to change, after they become feminists. Stanley and Wise also highlight the fact that there is no single, unitary feminist consciousness; feminists have many different ways of understanding the world and their place within it. These are important points, and are perhaps some of the reasons why feminist writers, particularly under the influence of the anti-objectivist, anti-essentialist thrust of poststructuralism, have shied away from using the concept of consciousness in recent years.

I would argue, however, that this theoretical baggage attached to the concept does not justify its abandonment altogether; we must just be wary of that baggage. Feminist theory in general, and feminist sociology in particular, still have need of a concept with which to describe and analyse the ways in which women understand the world and their own place within it. In addition, and approaching the concept from a slightly different angle, it is important not to allow changes in consciousness to be seen as the be-all-and-end-all of feminist political action. The pursuit of consciousness, in MacKinnon's (1989) words, must not be seen as the sole legitimate activity of feminism, because changing consciousness does not necessarily and inevitably result in other social changes. As Bartky recognizes, 'the apprehension of some state of affairs as intolerable, as to be transformed, does not, in and of itself, transform it' (1990:15).[8]

Identity

Like the concept of experience, 'identity' has in recent years come under sustained scrutiny within feminist thought. The influence of the poststructuralist feminism of writers such as Chris Weedon (1987), Judith Butler (1990, 1992, 1993) and Joan Scott (1992, 1993a,b) has been such that it has become something of a truism that, until their interventions, feminism had tended to operate with the humanist assumption of the existence of a unified authentic subject, and that identities in general, and gender and sexual identities in particular, are essential and given. According to this construction of the history of feminist theory, poststructuralism is currently rescuing feminism from this naïve essentialism which saw women as a fixed and unified category, and assumed that women shared a common identity, which may be buried by patriarchy, but which could be uncovered to form the basis of feminist politics.[9] In opposition to this, poststructuralist feminists propose that identities are discursively constructed, and that they lack any essential nature; rather identities are unstable, fluid, often contradictory, and always in process.

There is undoubtedly a real tension within feminism 'between the notions of "developing" an identity and "finding" an identity' (Fuss 1989:100), which in many respects parallels that between social constructionism and essentialism. However, the polarization between the two sides of these positions can be overstated (Franklin and Stacey 1988; Fuss 1989; de Lauretis 1990), and I would challenge any argument, such as Weedon's (1987) which suggests that essentialism has been a widespread position within feminism (particularly radical feminism).

The vast majority of feminist theory has long been determinedly anti-essentialist, and even in the 1970s feminist activists paid considerable attention to differences within the category 'woman' and to the problem of constructing a politicized collective identity as women.

In this tradition, my use of the concept of identity falls firmly on the side of identity as 'developed' and socially constructed, rather than seeing it as fixed, given, and essential. Conceptualizing identity as achieved and recognizing that it changes over time does not mean abandoning the concept altogether, as advocated by the radical position of Julia Kristeva (1986).[10] The identity of 'woman' is crucial for feminism, even as it is pulled between, on the one hand, 'the need to tear down the very category "woman" and dismantle its all too solid history' and, on the other hand, 'the need to build the identity "woman" and give it solid political meaning' (Snitow 1990:9).[11] But this 'building' of the identity 'woman' must go hand in hand with its deconstruction, which together serve to open up the possibilities of change. As Judith Butler (1992:16) puts it:

> Paradoxically, it may be that only through releasing the category of women from a fixed referent that something like 'agency' becomes possible. For if the term permits of a resignification, if its referent is not fixed, then possibilities for new configurations of the term become possible. In a sense, what women signify has been taken for granted for too long, and what has been fixed as the 'referent' of the term has been 'fixed', normalized, immobilized, paralyzed in positions of subordination. In effect, the signified has been conflated with the referent, whereby a set of meanings have been taken to inhere in the real nature of women themselves. To recast the referent as the signified, and to authorize or safeguard the category of women as the site of possible resignifications is to expand the possibilities of what it means to be a woman and in this sense to condition and enable an enhanced sense of agency.

In parallel to deliberations about the identity 'woman', that of 'lesbian' has been the subject of much discussion by feminist and lesbian theorists. The essentialism/social constructionism debate has also raged furiously in the field of sexuality research, focusing particularly on the question of definitions of 'lesbian'.[12] Recently there have been signs of a growing interest in examining the contexts within which, and the processes by which, the identity of lesbian is constructed (e.g. Jenness 1992; Schuyf 1992).

What I now propose to do, then, is examine how dominant modes of consciousness and hegemonic constructions of the identities of 'woman' and 'lesbian' were transgressed and transformed within the historically specific experiences of involvement with Greenham. Living at Greenham and engaging in political action there did not *directly*, or automatically, give rise to new forms of consciousness or to new identities. Rather, this provided the occasion and the challenge which demanded that women engaged in an active process of rethinking and reconstructing their ways of understanding the world and their sense of themselves, making use of the discursive material to which they already had access, but not bound by this. Many of the experiences of Greenham did not make sense within, and could not be assimilated into, women's pre-Greenham consciousness. There was often a lack of fit, a 'discursive dissonance', between the discourses with which they understood the world and the new experiences they were living through. Even those women who had previously been active as feminists or in other forms of radical politics found that their old discursive frameworks needed remoulding. Women also found that their old identities were questioned by these new ways of thinking, and that they were thereby opening up new ways of being and new identities for themselves.

Greenham was a liminal place, outside many of the structures and routines of everyday life under patriarchy and capitalism. In going to Greenham, particularly for any length of time, women were leaving home both physically and emotionally, and were abandoning many of the securities of their previous lives. They were thereby displacing themselves, and relocating themselves into a new environment in which new ways of thinking and being became possible. The liminality of Greenham was expressed very clearly by Carmel Cadden, who related it, in part, to Greenham being outdoors:

> [You'd] get this sort of freedom to let your mind wander outside its normal confines, which you can't do if you're confined by a building, and your thoughts are shaped by that building. If you sit around a fire, it's dark, and after a while you could be living in any century, and any country, and your whole being is totally free from those restrictions [. . .]. [W]omen felt outside normal behaviour.

> (Carmel Cadden, 30, camper)

To suggest that Greenham wrought major transformations in the consciousness and identities of the women involved is not to say that there was a uniform product of Greenham, which emerged after six months or a year with a particular set of ways of understanding the world or a cloned identity: there was not. The women who constituted Greenham began as a heterogeneous collectivity, remained so throughout, and left Greenham still with many differences in political orientation and self-identity between them. In particular, there was a relationship between the amount of time spent at Greenham, and whether this was as a camper, stayer or visitor, and the degree to which women experienced changes in their consciousness and identity.[13] None the less, the research suggests that there were many commonalities in the effects of involvement with Greenham on women's consciousness and self-identity.

Transformations in consciousness

The social environment of Greenham was one of often intense interaction and rapid change. Most women chose to take time alone or away from the camp to reflect upon their experiences at Greenham, attempting to integrate them into their consciousness. This inevitably individual process was accompanied and assisted by the collective consideration of these experiences. Women living at and visiting Greenham, as well as those working in the close-knit local groups which met frequently, engaged in a great deal of discussion. Besides meetings in which the politics of actions, both internal and external, were discussed, much time at the camp was spent sitting around the fire talking about politics and personal experience. This was a far more informal process than occurred within the consciousness-raising groups of the 1970s, where there would often be a topic chosen for each meeting, but fireside discussions often worked as consciousness-changing sessions. The process of pooling ideas in discussions of particular events or experiences involved individual women drawing on the discursive resources with which they arrived at Greenham, and this often led them to new understandings of the world.

In addition the range of ideas and discourses available to women at Greenham was continually broadened by the influx and through-flow of new women from all over the world from a wide variety of backgrounds. These women brought with them information and enthusiasm about political campaigns in which they were involved, ranging from feminist work in women's refuges and rape crisis centres, to campaigns about uranium mining and Aboriginal land rights in Australia, nuclear testing in the Pacific, and US intervention in Nicaragua and El Salvador. There were frequent visitors from radical political groups, particularly women's groups, including from the African National Congress and AMNLAE, the Nicaraguan women's organization, and women from the Pacific Islands. Greenham received newsletters and information from all over the world, and Greenham women were invited to speak in dozens of countries, including Eastern Europe and Latin America. This served to induct women into a global network of social movements and introduced to them a wide range of political ideas.

Changes in consciousness through Greenham occurred in four main areas: consciousness about women's oppression, about the environment, about global issues, and about the state. All of the women interviewed experienced some change in consciousness about women's oppression, which, not surprisingly, was in the direction of an increasingly feminist consciousness. Most of the women interviewed also experienced changes in each of the other four areas. Here many of the changes involved the development of feminist ways of understanding these issues, but for some, it was more a matter of general politicization and the development of a critical perspective which was not specifically feminist. In discussing the range of experiences which, filtered through the discursive resources available, provoked changes in these areas of consciousness, I look first at the experiences of being part of Greenham itself, and then at the experiences of being on the receiving end of the responses of others to Greenham.

Greenham's internal mode of action and transformations in consciousness

Being part of the community and/or wider network of Greenham, had a profound impact on the consciousness about women's oppression of those involved.

First, at Greenham many women experienced, often for the first time in their lives, a sense of real participation in decision making and social life, a feeling that their opinions mattered, deserved expression and would be taken seriously. It was, as I suggested in Chapter 4, an important part of the ethos of Greenham that there were no leaders, that decisions should be made collectively and hierarchies opposed, and that the contribution of each individual should be respected. Although this ideal was not always achieved, the contrast between Greenham's attempts to put it into practice and the organizational structures of other institutions in which women were or had been involved was sharp.

> Very often there was really good argument, really good debate, with women treating each other with enormous respect, and listening to each other. God, that was the difference I saw between the mixed politics and Greenham. All right, women may not always get it right, and occasionally they'd end up shouting each other down, but the assumption was, from the beginning, that you should be listening to each other.
>
> (Carol Harwood, 36, stayer)

> I felt the opportunity was there to put in anything I wanted to [. . .]. The format of meetings at Greenham was very different to anything that I had been involved in before, inasmuch as everybody had an opportunity to speak, and there was no formal meeting structure.
>
> (Kim Smith, 25, camper)

For many women, reflection on this, mediated by the feminist discourses to which they became exposed at Greenham, contributed to a new consciousness of men's domination of political and social life, even within the peace movement and radical groups. Combined with this, there often emerged an awareness of how they had tended to defer to the men in their political groups, and were thereby contributing to the problem. Jenny Heron, for instance:

> Before Greenham came along I was involved in CND as a silent female member, being part of a very erudite male group, who did all my talking for me, which was quite fine by me, and I thought we'd got to get rid of the bomb, and feminism, we'll sort that out when we get rid of the threat to the planet.
>
> (Jenny Heron, 30, camper)

Similarly, Carola Addington had been working in a mixed co-operative language school before Greenham:

> I'd never been involved with women's groups before, although I was concerned with women's issues [. . .]. There were awareness groups going on, which I hadn't been involved with. I thought I didn't need them because at college I was with women all the time, and I hadn't felt that I was put down at all, particularly. And I was working in a cooperative, which had lots of strong women being very vocal and so on. And there wasn't any need for

that. But then after Greenham I realized how in fact I was putting myself down on occasions. Simply because there were men around I wasn't verbalizing my thoughts enough. I wasn't coming forward. And at the time I just thought, well maybe this is just my lack of experience or lack of confidence or whatever. But I realized that the men were dominating, and I was allowing them to dominate me.

(Carola Addington, 29, camper)

Second, the experience of living and working in a women-only community which, to a large extent, cohered through the strong affective bonds which developed between the women involved, had an important effect on their consciousness. All of the women interviewed spoke of developing close friendships with the women they lived with at camp or worked with in local groups, and suggested that these friendships often had an intensity and depth they had not experienced before.

I've made friends who are the most important people in my life [. . .]. And I know that it will carry on being like that for ever and ever [. . .]. I've had lots of friends in my life but I've never really held on to any of them. I haven't had that quality of friendship with anyone else. They're quite intense friendships.

(Penny Gulliver, 22, camper)

I found out what it was like to be really close to women and to be really friends with women, and how good women are together. All that was new to me.

(Barbara Rawson, 52, camper)

As a result, and within the context of Greenham's pro-woman, or woman-centred, ethos, many women came to realize that they had learnt not to value other women's company, and that their social orientations had been constructed as heterorelational (Raymond 1986).[14]

I'd never really had friendships with women on their own. When you're married, you have friendships with another couple [. . .] When we first formed the group in Derby it just opened my eyes. I'd never seen anything like it. It was amazing. [. . .] It was the way that women could be together and be friends and talk about things and do things together. It was something I hadn't encountered. I'd been brought up to think that anything that you did with women was really secondary, your marriage was the thing and your husband, and the things you did with your husband. If you went and had coffee with another woman that was just a bit of frivolity. It wasn't your real life.

(Leah Thalmann, 53, camper)

So many women said to me, it's so nice living with women. I never thought it would be. And it was clear that they had these concepts that obviously patriarchy fosters, that women together are just a disaster, that they squabble and fight, and they can't get anything done.

(Katrina Allen, 31, camper)

Third, as a strongly lesbian community, Greenham was a place where heterosexual women were challenged to think about lesbianism, often for the first time. In Britain in the early and mid-1980s many women, particularly those who had not previously been involved in feminist political action, had never knowingly encountered lesbians before, were not conscious of their oppression or of the possibility that lesbianism could be a positive identity.

> It just made me realise how excluded lesbians are, how invisible they are in day to day life. And that for women to meet each other you have to make a conscious decision and effort to do it. But there is a whole world there and networks and support. I was aware that I had missed out on so much. But I was happy to have come into contact with it, and know it's there. And I still do know it's there, and where to go to find other women and to be with them and so on. That is tremendously exciting to discover.
>
> (Carola Addington, 29, camper)

> I remember the first time I heard two women talking about planning to have a baby and the methods they might use, and I was amazed. I sat goggle eyed, listening to it all. When I first went to Greenham I had lots of my assumptions knocked. The first time I saw two women kissing each other, I remember, was the second time I went. I remember thinking they shouldn't. My assumption was to say, 'Ooh, you don't like that sort of thing?' But underneath I think part of me was thinking, 'it's all right'.
>
> (Leah Thalmann, 53, camper)

Ann Armstrong described how her attitude towards lesbians changed from wanting to deny their existence in order to promote an image of Greenham women as respectable heterosexual mothers, to later coming to value lesbians positively.

> I can remember first coming across lesbians [. . .]. At first I suppose I thought it was a bit odd, but it soon got to be the norm. It didn't worry me. I suppose at one time there was an awful lot in the press, Sun journalism, about lesbians, you'd be saying, they're not like that. You know, this is my friend from Greenham who's got six kids. One tended to overemphasize the normal ones. But it very soon just made no difference at all. Whereas now I suppose, you meet somebody and if you hear somebody is a lesbian, you think, good, she's right on, you know. It seems to have gone completely the other way. I remember my aunt telling me her daughter was, well, I think she's a lesbian mostly, you know, and I was really pleased. I thought, ahh, isn't that nice. A while ago I'd have thought, oh how funny.
>
> (Ann Armstrong, 44, stayer)

In addition to contributing to consciousness about patriarchal oppression, life at Greenham prompted many women, particularly campers, to develop new ways of thinking about the environment. Influenced by the politics of environmentalism which had been growing in Western industrialized societies since the early 1970s,

Greenham developed a collective ethos of concern for the ecology of the Common and a wider ecofeminism, which inevitably had an impact on the individual women involved with the camp. In particular, the experience of living outdoors, gathering firewood, and building benders from saplings, meant that women at Greenham were in direct contact with the natural environment in a way which is unusual in the 'developed' world. Many women spoke in their interviews of how they had loved living on the Common and walking in the woods, and had come to value the natural world through this. This, together with witnessing the transformation of the base during the preparation for Cruise, which involved the felling of hundreds of trees and the displacement of wildlife, worked both on an emotional level and an intellectual level to make women at Greenham increasingly sensitive to the impact of their presence on the ecosystem.

For instance, two women whose previous political orientations had been strongly socialist feminist, and who had been either hostile to, or uninterested in environmentalism, underwent a volte face at Greenham:

> I've completely come round. I used to think that people who were into trees and nature and all that kind of thing were wet people, who were middle class and had nothing better, nothing more relevant to their lives to worry about than trees. And I've actually come round completely to think that dealing with those things is much more important, is as important as other issue-based things. Greenham extended my viewpoint. The fact that capitalism in Bangladesh means that they go in and they chop all the trees down and it means 4 million people drown the next summer. And why should women here being battered be more important than women drowning in Bangladesh? [. . .] I think I've managed to integrate things much more because of Greenham.
>
> (Penny Gulliver, 22, camper)

> I think where it changed things for me was learning about how we treat the land. I don't mean in a quasi-religious sense. I think I became less empirical and less demanding of empiricism, and understand a lot more about the environment.
>
> (Penni Bestic, 31, camper)

Finally, living at Greenham or being involved in the wider Greenham network was the catalyst for many women for the development of a global consciousness. Many of the women interviewed spoke of having had a fairly narrow, British or Western European orientation to politics when they first got involved with Greenham. This was broadened through contact, as described earlier in the chapter, with visitors to the camp from all over the world, and by the camp's growing collective interest in global issues, which was manifested in both informal discussions around the fire and meetings about connections between political struggles in different parts of the world.

> Whilst you were there a lot of other issues would click. There was the miners' strike and a lot of miners' wives used to come down and bring

bottles of vodka and sandwiches and chocolate, and crisps and everybody would go off to the pub with them. And they'd ask us to go to the strike meetings and talk about nuclear weapons and the connection with the pits. And there was the American Indian from the Indian reservation. And he did a slide show about the uranium mines where they lived. And there were delegations from South Africa. And we were just dead ordinary working class women from the inner cities and we were talking to people who were directly involved in struggles from all over the world.

(Trisha, 20, camper)

It made me feel connected to women from other places and other countries [. . .]. I met and spent time with women who were from other countries and had worked on connected issues.

(Barbara Rawson, 52, camper)

Greenham's external mode of action and transformations in consciousness

As I suggested in the previous chapter, women's externally focused action at Greenham provoked a range of reactions amongst individual and collective actors, and from the state, which were, either directly or indirectly, challenged by them. Mediated by the various discourses, particularly of feminism, anarchism and, to a lesser extent, civil liberties, which were in evidence at Greenham and within wider society, the experiences of these reactions contributed to significant shifts in consciousness about women's oppression and the state.

No woman involved with Greenham could avoid the realization that there was considerable opposition to the camp's women-only policy. This opposition was not confined to the few men who were asked to leave the camp at the time that the women decided it should be women-only, nor to the few women who had been involved in the original march who objected to the decision. The mixed peace movement debated Greenham at great length, the letters pages of *Sanity* and *Peace News*, its two main journals, featured regular correspondence about the issue, and local CND and peace groups spent considerable time discussing it.[15] Those who opposed the policy argued that it was divisive, served to weaken the peace movement, and prevented the full extent of opposition to Cruise being demonstrated at the base which was to receive the first missiles. A report commissioned by CND in 1983 fuelled such antagonism in its suggestion that:

> The Greenham women are burying a potentially popular cause in a tide of criticism levelled against them on personal grounds. They are discrediting a cause to which they profess allegiance.

(CND 1983:23)

Women who lived and stayed at the camp found themselves having to defend Greenham being women-only repeatedly to visitors who came to have a look at the camp, and often to argue. Those who did 'speaks' to CND groups and other local peace groups were usually required to spend more time fielding hostile questions about the subject than talking about Cruise or the actions being taken at Greenham. And women involved in the wider Greenham network, some of whom were also active in CND, were similarly assailed by antagonism and criticism.

Reflecting on these expressions of hostility, again through the lens of feminism, many women came to understand them as the result of the challenge posed to patriarchal power by women's autonomous action and by women's affective bonding with each other. For example, Helen Mary Jones, a visitor to Greenham who was active in her local CND group, faced regular arguments about whether men should be allowed to travel on the group's coaches to the camp for the annual December gatherings, which were always publicized as women-only. She came to interpret this as follows:

> [M]en who are less aware, or perhaps less confident about their own masculinity and their own sexuality, are very frightened of women being together, they are terrified of it, and I think that was why the whole, right from the men in our CND group right through to my husband, to the media, why Greenham was so frightening, it was women on their own. And the women on their own were managing perfectly well without men, thank you very much. And the huge demonstrations that we were able to have, the number of women. That was scary. And when women choose to live on their own with other women, for a political reason, that leads to questioning about the way that our society is structured. No wonder they were frightened. And I think that's absolutely true of the government reaction and the media reaction and of why the police became more and more hostile – because it wasn't a one-off. It wasn't a girls' night out. It became a way of living. A girls' night out where the girls came back very different from when they went.
>
> (Helen Mary Jones, 23, visitor)

Carola Addington came to similar conclusions:

> Through Greenham I understood the need for women to have their own space, which I hadn't realized before [. . .]. There is a tremendous fear of women doing anything on their own, surviving without men, particularly surviving in the great outdoors.
>
> (Carola Addington, 29, camper)

The reaction of Helen Mary's husband to Greenham mentioned above was a common experience for heterosexual Greenham women. Eighteen of the women interviewed were in long-term relationships with men when they first got involved with Greenham. All of these men ostensibly shared the anti-nuclear politics of their women partners/wives, and almost all considered themselves supportive of their involvement in Greenham. However, all eighteen women said that their relationships had been put under strain by their involvement with Greenham (only five relationships were still ongoing at the time of interview), and all but two of the eighteen spoke of their husbands'/partners' difficulty in accepting their commitment to the camp. Many male partners expressed more or less open hostility to Greenham, in the form of sarcastic remarks, mocking criticisms, or 'meaningful silences'; others refused to take responsibility for childcare or domestic tasks to enable women to participate to the extent they wished. A few made frequent visits to Greenham in attempts to 'share' it with their women. A number of women recounted how their husbands'/partners' reactions were, in part, due to the changes that they were undergoing as a result of being involved with Greenham, which the men found threatening.

> *Ann:* You'd be so full of it [Greenham], and what you'd done. And quite often you've described some stupid thing that you'd done, which really had made you laugh so much, and everyone else, and Ray would say, 'Oh yes, I bet that will get Mrs Thatcher worried'. And you think, well, of course it's silly, but it is important [. . .]. My husband always felt jealous because he would have liked to come and spent his nights sitting round a fire, laughing and joking and drinking alcohol. And during the Ten Days [action in 1984, see Chapter 6] he would come down and bring things. I used to be very embarrassed because I couldn't get rid of him. [. . .] I never liked him being there.
>
> *Sasha:* Because it was your place?
>
> *Ann:* Yes, our place.
>
> *Sasha:* Has that put a strain on your relationship? Did it at the time?
>
> *Ann:* Occasionally. I mean I think probably more from my feminism, which I got from Greenham. [. . .] I think I used to be a lot more amenable than I am now. I used to do as I was told. [. . .] When I was young I definitely let men walk all over me, Ray particularly. He didn't think so, but I always did everything he wanted, which I don't do now. Which is to the detriment of our relationship.
>
> (Ann Armstrong, 44, stayer)

I had him [male partner] bobbing in and out, upsetting the apple cart and panicking because I was getting visibly stronger by the day, and the stronger I got, the more he tried to cut that down and refused to baby sit [. . .]. Or he'd discover something really important to talk about just as you were putting your coat on to go out to a meeting and he knew perfectly well you'd only got 5 minutes and you couldn't actually deal with whether we were going to move in 5 minutes. It was that sort of thing. It took me a while to notice the pattern and then I ignored it. He definitely did try to prevent me getting involved [. . .]. It was the kiss of death to our relationship [. . .]. The public face was that he was incredibly supportive and incredibly helpful [. . .]. I think he was living vicariously through my experiences [. . .]. I had to come back and he would take these interesting experiences and live off them. But it took me quite a while to recognize that. It just felt to me like he wouldn't leave me half an hour just to adjust to being back at the house. I used to think, if only he would leave me half an hour, I'd probably be all right about it. But it became more and more oppressive. It built up to the point where I was dreading coming back.

(Pat Paris, 33, camper)

On the surface of it he thought it was a good thing because his politics were the same as mine and he fully supported doing something. But actually underneath there was a lot of resentment. With hindsight I realized a lot of the things I said and did at Greenham he treated like little girls playing in the woods and having good fun, but nothing really very serious [. . .]. He didn't try and stop me going – not specifically. He didn't make a huge fuss about it [. . .]. And yet, there was quite a lot of resentment really.

(Leah Thalmann, 53, camper)

Nor was a negative reaction confined to the partners/husbands of women who went to live at Greenham, or who spent significant periods of time staying there. Helen Mary Jones, who only visited Greenham on a handful of occasions, describes her partner's response:

He was intellectually committed to feminism and very supportive and a very good socialist and whatever [. . .] He knew that it was politically extremely incorrect to feel threatened by it. But he did. He felt, and he had reason to feel, threatened by my involvement with women.

(Helen Mary Jones, 23, visitor)

Women who recounted such behaviour by their partners tended to have become conscious of it slowly, accepting for a long time their partners' declarations of support as reflecting their 'true' attitudes. Often these women only developed a critical perspective on this behaviour, and an understanding of it as an attempt to exercise control over their involvement with Greenham, when they mentioned what was happening at home to other women at the camp. The feminist analyses proffered by their friends contributed to increasing awareness for many women of how they were, or had been, dominated by men in their intimate relationships.

The experience of the often sexualized violence of soldiers, policemen, and local men also served to raise awareness about the role played by men's violence in controlling and punishing women who stepped out of line. There was considerable discussion at Greenham about violence against women, with particular input from women who had been involved in feminist work on the issue. Penny Gulliver talked of how, in the small-group environment of the camp in winter, at a time of considerable vigilante harassment and violence from soldiers, the subject of women's previous experiences of violence and abuse arose:

Over the winter, because it was such a small group, people just started talking about themselves, you know. And people were saying, oh god, I've never talked about this. I remember one night when there were five of us at camp and we were really depressed and we went to bed and actually somebody started talking and the subject got onto incest. We were talking about sexual assault. Three people in the tent said, god, I've never told anybody about this, and they actually came out to each other. And everyone was bawling their eyes out. But everyone was really happy. That's quite an extreme case, but things like that happened all the time, about all sorts of things.

(Penny Gulliver, 22, camper)

Being on the receiving end of violence and abuse from state employees, particularly soldiers and police, was also a shaking experience for the many women who came to Greenham believing that the state was a neutral arbiter of conflicting interests within society. Penny described seeing these processes of consciousness-change about the operations of the state in other women:

Lots and lots of women came to camp as visitors or for a night or a couple of nights, who were anti-nuclear but really probably that was as far as they were political. A lot of them would say they weren't political, they just knew nuclear weapons were wrong and they had children, that sort of thing. And then they'd walk along the fence, especially that time when there were the Paras there, and they'd be saying things like, 'God, I wouldn't mind fucking you, darling', you know, that sort of thing. And they were absolutely horrified. And up until then they'd seen the police and the army as people in the middle, doing their jobs, and suddenly it wasn't like that at all.

(Penny Gulliver, 22, camper)

The experience of the court process, which, given the thousands of arrests made at Greenham over the years, involved substantial numbers of women, was also significant in provoking new understandings of the state. Of the women I interviewed, all of the campers and stayers had been arrested, many on numerous occasions, as had two of the visitors. Many of these women spoke of their initial shock that the police regularly lied in court about what had happened. Women found this particularly strange, as more often than not, they were only too happy to admit it, if they had actually done that with which they were charged.

The thing that struck me most was the way that the police lied. And the thing that irritated me was that there was no need to lie [. . .]. It's not as if we were saying, I didn't do it. They're saying, I did it, but I did it to defend myself against a nuclear holocaust [. . .]. [I]n our situation, it's not actually such a worry, because actually we're fighting on a completely different ground anyway, but the fact that this is obviously how they proceed in any situation, that they just lie and it is completely acceptable [. . .]. It's always a bit of a shock to be involved in it yourself [. . .]. It's something I'd always suspected, but I'd never actually put my finger on.

(Katrina Allen, 31, camper)

The other thing [Greenham did], was the thing about the trials, the thing about the police lying [. . .]. The out-and-out lying of the police was just so unmistakeable. The way the justice system was shown up to be such a load of crap. Policemen *do* lie. And I think for hundreds of women that must have been quite a thing [. . .]. And seeing policemen break women's arms, and things like that [. . .]. I was brought up with a respect for authority.

(Rowan Gwedhen, 24, camper)

Before I got involved in it, I used to think that the law had something to do with justice. I realized once I'd been involved in it, the law is just the law. It doesn't actually have anything to do with morality at all.

(Ann Armstrong, 44, stayer)

It was like walking into the lion's jaws, finding out that it wasn't a democracy. That was a shock to me, and that there was no justice. And that it was as bad as we all thought, and worse.

(Susan Lamb, 28, stayer)

It's changed me. I don't ever trust any policeman.

(Barbara Rawson, 52, camper)

Finally there was the experience of imprisonment. Whilst not everyone chose to go to prison for every offence of which she was convicted, on some occasions women had no choice, and on many more they refused to pay fines. Women were often profoundly shocked by the treatment of women in prison, and by what they learnt about why they were there.

It was horrible. I think it was just the most demeaning and degrading and awful place. It was also a lot of learning. And I certainly became aware that the vast majority of women who were there were in because of debt, you know, and some outstanding cases. We were waiting about 8 hours in the receiving room at Holloway because they were taking their time processing everybody, and there was one woman there who was 8 months pregnant who'd got 6 weeks for shoplifting around December. She had five other kids. This was her sixth. And in the same court, on the same morning was the man who said he'd been shoplifting while drunk and actually got off, and she'd been put in prison and her child would be born in prison. And it was so obvious that she'd been shoplifting around Christmas, and I don't care whether she'd been shoplifting for food or shoplifting for clothes or shoplifting for presents. I just felt that the system that would imprison her and let that bloke go free was completely wrong. And most of the people that we were in there with, there were a few in for drugs, and there were a few in for murder, but the vast majority were in for doing credit cards and for not paying fines. It was just the financial punishment for being poor. That was so clear, and it was so degrading and so awful. I think you can minimize what a horrific situation that is [. . .]. I found it a really shocking experience, and it confirmed for me the validity of breaking the law, actually. Cos I just thought, all these women are in here, and they've done nothing, most of them have done nothing. Most of them are poor, or disorganized or both, and so they've ended up trying to cheat the system, and they've been caught. Tax evaders are among those who are judging them and they're not going to prison. I think the system stinks.

Sasha: Was this a revelation?

Katrina: Yeah. Yeah it was. It clarified a whole lot of things in a very shocking fashion, in a way that really woke me up. I think actually it was really good for me, it was really useful in terms of making me understand more fully the way the world works and how it penalizes people who are poor. That's something I'd appreciated intellectually, I suppose, but never really had the guts of it pointed out to me.

(Katrina Allen, 31, camper)

The final sentences of this extract raise an important point concerning the transformations in consciousness which women experienced at and through Greenham, with which I conclude this part of the discussion. Experiences at Greenham, whether of the joys of gyn/affective bonding, of men's hostility to autonomous action by women, or of state violence in its many forms, led women to engage in significant restructuring of their ways of understanding the world. To a large extent this was because of the immediacy and emotional impact of the experiences. In some cases women already had an intellectual appreciation of patriarchal or state oppression, but experiencing them in new ways, and first-hand, qualitatively changed their previous consciousness.[17] Within the discursive context of Greenham which valued the emotional as a source of knowledge, these experiences could contribute to the creation of new forms of consciousness.

Transformations in identity

The actions of women at Greenham constituted a powerful challenge to hegemonic constructions of 'woman'. Even within late twentieth century public patriarchy (Walby 1990a,b), in which women are formally equal citizens and most women are paid workers, women are still expected to be domestic creatures first and foremost; as wives, mothers, and grandmothers to put the needs and interests of others before their own. The woman who does not is castigated as selfish and unnatural. Women are still expected to adorn their bodies with fashionable clothes and cosmetics (though this is now supposed to be for women themselves, and less for men) and to carry themselves with feminine grace. Their bodies are not expected to be strong, and they are not thought to be competent at manual and practical tasks. Above all, 'woman' is still constructed as the complement of man, as existing only for and in relation to man, as heterorelational and heterosexual.

Greenham was an arena in which this 'woman' was deconstructed and rejected, and alternative notions of 'woman' were formed. The woman of Greenham was different in many respects from the woman of patriarchal creation. She was a woman who transgressed boundaries between the public and private spheres;

she made her home in public, in the full glare of the world's media, under the surveillance of the state. She put herself and other women first, acting according to her conscience, taking responsibility for her own actions. She dressed according to a different aesthetic, in warm, comfortable clothing, removing many of the markers of femininity, but often adorning her body in ways which celebrated her independence of fashion. She was confident and assertive in the face of authority, rejecting its power to control her behaviour, testing it and taunting it. She developed close friendships and often sexual relationships with other women. This woman was stepping outside many of the restrictions of patriarchy.

At Greenham, women created new identities for themselves, and in so doing, became different people. With only one exception, the women interviewed said that through Greenham they gained new identities as individuals with agency. In the face of the disempowering threat of nuclear war, and against constructions of women as victims, as those who are 'done to' by men and governments or who are 'fought for' by armies, women at Greenham came to perceive themselves as powerful. Connected to this sense of personal power was a sense of collective power as women, as the new identities created through Greenham were gendered identities, forged through the gendered experiences of Greenham.

> I think it has changed me. I mean, I think it's meant something to me in terms of the power that women can have. And that I have power [. . .]. I think it's almost for me, once you become aware of that, that feeling never goes away. That feeling of power, that women can have.
>
> (Bridget Evans, 23, camper)

> It's made me brave. I deliberately use it sometimes if I feel afraid [. . .], I think, come on, you're a Greenham woman. So that aspect of it was important to me. It dragged me up a bit more, out of doing as I was told and thinking everyone else knew what to do and not me.
>
> (Barbara Rawson, 52, camper)

> I think Greenham changed me enormously [. . .]. I felt at the beginning that I could push the world over, almost. I felt less afraid than I'd ever been.
>
> (Margery Lewis, 64, visitor)

> I've become more autonomous. I am less fearful of doing what I want to do, if it's not what society would approve of. I understand the consequences of that sort of action more fully than I ever did. But in a way having braved those consequences, I am more prepared to do what I want to do. I sort of feel like I can weigh that thing up and decide, yes, I actually need to do this thing. And I need to do it either openly and probably get caught, or I need to try and get away with it. But either way I'm more clear about what I might need to do and more able to weigh it out. Instead of saying, oh I can't do that, it's against the law, I sort of think, that's only one factor, and there might be other things that are more important.
>
> (Katrina Allen, 29, camper)

Jinny: I'm a completely different woman.

Sasha: How are you different?

Jinny: Stronger, for sure. And I don't mean in terms of putting up with the rain. I learnt to believe in myself, and before I went I wasn't too sure about who I was.

(Jinny List, 20, camper)

The women who underwent the most dramatic transformations in identity were those whose motivation to get involved with Greenham had been strongly maternalist, and who had begun by identifying as 'ordinary women' and mothers.

A hell of a lot of women grew through Greenham, in all sorts of ways. Your awareness of your own power and abilities. It broke our images of ourselves. We went with housewives' values, the values of real narrow-minded, narrow, narrow-minded women from the Rhondda, and we broke this image of what we were. And then anything was possible.

(Christine King, 27, stayer)

I discovered a side of me that I hadn't even realized existed. A very effective and good side. And that was something that I think a hell of a lot of women discovered about themselves. You know, they tiptoed in timidly, and became bold human beings.

(Helen John, 34, camper)

Jenny: We leafleted and fly-posted. We did a poster with a picture of a baby – it was not terribly right-on these days, because it was all about protecting our children.

Sasha: How do you feel about that now?

Jenny: It was not women-centred. It was women's role-centred, not women as individuals. But that was where we were at, and it was vehicle in a way that led us on to being able to do our own thing, and to break free from the roles and the men [. . .]. Greenham was a catalyst that changed women's lives. Most women that went there have been changed radically, to some degree or other, and have never been the same since [. . .]. It's given me more sense of self-pride and self-liking.

(Jenny Heron, 30, camper)

As well as being a place in which the identity of 'woman' was created anew for many thousands of women, Greenham facilitated for many women the construction of new identities as lesbians. There were lesbians involved with Greenham from the earliest days, although it was only after the decision that the camp should be women-only that lesbians really became visible in any number. By the end of 1982, the majority of women living at Greenham were lesbians, and many women who arrived at Greenham thinking of themselves as heterosexual came to question their sexuality and embarked upon sexual relationships with other women. Greenham opened up the possibility of a positive lesbian identity, both for previously heterosexual women, and for women who were already 'doing' lesbianism without 'being' lesbians, or without being happy with a lesbian identity.

Problematic though such figures are (see Appendix II), it is worth giving some indication of the overall picture of transformations in sexual identity amongst the women interviewed. Of the 35 women interviewed, 20 were heterosexual prior to involvement with Greenham and 14 were lesbians, though many of these women were not happy with a lesbian identity. At the time of interview, 12 identified as heterosexual, 21 as lesbians, and two were self-consciously ambivalent. Whilst one lesbian had entered a heterosexual relationship since Greenham, she was reluctant to give up her lesbian identity, overwhelmingly Greenham contributed to shifts from heterosexual towards lesbian identities.

There were several reasons why Greenham was a crucible for the construction and reconstruction of lesbian identities. First, the sheer number of lesbians at Greenham rendered lesbianism completely 'normal' there. There was, in contrast to the rest of society, an assumption of lesbianism amongst the women who lived at the camp. At many gates the effect was that women almost had to opt-out of lesbianism; they had to 'come' out as heterosexual. Lesbianism was treated matter-of-factly, needing no explanation or justification, and was the material of everyday conversation, discussion, and humour. As Penny Gulliver explained it:

> I used to have to kick myself because I used to take it that everybody that arrived at camp was a lesbian after I'd been there for about five minutes, and I was really shocked when people would say, of course my boyfriend Rodney, and I'd think, god, it's not a lesbian camp. There were so many lesbians there you did start to forget what was the norm [. . .]. After a while I forgot that women could be heterosexual. When I think about it now I can't believe how I felt like that because it's completely gone again, because you feel completely isolated. There's so much of your life that you censor and so many things you can't do, that people take for granted. It was a very odd situation, there you are, in a muddy bender on the outskirts of the common, but to be sort of normal and to get to the point where you're shocked because somebody's heterosexual.
>
> (Penny Gulliver, 22, camper)

> I'll tell you when I realized what an influence it had. I'd been staying at the camp and it was some Easter action and I went with Rebecca to Burghfield. We were going to deliver leaflets or something, and there were a man and a woman kissing, and I was really shocked.
>
> (Carol Harwood, 36, stayer)

Because of the normality of lesbianism at Greenham, it became a 'thinkable' practice and identity, available to all women at Greenham.

Second, there was considerable diversity in ways of being a lesbian amongst those at Greenham; lesbians there ranged in age from 16 to 60, some had long lives as heterosexual wives and mothers behind them, others were 'life-long' lesbians, some maintained long-term monogamous relationships, others had short, serially monogamous relationships, and still others were rampantly non-monogamous. There were many working class lesbians, and a wide variety of political orientations amongst lesbians at Greenham. The experience of this diversity of lesbian lives increased the availability of a lesbian identity to many heterosexual women who came to the camp, allowing women to see themselves, or women like themselves, as lesbians.

Third, the meaning of lesbianism at Greenham was positive. The evident pleasure and happiness that being a lesbian brought to many women at Greenham served to counter hegemonic constructions of lesbians as sad, lonely women who could not get a man. Many women encountered women whom they considered to be positive lesbian role models for the first time in their lives. Moreover, as was the case with transformations of consciousness, actually *experiencing* the collective strength of lesbians, and the pleasure of being surrounded by lots of other lesbians had a significant impact on women's identities as lesbians:

> We live in a homophobic society that told me for so long women and lesbians were bad news, whether that included me or not, that something had to show me that wasn't right. And Greenham did that, that's for sure. I don't care how politically right on, or politically correct you are, or whether you read the right books, if you're an isolated lesbian, how much do you believe about women's strength? If it's there, in your face, you learn, pretty damn quick.
>
> (Jinny List, 20, camper)

At Greenham being a lesbian seemed to be about more than just having sex with women; it seemed to be a way of being in the world, an assertion of independence and personal autonomy and a statement of women's strength.

Finally, within the women-only community of Greenham, in which women's emotional and sexual relationships with each other were highly valued, many women experienced great pleasure in women's company, often for the first time in their lives. The affective bonding between women living at Greenham was heightened by shared experiences of the excitement, fear, and adrenalin-rush of doing actions, and was expressed in a far higher degree of physical intimacy than is common in British society. Thus many of the social and psychological barriers to the expression of affection in bodily contact between women were removed. In this context liking and love for another woman could more easily cross boundaries into sexual desire and eroticism.

For those women who already identified as lesbians at the time of getting involved, Greenham offered a unique lesbian community in which they could be completely open about and at ease with their sense of self. An example of this group was Penny Gulliver, who had come out whilst at drama school, and had been living in a women-only squat before moving to Greenham:

> I think the most important thing for me was that I was actually surrounded by a lot of lesbians. That was really nice and really important. Because you

could be open about it was better fun. We didn't talk about being a lesbian, we talked about things to do with the fact that you were a lesbian. And that was really nice because when people find out that you're a lesbian they want to talk about it all the time. If you come out to people, they want to know, they ask all sorts of questions. It was moving on from that level of talking about it, being able to talk about things which are on a much deeper level, or things that are much more subtle about being a lesbian, which other lesbians know, but you don't talk about. You recognize a lot more. Suddenly people say something and you say, yeah, that's right, and you find that you've got a lot more in common than you thought, and things are much more complicated about being a lesbian than actually it just being difficult. The subtleties of being a lesbian, the things that you learn to do so that you're not recognized, or so that you don't get into trouble, and things that you don't even realize that you do. You suddenly twig, yes I do that and I have done that since I came out, and you realize what a strange state you have to live your life in.

(Penny Gulliver, 22, camper)

For the larger group of women who prior to going to Greenham were 'doing' lesbianism, that is who were involved in sexual relationships with other women but who did not have strong or positive identities as lesbians, Greenham was a place in which they could develop such identities, supported and encouraged by the women around them. Sarah Benham was one such woman, who had been involved in a two-year-long sexual relationship with another girl at her school:

I came across all her letters the other day and it was full of this stuff, we're not really gay, we're just very special friends to each other. We were completely closeted. And then that time that Jane said, I'd say that about 80 per cent of the women here are lesbians I was just very shocked by it. It hadn't occurred to me. I think Greenham was about [. . .] realizing I was a lesbian. I wouldn't be where I am today. I wouldn't have come out as a lesbian at 17 if I hadn't been to Greenham, and if I wasn't a lesbian I wouldn't be me. I'd be floundering away trying to make it work in relationships with men, I should imagine. Instead of floundering away trying to make it work in relationships with women!

(Sarah Benham, 17, stayer)

Rowan Gwedhen had thought of herself as 'gay' before her involvement with Greenham, the identity of 'lesbian' not having been available to her:

When I was growing up male homosexuals were visible. You had a stereotype in every television situation comedy. You had Oscar Wilde. When I was growing up I got hold of gay male culture because there wasn't a lesbian culture. The word 'lesbian' never came up. I started out calling myself 'gay', a word which I now abhor [. . .]. There was no visible lesbian culture. There were no visible lesbians. So the only culture one could snatch at was gay male culture. And yes, you ended up reading biographies of Oscar Wilde

[. . .]. I think that Greenham helped towards the whole lesbian culture that has built up. And it's a fact that now there is a lesbian culture.

(Rowan Gwedhen, 24, camper)

For women in both of these groups Greenham was a place for the exploration of the meaning of a lesbian identity in a community in which they had to be neither defensive nor on their guard for abuse and violence from those around them (although there was a sharp contrast once women left the camp to go into New-bury). Lesbians at Greenham created their identities in opposition to the hetero-sexual world around them, and by developing distinctive ways of being. Many women, particularly but not exclusively younger women, engaged in what would now be called 'queer politics' – bold, brash, and deliberate in-your-face assertions of their sexuality, which were designed to outrage and shock and to challenge heterosexual hegemony. Women would passionately kiss their lovers in pubs and cafés in town, talk loudly about lesbian sex and make jokes about heterosexuality, daring those around them to respond. Paradoxically it was both the strength derived from the normality of lesbianism at Greenham and the knowledge of the uniqueness of this, which fed such performances. An identity was also constructed through modes of dress and bodily display. Many lesbians at Greenham cut their hair very short, some wore it partially or completely shaved, and died it pink or green. Women deliberately presented themselves as outside conventional hetero-sexual femininity. As Liz Galst put it:

We were scruffy. It was partially circumstantial, I mean, how could you not be? But a lot of us had a different aesthetic than the mainstream, what a nice girl's supposed to look like, or supposed to be.

(Liz Galst, 20, camper)

The other group of women whose sexual identities were affected by their involvement with Greenham were the eight women interviewed who were in hetero-sexual relationships pre-Greenham, and who left marriages and relationships with men and became lesbians.[18] Five of these women embarked upon relationships with women whilst at Greenham or involved in the Greenham network, which resulted in the ending of their relationships with husbands/partners and the adoption of lesbian identities. Two began a process of self-questioning at Greenham, which later resulted in decisions to finish their relationships with their husbands/partners and the more or less contemporaneous start of relationships with women.

Leah Thalmann, for example, had been unhappy in her marriage for some time, but did not leave her husband and begin a relationship with a woman until after her involvement with Greenham was over:

Going to Greenham was a sort of catalyst for what was going to have to happen anyway. It sort of set me on that track. And when I went to Greenham I knew nothing about lesbians or anything, and when I first saw them, my assumptions were, mmm, I'm not sure about this.

(Leah Thalmann, 53, camper)

Helen John, who was on the original walk from Cardiff to Greenham, and whose motivations for involvement had been strongly maternalist, also underwent significant transformation in identity through Greenham, entering a relationship with another woman for the first time whilst living there.

> I went there because of the nuclear weapons and so forth and changed my opinion on a whole load of other things and my lifestyle. It was really an incredible time, it was just an enormous change in my life. My whole life stood on end, you know. It was really an incredible experience. And it was absolutely the right thing to do, to acknowledge that side of myself and not run away from it, as I could have done.
>
> (Helen John, 34, camper)

Jenny Heron, who was quoted earlier in the chapter as also having a maternalist orientation when first involved with Greenham and who was a committed environmentalist, had never before met lesbians to whom she could relate. At Greenham she fell in love with a woman, and eventually left her husband. Here she cites the importance of the existence of positive lesbian role models at Greenham:

> I knew [J.] and [L.], but they were so much into roles. Their style of life wasn't at all eco. When I got to Greenham there were all these women who cared about the environment. You'd see a certain intimacy going on between certain women and every day you'd notice it was going on with nearly all of them. It was marvellous because it was so positive. It was so uninhibited. There were no great heartbreaks going on at the time. It was all such positive role models. There haven't been such positive role models anywhere before or since. Certainly before that, you could meet perhaps a couple or two couples, but there you'd got hundreds of them, and you couldn't resist it really. You'd just got to go along with them.
>
> (Jenny Heron, 30, camper)

The new identity of 'woman' created at Greenham was closely connected to the possibility of a new identities as lesbians. As women disengaged from dominant constructions of femininity, they also saw possibilities of new sexual identities. As Pat Paris who had got involved with Greenham out of a concern about the future of the world following the illness and fragility of her baby daughter, explained:

> There must be thousands of dykes in this country who would never have been, if it hadn't been for Greenham, because it was a safe place to explore that, because we felt we could do anything. I mean, I remember thinking when I was sitting at camp, if the car didn't work, then you had somebody who knew bits about it and you learnt things and you fixed it. And we were really totally self-sufficient, in almost every way you could think of. I think a lot of women became very strong at Greenham just through seeing other women like that.
>
> (Pat Paris, 33, camper)

To conclude, Greenham was a place of transformations and transgressions. At Greenham, and through Greenham, women created for themselves new forms of consciousness and new identities. Drawing on the discursive resources available to them at Greenham, which were forged from, but by not limited by, the counter-hegemonic political ideas and theories of the time, women actively interpreted the experiences of involvement. Through this, women developed new understandings of their oppression, often producing shifts from maternalist and female conscious-ness to feminist consciousness, or changes within feminist consciousness, expand-ing it globally and adding new knowledge about the state. Linked to this, women at Greenham built the collective identity of woman, making concrete solidarity between women, whilst simultaneously transgressing patriarchal constructions of woman, and giving to it new meanings. At an individual level, women reflexively produced themselves as changed in significant ways, and sensed themselves, often for the first time, as possessing agency.

Conclusion:
disarming patriarchy

The end of Greenham

Just as the making of Greenham has to be understood both within its macro-structural context and in terms of the aggregated decisions of thousands of individual women, so too does the ending of Greenham.

At the level of geopolitics, much has changed since the deployment of Cruise in 1983. The latter years of the 1980s saw rapprochement between the United States and the Soviet Union, initiated by President Gorbachev. This gave way to a new period of détente, followed by a clear end to the Cold War. In 1987 Gorbachev and Reagan signed the Intermediate Nuclear Forces Treaty, which provided for the removal of Cruise, Pershing II and SS-20 nuclear missiles from Europe. In 1988 the Soviet Union made unilateral cuts in its conventional forces and began military withdrawal from Eastern Europe. Then, in 1989, in a series of largely non-violent revolutions across Eastern Europe, the Communist bloc dissolved.[1] This was followed by the ousting of the Communist Party in the Soviet Union, and the break-up of the Union. By early 1990, the United States was prepared (and needed) to cut its defence budget, and as part of a programme of military reductions, announced the withdrawal of five thousand troops from Britain, and the closure of the base at Greenham. During the first half of the 1990s there have been further multilateral agreements on reductions in nuclear weapons and substantial cuts in military personnel in the former Soviet Union, the United States and other NATO countries, including Britain. The former Cruise missile silos at Greenham are, in 1995, being leased out by the Ministry of Defence to small businesses at low rents, whilst all but the hundred acres of the base surrounding the silos (which have to be maintained for inspection by the former Soviet Union under the terms of the INF treaty) is being sold to Newbury District Council in order that it be returned to open common once more.[2]

Even after 1987, when it became clear that Cruise was to be removed, women continued to arrive at Greenham for the first time; most were young women, for whom Greenham had long been a part of the fabric of their political world, but who had not been old enough to have been involved when it was at its peak. The last Cruise missile was flown back to the US in March 1991, and on 4 July 1991 a large gathering was held to celebrate 'Greenham's Independence Day', bringing thousands of women back to Greenham for the first time in years. A small number of women maintained the camp for a further three years, making regular incursions and monitoring the decommissioning of the base. Then, in February 1994, the women at Blue Gate, the last remaining camp, decided to leave, and the camp was disbanded.[3]

Most of the women interviewed in this research, and the vast majority of the tens of thousands who had been active as campers, stayers, and in the wider Greenham network during the early and mid-1980s, had ebbed away before the INF treaty was signed.

Women who had made Greenham their home for months or years tended to leave the camp in stages, gradually spending more time away from the camp to recuperate until they decided to move away completely. The explanations given by the women interviewed for leaving generally involved a combination of negative and positive reasons. Although the response of the state to Greenham took its toll on women who lived there, and often reduced the length of time they would spend at the camp before leaving permanently, it was rarely enough on its own to make women leave. Other factors, internal to the dynamic of Greenham, combined with the impact of the state harassment.

The most frequently cited negative reason was physical and emotional exhaustion, or 'burnout', as a result of the stress of living with regular evictions, harassment, court appearances, and for some, prison sentences. Living at Greenham was, for much of the time, 'living on the edge', and from 1984 onwards, involved regular nights of disrupted sleep when the convoy was taken out of the base. Some women became physically sick, which they attributed to 'zapping', and were unable to spend time in the vicinity of the base. In addition, the intensity of the affective bonding within the camp, together with the transience and lack of stability was experienced by many women as emotionally draining, and contributed to decisions to return to the 'normality' of house-dwelling.

The other main negative reason for leaving was financial. As the 1980s went on, unemployment rose and the Conservative government committed itself to expunging 'scroungers'. The DHSS therefore increased pressure on those claiming benefit, which included most of the women living at Greenham, to take up work or training places. Women generally resisted this for a long time, believing that their activity at Greenham was more important than paid work, and that they were entitled to state support, when it was the state that was pursuing policies of nuclear militarism. However, for those women who were living at Greenham whilst maintaining a flat or house elsewhere, this pressure eventually contributed to their decisions to leave.

The positive reasons that women gave for leaving Greenham concerned changing political and personal priorities. Generally this involved a shift in political focus away from Cruise missiles, towards feminist work in organizations such as Women's Aid, Rape Crisis, and women's centres, or to work in international solidarity campaigns, such as the Greenham-originated Women's Network for a Nuclear Free and Independent Pacific.[4] Many women spoke of believing that they should return to their home towns to engage in political action 'in the community', taking with them the personal strength and knowledge that they had acquired at Greenham. Other women decided that they wanted to enter further or higher education (two of the women interviewed embarked on midwifery training, and six went to university as mature students), or to train in a new skill (most frequently a manual trade such as carpentry or car mechanics).

For those who did not live at Greenham, the process of disengagement tended to be even more gradual, as they did not have to make a decision to physically leave the camp. Like the campers interviewed, most slowly developed different foci, which meant that they had less time, and less desire, to go to Greenham or to be involved with their local women's peace group. Most groups continued to function, albeit at a much lower level of activity and with far fewer active members, until about 1987. However, over time their orientations generally shifted away from Greenham and the issue of Cruise, in line with the changing consciousness of the women involved. Some groups, as they contracted in size, also became more closed and insular, functioning above all as friendship groups, and did less and less to attract or welcome new members. Often the point at which a decision was made to disband the group was the moment when this was articulated within the group.

Above all though, for campers, stayers, and visitors, the intense level of fear which had initially activated many, or which had arisen once already involved, gradually ebbed away during the 1980s. Partly this was just the effect of time – the degree of passionate urgency and intense activity which characterized Greenham in its first three years could not be sustained indefinitely.[5] But also, as the new détente broke out, the imminent danger of nuclear war seemed to recede, and Greenham began to lose its place of primary importance in women's lives. In effect, Greenham sowed the seeds of its own ending. The transformative impact of involvement in Greenham at the level of the individual meant that it was almost inevitable that women should seek new directions for their political energies. The cognitive praxis of 'making connections', and the process of politicization which women experienced at Greenham led them into new areas of political action, and the transformation of identity and sense of personal empowerment engendered, opened up possibilities of travel, new careers, and education. Greenham made women desirous of ongoing change, both personal and in political action, and when they felt that Greenham had become routine and no longer offered them new experiences, or that they were not contributing positively to Greenham any more, they tended to withdraw.

I started to get really nasty and cynical, and it wasn't very nice because there were some women who hadn't been there before and it was still really exciting for them. I just started to feel that the record had got stuck. And I didn't feel that I was putting anything new into it.

(Clare Hudson, 25, stayer)

I came to the point where I felt I wasn't giving enough or getting enough. I wasn't putting any more energy in, and I wasn't taking any more energy from Greenham. It just felt that it was becoming the same.

(Leah Thalmann, 53, camper)

In the same way that withdrawal from Greenham did not mean deactivation for individual women, the contraction of Greenham as a social movement did not mean an end to women's anti-militarist activism. Some women remained involved in the Women's Network for a Nuclear Free and Independent Pacific, continued to campaign against Rio Tinto Zinc, held monthly weekend camps outside Aldermaston, and went to Nevada to disrupt US nuclear testing. To publicize the land rights claims of the Shoshone people, who have been displaced by nuclear tests in the US, a dozen women climbed into Buckingham Palace in 1993. Large numbers of women have also been reactivated at times of international crisis. Thousands rapidly came together after the US bombing of Libya in 1986 for demonstrations outside the US embassy, and again during the Gulf War, when a women's peace camp was set up outside the Foreign Office in Whitehall for several weeks, and women disrupted parliamentary debates about British involvement. The wars in Croatia and Bosnia led ex-Greenham women to form 'Women's Aid to former Yugoslavia', and lorries containing aid were driven to women in refugee camps. They also contributed to campaigns about sexual violence perpetrated against women on all sides during these wars, and raised money to finance practical assistance with the training of rape crisis counsellors. Finally, since closing the last camp at Greenham, women from Blue Gate and others have set up women's peace camps at Menwith Hill, the US National Security Agency surveillance centre in Yorkshire, and travelled Britain doing actions at military bases on the 'Women on the Road for Peace' tour.

Disarming patriarchy?

So, by the end of its twelve and a half years of existence, what had Greenham achieved? What has been its political, social and cultural impact, and what is its legacy?

The challenge to militarism

Evaluating the influence of Greenham on nuclear policy is fraught with difficulty, not least because it conjures a cause/effect mode of thinking which is inherently problematic. The impact of Greenham, in this area, is hard to disentangle from that of the wider peace movement, and in social life, controlled experiments (the world with Greenham compared with the world without Greenham) are impossible. Moreover, as Randle points out (1987), commenting on non-violent direct action in the late 1950s and early 1960s, the secrecy which surrounds all government decisions, particularly about nuclear weapons, means that it is seldom possible to demonstrate beyond doubt that changes in policy may be attributed to social movements. None the less, it is vital to put forward, at the very least, speculative answers to these questions in order to claim the agency of movements, particularly of women's movements. Official histories, the rhetoric of politicians, and mainstream discourses of international relations, in their state-oriented world view, all overwhelmingly erase the existence of social movements and attribute geopolitical change to state actors and 'great men'. Peace movements, in particular, have historically been subject to this treatment (N. Young 1990), and women's peace movements more so, suffering erasure even from those who have sought to repossess the history of radical social movements (e.g. Caedel 1980).[6]

Obviously, Greenham did not achieve its initial aim of preventing the deployment of Cruise missiles in Britain. Unlike the Dutch and Belgian governments, the British government pushed ahead in 1983, unheeding of the mass protests and the opinion polls. But within four years of deployment, agreement had been reached between the superpowers to scrap Cruise, and within 10 years of the establishment of the camp, the last missiles were removed. Undoubtedly the most important factors which led to Gorbachev's disarmament initiatives were internal to the Soviet Union, and were primarily economic; the arms race was just not sustainable indefinitely. Commentators on the impact of the peace movement as a whole on this process are generally cautious, but argue that it contributed in a number of ways. First, the peace movement heightened public consciousness about nuclear weapons, the arms race and NATO policy, galvanizing opposition to Cruise, which, according to opinion polls, ranged between 40 and 60 per cent.[7] The movement thereby contributed to the democratization of debate about defence (Carter 1992; Wittner 1988). Its assertion that people had a right to information and to form opinions in this area constituted an important attack on the geopolitical privacy of the state (Shaw 1991). Second, in promoting debate about nuclear weapons and the probable effects of their use, the peace movement served to delegitimize them; Reagan's notion of a 'winnable' and limited nuclear war in Europe was publicly challenged, and its implications for Europe exposed. Wittner (1988:287) suggests that this put a brake on the arms race and made nuclear war less likely.[8] Gleditsch (1990) concludes that the overall effect of the peace movement was to exert significant pressure on governments: 'it is questionable whether the breakthrough in the disarmament negotiations in 1986–7 would have occurred without the widespread moral revulsion against the nuclear arms race championed by the "new" peace movement' (Gleditsch 1990:73). Shaw (1991) is more specific about how this worked, suggesting that the movement indicated to Gorbachev that Brezhnev's European policy was outdated, and that there was a significant constituency in the West which was not actively hostile to the Soviet Union. This may well have contributed to his willingness to make the substantial concessions in the arms negotiations that eventually led to the INF treaty. The strength of the peace movement meant that NATO was impelled to listen seriously to Gorbachev. Finally, the Western peace movement, particularly European Nuclear Disarmament (END), stimulated the growth of the underground peace movements of Eastern Europe, contributing pressure for 'détente from below', and preparing the way for the revolutions of 1989 (Jahn 1989; Shaw 1991).[9]

Greenham's role within the British peace movement was that of its most radical wing. Whilst Greenham's women-only policy was the subject of fierce debate within the peace movement, and was extremely unpopular in some sectors, Greenham undoubtedly influenced the forms of action in which other participants engaged. Mixed peace camps were set up at many other nuclear bases around Britain (Molesworth, Faslane, and Upper Heyford were the largest), following the model of Greenham, and gatherings and blockades became regular types of action there. CND initiated demonstrations which sought to replicate Greenham actions, such as the Aldermaston to Burghfield human chain of Easter 1983, which imitated Greenham's 'Embrace the Base' gathering. The peace movement as a whole was never split over the issue of non-violent direct action in the way that it had been in the 1950s (see Randle 1987), and even the cutting of fences around military bases ('snowball actions') became a widespread practice in the years after it was first done at Greenham.

It was also Greenham, spotlighted by the media during 1982 and 1983 because it was women-only and because of its imaginative and unusual forms of action, which seemed to be particularly effective at raising public awareness of Cruise. In 1980, 41 per cent of those surveyed in Britain did not know that there were nuclear weapons in their country (Hastings and Hastings 1982:330), but by 1983, only 6 per cent had never heard of Greenham (Hastings and Hastings 1984:323). Whether Greenham made the public more or less likely to oppose the deployment of Cruise is debatable. Byrd (1985) suggests that there was a 'Greenham effect' on women, citing the significant gender gap in attitudes to Cruise, and the 32 per cent of women who said that they had become more sympathetic to the campaign against Cruise as a result of Greenham, as against 50 per cent who were unaffected (*Sunday Times*, 23 January 1983). A small non-random survey of women in *Spare Rib* also reported that 1 in 3 women had become more favourable to nuclear disarmament or more aware of the issue because of Greenham (*Spare Rib*, May 1984). In contrast, Rochon (1990:107) refers to the 54 per cent of the public who had an unfavourable opinion of Greenham, and to the finding that of those who said that the camp had affected their attitudes to Cruise, one-third said it had made them less supportive of the peace movement. (He ignores the two-thirds of those affected who became more sympathetic.) Similarly, Rootes (1989) argues that Greenham posed a serious problem for CND, because the public found it difficult to distinguish the two, and Greenham 'incurs the disapproval even of those members of the public who are in general sympathetic to CND's message' (Rootes 1989:98).

However, the question of whether the public approved of Greenham is framed within a problematic which Greenham rejected. Greenham women were well aware that their methods of protest were considered illegitimate by most people. Barnes *et al.*'s (1979:544–6) five-nation study of attitudes to unconventional political action found that whereas 85 per cent approved of petitioning (an activity in which Greenham as a collectivity never engaged), less than 5 per cent supported occupations, blocking traffic, painting slogans, and damaging property, all of which were regular actions in Greenham's repertoire. Very few women ever expressed concern about possible public disapproval of particular actions, such as fence cutting, and debates about forms of action tended rather to focus on issues of non-violence and the likelihood of women being injured. Moreover, the extremely hostile attention paid by the media to the existence of lesbians at Greenham provoked neither attempts to downplay their numbers nor conciliatory and liberal efforts to change public opinion. On the contrary, women reacted with defiance: after *The Sun* labelled them 'militant feminists and burly lesbians' many women took to sporting 'Burly Lesbian' badges, and Blue Gate women painted 'Beware Dirty Dykes' on their van.[10] Greenham was not a pressure group, concerned to be integrated into the political process, but rather sought to undermine from outside the legitimacy of a political order which promoted militarism and excluded women.

The significance of this challenge can, in part, be gauged by the energies expended by the state in opposing Greenham. As I have shown in Chapter 7, a panoply of measures, official and unofficial, were activated to harass and intimidate women at Greenham, in order to destroy the camp. Co-ordinated strategies were developed by various arms of the state, and huge resources of time and money were poured into campaigns against Greenham. The actions of women at Greenham slowed down and hampered preparations at the base for the installation of Cruise, and later repeatedly demonstrated both the insecurity of the base and (together with Cruisewatch) the vulnerability of the missiles whilst on exercise. I would suggest (though it is unlikely that documentary evidence will ever be released to support my contention) that Greenham's monitoring and disruption of Cruise demonstrated strategic weakness inherent in the weapon system, and thereby significantly contributed to the willingness of the United States to agree to its withdrawal in 1987.

The challenge to patriarchy

In the same way that the challenge posed by Greenham to military policy can be evaluated by examining the response of the state, its challenge to patriarchy can be analysed by looking at the reactions of patriarchal actors. After a very short period, during which Greenham was understood and represented by the media as composed of heroic mothers seeking to save the world for their children, the criticisms, hostility, harassment, and violence began. Attention turned to Greenham as a women-only community and protest, as it increasingly vociferously refused its earlier representation. Whilst many men directly affected by women's involvement with Greenham were critical or even angry because Greenham appeared to be consuming time and emotional engagement which had previously been available to them, Greenham's impact was far wider than this. It operated primarily at a symbolic level, conveying messages about women's independence, autonomy and agency.[11] For women to leave their homes, and in some cases husbands and children, to pursue a political and personal project constituted an outrageous symbolic affront to men's power to control women's actions, and to women's confinement by domestic responsibilities. For women to *choose* to live and work only with other women, and to deliberately and consistently refuse to allow men to join in, was shocking. For women to be devising and undertaking daring and sometimes dangerous actions against the nuclear state, without male protection or assistance, was new. For women to occupy public space in such numbers, over such a long period of time, and with no concessions to the patriarchal gaze in their mode of dress, bodily comportment, or standards of domestic order, was unprecedented. And for women to do all this, and to appear to enjoy it, to refuse the status of martyrs for a higher cause, was deeply troubling.

Greenham thus disrupted many discourses which are central to contemporary constructions of womanhood. Greenham women refused to perform gender as they should, above all resisting the heterorelational imperative of patriarchy which demands that women exist first and foremost for men.[12] Many challenged this as lesbians, developing erotic and sexual connections with other women. But, lesbian or heterosexual, Greenham women in their thousands symbolically and practically put women first in their political and daily lives.

Contrary to the predictions of some radical feminists, Greenham did not destroy the women's movement or undermine feminism. It did not long remain 'the acceptable face of women-only actions, legitimized by its falling into women's traditional role of concern for future generations' (Green 1983:7–8). It did not employ 'reformist methods', have 'considerable faith in parliamentary democracy' (Laws 1983:42) or 'petition men to change' (Mohin 1983:24). Nor did it 'divert' women's attention away from their own oppression and from male violence (Bellos *et al.* 1983:20). Instead Greenham both quantitatively and qualitatively *extended* feminist consciousness, at both a collective and an individual level.

Whilst Greenham began partially from within a maternalist discourse, as a collectivity it became increasingly feminist over time. It did not adopt wholesale any one of the 'brands' of feminism on offer to it, and never developed a single, unified analysis of women's oppression or of the relationship between patriarchy and militarism. But the ethos it created drew on previous feminist practices, as well as anarchism, to create a distinctive approach to feminist political action. Thousands of women who had been untouched by the women's liberation movement, or who had not known how to get involved, were introduced to feminist ideas for the first time at Greenham. Precisely because Greenham had no 'line' for which prospective participants had to sign up in advance, it was a place where women could make major changes to their lives. Greenham allowed women to start a process of personal transformation from where they were: whilst some women were drawn to Greenham as mothers with a concern for the fate of their children, many others were attracted by the loud, brash community of lesbians. Occupying space outside the restrictions of patriarchal society, Greenham was a place where women felt able to construct for themselves new identities.

Greenham was far from being a harmonious, tranquil idyll, in which some innate womanly peacefulness reigned supreme. A community of strong-minded women, who grew stronger over time, there were many differences of opinion, often vociferously expressed. Conflict sometimes rocked the camp, and arguments about money, hierarchy, class and, to some extent, race, created real divisions. But Greenham's longevity rested in its adaptability and fluidity, its openness to change, and its ongoing creation and recreation by women who were committed to its ethos of anarchistic feminism and, above all, to each other. Greenham survived against all the odds, and despite dozens of premature obituaries, because there were women who chose to make it.

Greenham's legacy

Although the women's peace camp has disbanded, Greenham has left a rich legacy. To other social movements, Greenham passes on a greatly expanded repertoire of action, replete with forms of action which are imaginative, theatrical, parodic, and non-violent. The humorous and eye-catching actions of OutRage and ACT UP and the Lesbian Avengers, as well as drawing on American queer politics (which in turn has been much influenced by the Women's Pentagon Action), have their precursors in Greenham.[13] It is no coincidence that the two most memorable actions of the campaign against Clause 28 – the lesbians abseiling into the House of Lords, and the lesbians who invaded the BBC News studio and chained themselves to the newsreaders' chairs – were ex-Greenham women.[14] The setting up of camps at protest sites also appears to have become a favoured form of action in very different campaigns: the Women's Pit Camps, outside collieries threatened with closure in 1993, and camps against road building on Twyford Down and Solsbury Hill. Increasingly environmentalists and animal rights campaigners are practising blockades and sabotage in scenes reminiscent of Greenham in the early and mid-1980s.

Greenham also bequeaths extensive networks of women, connected by strong ties of friendship, who continue to engage in the everyday business of living and working as feminists, lesbians, and radicals. These women, whose anarchic, passionate political action defied patriarchy and nuclear militarism, remain to be re-activated as a collectivity should the occasion arise. For future generations of women, Greenham leaves a history of resistance in the late twentieth century which demonstrates women's agency and offers hope of the ultimate disarmament of patriarchy.

Appendix I
Characteristics of the interviewees

	Age[1]	Date[2]	Gate[3]	Level[4]	Class[5]	Sexuality b[6]	Sexuality a[7]	Employment[8]	Children[9]	Education[10]
1	29	1982	Y/O/V	camper	middle	het	het	part-time	0	degree
2	31	1983	G/V	camper	middle	lesbian	lesbian	travelling	0	post-grad
3	44	1981	V	stayer	middle	het	d/k	self-employed	2	post-grad
4	52	1982	G	camper	working	het	het	part-time	3	school
5	17	1982	Y/G	stayer	middle	lesbian	lesbian	student	0	school
6	31	1983	O	camper	middle	lesbian	lesbian	self-employed	0	degree
7	30	1981	V	camper	middle	het	het	part-time	0	degree
8	33	1982	O	visitor	middle	lesbian	lesbian	self-employed	0	degree
9	41	1982	O	camper	d/k	het	het	housewife	2	school
10	20	1983	I/O	camper	middle	lesbian	lesbian	travelling	0	school
11	22	1983	B	camper	working	lesbian	lesbian	unemployed	0	degree
12	36	1982	Y/O	stayer	d/k	d/k	lesbian	student	3	post-grad
13	30	1983	G	camper	middle	het	lesbian	unemployed	1	school
14	25	1981	O	stayer	middle	lesbian	het	self-employed	0	degree
15	34	1981	Y	camper	working	het	lesbian	housewife	5	nursing
16	23	1982	O	visitor	middle	het	d/k	full-time	0	degree
17	64	1981	O	visitor	middle	het	het	retired	4	school
18	23	1983	B	camper	middle	lesbian	lesbian	unemployed	0	degree
19	20	1982	B	camper	middle	lesbian	lesbian	unemployed	0	school

Continued over

	Age[1]	Date[2]	Gate[3]	Level[4]	Class[5]	Sexuality b[6]	Sexuality a[7]	Employment[8]	Children[9]	Education[10]
20	71	1981	Y	stayer	working	het	het	retired	3	school
21	52	1983	O	visitor	middle	het	het	carer	2	degree
22	33	1983	B	camper	d/k	het	lesbian	unemployed	2	school
23	24	1982	Y/R/V	camper	middle	lesbian	lesbian	unemployed	0	school
24	25	1983	G	stayer	middle	lesbian	lesbian	travelling	0	degree
25	25	1982	Y/G	camper	middle	lesbian	lesbian	unemployed	0	degree
26	53	1982	G/E	camper	middle	het	lesbian	full-time	5	degree
27	36	1981	Y	stayer	d/k	het	lesbian	housewife	2	degree
28	25	1982	G	stayer	middle	het	lesbian	full-time	0	degree
29	28	1981	Y/O	stayer	working	het	het	housewife	2	school
30	27	1981	Y/O	stayer	working	het	het	housewife	2	school
31	27	1981	Y/O	stayer	working	het	het	full-time	0	school
32	22	1981	Y/O	stayer	working	het	het	full-time	0	nursing
33	19	1983	B	camper	working	lesbian	lesbian	full-time	0	school
34	20	1983	B	camper	working	lesbian	lesbian	unemployed	0	school
35	22	1983	B	camper	working	het	lesbian	full-time	0	school

1 Age at first involvement.
2 Date of first involvement (at any level).
3 Primary gate(s) of association: Y, Yellow/Main Gate; G, Green Gate; E, Emerald Gate; B, Blue Gate; I, Indigo Gate; V, Violet Gate; R, Red Gate; O, Orange Gate.
4 Level of involvement (see Appendix II for discussion).
5 Self-defined class: middle, working and don't know (d/k) (see Appendix II).
6 Sexuality before involvement: heterosexual (het) or lesbian (see Appendix II for discussion).
7 Sexuality at time of interview: heterosexual (het), lesbian, don't know (d/k) (see Appendix II).
8 Employment status at time of first involvement (self-employed includes freelancers and agency workers).
9 Number of children at first involvement.
10 Highest level of education completed at time of first involvement.

Appendix II
Commentary on the sample

Thirty-five women were interviewed between 1989 and 1991. As there was no ready-made sampling frame to enable a random sample, the sample was purposely selected to maximize diversity; commentary on its representativeness of the population of Greenham women as a whole is significant, but speculative.

Age at time of getting involved

Age	Number of women
17–20	5
21–30	16
31–40	7
41–50	2
51–60	3
61+	2
total	35

I would suggest that this distribution of ages in the sample provided a good reflection of the ages of Greenham women as a whole. It is certainly not unrepresentative to have a scattering of women in their 40s, 50s, and 60s; the range of ages at Greenham was wide, although the majority were in their 20s and 30s.

Date of first involvement
The sample was composed entirely of women whose first involvement with Greenham was between 1981 and 1983: 11 women first got involved in 1981, 12 in 1982, and 12 in 1983. First involvement refers to a woman's first visit to Greenham (even if she did not then return for a year or more) or to her first involvement in the wider Greenham network.

It would have been possible to deliberately seek out women who got involved later than 1983, but this was rejected as a strategy because a decision had been made to focus on Greenham at its peak of mobilization. Initially I attempted to gather data on length of involvement, but this proved problematic and was abandoned. Very few women could identify an end date of involvement; those who could tended to be women who had lived at the camp for a long period of time and then never went back. By far the majority gradually became less and less involved over the years, moving for instance from living there, to staying there a few times a year, then perhaps not visiting the camp for three years, before returning to stay for a few days again.

Gate of association

In the snowballing of the sample, a deliberate attempt was made to maximize the variety of gates with which interviewees had been associated. The reasons for this were two-fold. First, my experience of Greenham told me that there were significant differences between the gates, in terms of the types of women who lived at them, the ethos of the gate, and the experience of living there, particularly due to the physical location of the gate. Second, the camp began at Main Gate, which was subsequently renamed Yellow Gate, and it tended to be to Yellow Gate that journalists went. Hence women at Yellow were often seen to be the spokeswomen for the whole camp, and this is not only reflected in newspaper reportage, but also in the work of Young (1990) and Liddington (1989). By 1983, the majority of women at Greenham were not living at Yellow Gate.

However it was not always a simple task to determine a woman's gate of association. Almost every camper and stayer had spent time at different gates, although most were able to identify themselves clearly with one particular gate. The absence of a Woad or Turquoise Gater reflects the short-lived existence of these gates rather than an inadequacy in the sample. That all the visitors associated with Orange Gate is due to the fact that they were all from Wales; there was a strong link between Orange Gate and Wales. Overall, a satisfactory distribution of gates of association was achieved across the sample.

Level of involvement

Level of involvement	Number of women
camper	19
stayer	12
visitor	4
total	35

The sample was deliberately skewed in favour of campers, and does not reflect the level of involvement of the population of women who were involved with Greenham, which over-whelmingly consisted of visitors. However, a deliberate attempt was made to interview women whose involvement with and commitment to Greenham had been of differing levels, as this was hypothesized as an important factor structuring the experience of involvement. The main problem with this, however, was the fluidity of forms and degrees of involvement in each woman's history. A three-fold classificatory scheme was devised consisting of the main types of involvement with the camp:

'camper', to designate a woman who, for a period of time greater than two months, made her home at Greenham;
'stayer', to designate a woman who stayed overnight at the camp either regularly or for a period of up to two months;
'visitor', to designate a woman who made daytime visits to Greenham and who may have stayed overnight on a few occasions.

The two-month period which differentiates 'campers' from 'stayers' is somewhat arbitrary but was chosen as reflecting approximately the length of time taken to integrate into the community of Greenham.

None the less, within these categories there remains considerable variation. For example, the category 'camper' contains women who lived at Greenham for between 2 months and 4 years; women who had no other home besides the camp and those who maintained a home away from Greenham whilst living there; and women who did not leave the camp for months on end, and others who went back to their place of origin every fortnight for a few days to sign on and rest, or even lived split weeks at the camp and at home (e.g. because of childcare). The 'visitor' category includes women who visited the camp anything between four and over forty times. Moreover the level of involvement category says nothing about the level of involvement in local women's peace groups.

Each woman was categorized by her highest level of involvement. Thus the number of visitors interviewed does not reflect the number of women in the sample who had experienced being a visitor.

Self-defined class

Class	Number of women
middle	19
working	11
don't know/no reply	5
total	35

Contrary to sociological wisdom on the new social movements and the peace movement, Greenham was not an overwhelmingly middle class movement (e.g. Parkin 1968; Cotgrove and Duff 1980, 1981; Taylor and Pritchard 1980; Offe 1987; Byrne 1988; Kriesi 1989; Mattausch 1989). The sample was purposively selected to include middle and working class women, though it would have been difficult for it not to have done, given the significant involvement of working class women in Greenham. The distribution of the sample by self-defined class is shown above, and is a reasonable representation of the population as a whole.

Class membership was self-defined, and when interviewees were asked to give their social class at the end of the interview, lengthy discussions about the problems of the meaning of class for women ensued, and about whether their class was defined by their education, their occupation, their father's class, mother's class, or husband's class. Many of the women who called themselves middle class did not have middle class employment; most were, however, university educated. Some university educated women described themselves as working class because of their family background. Five women were unable to self-define and rejected the applicability of the concept of class.

Sexuality at time of getting involved

Sexuality before	Number of women
heterosexual	20
lesbian	14
don't know	1
total	35

Sexuality at time of interview

Sexuality after	Number of women
heterosexual	12
lesbian	21
don't know	2
total	35

Sexual identity and the self-conscious claiming of both lesbian and heterosexual identities are complex matters (Wilkinson and Kitzinger 1993). Some women found it difficult to describe themselves as lesbian or heterosexual, before or after involvement with Greenham. For instance, some women were or had been involved in lesbian relationships before Greenham but had not consciously identified as lesbians. Some were in the process of coming out as they got involved with Greenham, making a clear cut 'before' and 'after' difficult to maintain. There is therefore a problem with applying a static label to pre- and post-Greenham sexuality, since for so many sexuality was fluid and changing.

However, despite its crudeness, I have chosen to allocate women to a three-fold categorization ('lesbian', 'heterosexual', 'don't know'), before involvement and at the time of interview, according to the accounts given of their lives in the interviews. No one interviewed gave an account of herself as bisexual. Of the three 'don't knows' one was married but involved in a lesbian relationship and two were celibate and self-consciously ambivalent.

Employment status

See discussion and table in Chapter 3.

Children

See discussion in Chapter 3.

Education at time of getting involved

Highest level of education completed at time of getting involved	*Number of women*
postgraduate degree	3
undergraduate degree	15
nursing qualification	2
school	16
total	35

I would suggest that the sample reflected reasonably well the population of Greenham, which had a higher representation of those with higher education than the general population of Britain (in this respect Greenham is similar to other 'new social movements'; Offe 1987; Rootes 1990).

Region of residence at time of getting involved

Of the 35 women interviewed, 19 were living in England, 13 in Wales and three overseas immediately prior to getting involved with Greenham for the first time. When the residents of England are broken down by region, four were living in London, four in the rest of the south, five in the Midlands, and six in the north of England. The residents of Wales were all living in south Wales, and of those from overseas, one was from Australia and two were from the United States.

By the time the interviews were carried out considerable geographical mobility had occurred. Interviews took place in: London, rural Kent, rural Wiltshire, rural Herefordshire, Norwich, Nottingham, Derby, Liverpool, Manchester, rural North Yorkshire, Cardiff, various towns in the Rhondda Valley, and in Cambridge, Massachusetts. Financial constraints ruled out interviews in Scotland, though there were considerable numbers of Scottish women involved in Greenham.

The representativeness of the sample in respect of region of residence at the time of getting involved is difficult to ascertain. Clearly there is a major deficiency in representativeness due to the decision not to interview in Scotland. Welsh women, on the other hand, are possibly over-represented in the sample, although there was a strong link between Greenham and Wales, which perhaps accounts for this.

'Race'/ethnicity

All the women interviewed were white, as I was unable to contact any of the small number of black women who had been involved with Greenham. When asked about their ethnic origin, twenty-one identified as white English, six as Welsh, three as Irish, and five as Jewish.

Notes

Chapter 1

1 My use of the concept of patriarchy recognizes the extensive debate within feminism about its usefulness (see Roseneil 1994a for a review, and, for instance, Barrett 1980, 1990; Rowbotham 1981; Acker 1989; Walby 1989, 1990a,b; Waters 1989). I use the term to refer to the systematic, regular and relatively stable, but historically specific, patterning of gender relations in the form of male domination and female subordination.

2 Whereas the largest suffrage rallies numbered up to quarter of a million demonstrators (Pankhurst 1977; Strachey 1978), the largest gatherings at Greenham numbered approximately 50,000 (though the suffrage rallies included men whereas the Greenham ones did not). However, at least a million women are estimated to have taken part in local demonstrations on International Women's Day for Disarmament, 24 May 1983.

3 I make this argument at greater length and within the context of a discussion of the general state of feminist sociology in Roseneil (1995). A similar argument is made by Davis (1991).

4 Exceptions include Banks (1986), Gerson and Peiss (1985), Dobash and Dobash (1992), Ryan (1992), Radcliffe and Westwood (1993). Examples of feminist concern with questions of agency outside the boundaries of feminist sociology include London Feminist History Group (1983), Hoagland (1989), Butler (1990, 1992, 1993), Hartsock (1990), Mahoney and Yngvesson (1992).

5 In feminist cultural studies see Gledhill (1992); on violence against women see Stanko (1990), Marcus (1992), Kelly, Regan, and Burton (1994); and on sexuality see Wilton (1993), Jackson (1994). For interdisciplinary perspectives see Griffin, Hester, Rai, and Roseneil (1994).

6 For discussions of Giddens' theory of structuration see Cohen (1989), Bryant and Jary (1991), Wolffensperger (1991).

7 See Chapter 8 for the development of this argument. My position here contrasts with that of Foucault, for whom it does not matter where discourses originate or how actors use them (Foucault 1984). For critical discussions of Foucault's theory of power and agency, see Ramazanoglu (1993).

8 Mouzelis (1989) develops an important two-fold critique of structuration theory. First, he argues that when actors distance themselves from the rules and resources of a social system, agency and structure exist in a dualism, rather than as a Giddensian duality. Second, he makes the point that some actors are more able to effect transformation of social systems than others, specifically those in positions of authority within hierarchical systems.

9 It will become apparent that I refer to Greenham both as an instance of 'political action' and as a 'social movement'. Implicit in this is a rejection of the existence of any clear distinction between 'the political' and 'the social', a distinction which the discipline of political science holds as fundamental. The concept of 'social movement' relates to one specific form of political action, which is, minimally, collective, non-institutionalized and value-orientated. I use the term 'political action' in the feminist sense, which significantly expands the notion of 'the political'. The various meanings are summarized by Scott (1993a:236): 'First, in its most typical definition it can mean activity directed by or at governments or other powerful authorities, activity that involves an appeal to collective identity, mobilization of resources, strategic calculation and tactical maneuver. Second, the term *politics* is also used to refer to relations of power more generally and the strategies aimed at maintaining or contesting them. Third, the word *politics* is applied even more broadly to practices that reproduce or challenge what is sometimes labelled "ideology", those systems of belief and practice that establish individual and collective identities, that form the relations between individuals and collectivities and their world, and are taken to be natural or normative or self-evident'. I argue that Greenham, which was a social movement, was 'political' in all three senses.

10 There are also a number of articles about Greenham: Jones (1983, 1987), Wallsgrove (1983), McDonagh (1985), Snitow (1985a,b), Finch (1986), Kirk (1989a,b), Emberley and Landry (1989). See also Kitzinger (1984) and Edwards' (1986) novel.

11 It is beyond the scope of this book to develop an analysis of the patriarchal character of militarism. Rather, attention has been focused on the practices by which women have opposed it.

12 See Summers (1988), Wheelwright (1989, 1992), Fuchs (1991), Chandler *et al.* (1992).

13 See for example Beales (1931), Driver (1964), Parkin (1968), Brock (1972), Caedel (1980), Taylor and Pritchard (1980), Minnion and Bolsover (1983), Mattausch (1987, 1989), Taylor and Young (1987), Taylor (1988).

14 For histories of women's opposition to militarism see Bussey and Tims (1965), Liddington (1983, 1989), Black (1984), Schott (1985), Wiltsher (1985), Early (1986), Eglin (1987), Roach Pierson (1987), Foster (1989), Oldfield (1989), Swerdlow (1989), Vellacott (1993).

15 Whilst recognizing that maternalist discourses may overlap with feminist discourses (and materialist discourses may do likewise), implicit in making this distinction is my position that feminism must be defined as, minimally, 'the desire for increased autonomy for women' (Black 1989:1). I favour a broad definition of feminism which encompasses a very wide range of different positions and recognizes the political and theoretical diversity amongst those seeking to extend women's power and autonomy and to end women's subordination.

16 Ruddick is firm about this point; maternal work can be done by both men and women, but it is in fact overwhelmingly done by women. The vast majority of male parents are

'fathers', a role which implies a very different set of practices and ways of thinking (1990:41–4).

17 For example, the Women's Christian Temperance Union (Bordin 1981).

18 Woolf (1982) argues that because women own only a tiny proportion of private property and land in the world (and this has been diminishing since the seventeenth century) they have no vested interest in wars fought over territory.

19 Cohn's work draws on that of Easlea (1983), which explores the contribution to the arms race of the culture of competitive masculinity which exists amongst nuclear scientists, and points to the gendered language of nuclear militarism.

20 Hartsock (1989) discusses how the 'masculine self', as a cultural norm, has been historically constructed as defined by the pursuit of heroism, the ultimate expression of which is found in death.

21 For a more detailed discussion of the methodological issues arising in this research, see Roseneil (1993).

22 I was to become, therefore, an 'opportunistic researcher' when I later embarked on a sociological study of Greenham, rather than being a 'convert' for the purposes of research (Adler and Adler 1987:67).

23 Examples of where researchers have done this include Krieger's (1983, 1985) study of a midwestern lesbian community of which she was a member, Hayano's (1983) study of poker rooms where he was already a regular player, Greed's (1990) study of women in her own profession of chartered surveying, and Hobbs' (1988) study of the entrepreneurial culture of the East End of London.

24 For discussions of positivism, see Giddens (1976), Alexander (1982), Giddens and Turner (1987), Wiley (1990).

25 My position is one which seeks to challenge the objectivism/subjectivism dichotomy within social science, and is unavoidably 'relativist' at the level of epistemology. For a more detailed discussion of my epistemological position, see Roseneil (1994b).

26 For a discussion of the organizational structure of Greenham, see Chapter 5.

27 The danger of 'elite bias' is much commented upon in the literature on qualitative research (e.g. Lofland 1971; Miles and Huberman 1984). The feminist literature on biographies emphasises the importance of challenging the 'great individual' approach to feminist history, which is a self-perpetuating cycle in which once someone has been singled out for mention in a study, she comes up again and again in future studies. This perpetuates the belief that only a few individuals have any influence within women's movements (Hannam 1985; Stanley 1985).

28 This does, of course, raise ethical/political issues about the responsibilities and loyalties of the researcher, and the possible exploitation of interviewees. See Roseneil (1993) for a more detailed discussion of this.

29 They were: Mid-Glamorgan County Archives (the Ann Pettit/Women for Life on Earth papers), Cardiff; British Library newspaper collection, Colindale; Schlesinger Library, Radcliffe College, (Seneca Women's Peace Encampment Papers); New York Public Library newspaper archive.

30 Strict adherence to the processes of grounded theory is recognized as problematic by Hammersley (1984) and Bulmer (1979). Bryman (1988) points out that very few researchers have actually made use of the approach in the exact form advocated by Glaser and Strauss.

31 Since Glaser and Strauss's *Discovery of Grounded Theory*, most writers on qualitative

research have advocated the simultaneous collection and analysis of data, recognising that data analysis actually begins even before the fieldwork does. For example, Burgess (1984); Miles and Huberman (1984); Hammersley and Atkinson (1983).

32 Touraine's (1981) method of 'sociological intervention' in social movements, in which he engages in a process of analysis and discussion with participants has sometimes produced a backlash from those he was researching and seeking to 'assist'. See Papadakis (1993).

33 For example, Hammersley and Atkinson warn against the 'more "sophisticated" inter-viewee' who moves away from description into analysis, as this means that 'the data base has been eroded' (1983:189). Their suggestion that description *can* exist uncontami-nated by analysis/discourse, is clearly problematic.

34 Oakley (1981) suggests that the problems of objectification and exploitation disappear for feminists researching women, because of the shared social structural position of the researcher and the researched. Wise (1987) and Bowles and Duelli Klein (1983) chal-lenge this, and point out that women researchers tend to occupy more privileged social locations than the women they research.

35 Finch (1984) and Stacey (1988) both suggest that the greater the intimacy and identification of the researcher and the researched, the greater the potential for exploitation.

36 A similar experience is noted by Wise (1987) and Hobbs (1988).

Chapter 2

1 For example, McCarthy and Zald (1973, 1977), Jenkins (1983), Oberschall (1973), Olson (1965).

2 For example, McCarthy and Zald (1977:1236) do no more than simply assume 'the modern American context' for their work.

3 This is not to say that no American sociologists of social movements are concerned with historical context. An obvious example is Tilly *et al.* (1975), and Tilly (1978), whose work is profoundly historical.

4 Bagguley (1992) is an exception. His critique of the new social movements literature focuses on its lack of explanatory power *vis à vis* feminism.

5 There is some disagreement about whether a significant division exists within the middle class concerning the new politics. Mattausch (1989) considers sector of em-ployment to be crucial, with the 'state class' of welfare workers constituting the base of the 1980s peace movement. In contrast, Kriesi (1989) argues that conflict within the middle class cross-cuts the public/private sector division; as the power of the technocrats (public and private sector managers and technical specialists) increases, the specialists (professionals and semi-professionals in teaching, medicine, social work, arts, and journalism) seek to defend their authority and autonomy, and thus constitute the primary recruiting ground for the new social movements.

6 See for example Ehrenreich and English (1979), Arditti *et al.* (1984), Cockburn (1985).

7 A similar point is made by Scott (1990), and Rootes (1991) about new social move-ments as a whole, and by Walby (1988) about labelling the women's movement a new social movement.

8 For example, Scott (1988) and Kelly-Gadol (1976).

9 I do not wish, however, to assert a causal connection between women's labour market

participation and political activism. Although a belief in such a relationship is widely held among political scientists (e.g. Duverger 1955; Campbell *et al.* 1960; Almond and Verba 1963; Andersen 1975; Flora 1977; Welch 1977), it has been effectively challenged by Thomson and Eichler (1985). In the case of Greenham I am not suggesting that participation is linked with paid employment at the level of the individual, but rather that the increasing possibility of women's economic independence was an underlying precondition of autonomous mass activism by women.

10 I think Mann (1987) overstates the argument that the modern state is characterized by a duality of domestic life and geopolitics. It is important to recognize the interconnectedness of the two, and particularly in this context, the relationship between events on the geopolitical stage and political mobilization. Whilst emphasizing linkages, I consider the two separately for the sake of clarity.

11 The history of this wave of peace campaigning is now well documented. For example, Driver (1964), Taylor and Pritchard (1980), Cox (1981), Minnion and Bolsover (1983), Randle (1987).

12 The roots of environmentalism, like other social movements of recent decades, can be traced back to the nineteenth century. However, the beginning of widespread public concern about the environment is typically dated from the early 1960s, in particular the publication of Rachel Carson's best-seller, *Silent Spring* in 1962 (Eckersley 1992).

13 On the environmental movement see, for example, Cotgrove and Duff (1980), Cotgrove (1982), Touraine (1983), Joppke (1991).

14 For example, Freeman (1975), Evans (1979), Bunch (1987), Jaggar (1988), Miles (1989).

15 For discussions of these feminist peace actions in the US see McAllister (1982), Jaggar (1988), King (1983), Harris & King (1989).

16 For example, the secrecy and absence of democracy surrounding nuclear decision making is discussed by Cox (1981), Kaldor and Smith (1982), Burke (1988), Elworthy (1989).

17 The neutron bomb was said to be a 'clean' weapon because it would kill people whilst leaving buildings intact.

18 The Belgian and Dutch governments later rejected the missiles, after intense peace movement opposition.

19 Kaldor (1982) argues that Soviet conventional superiority was a myth, and that NATO and the Warsaw Pact actually possessed a rough balance of weaponry in Europe in the early eighties.

20 I have placed inverted commas around the word 'generation' in recognition of its role in familiarizing nuclear weapons, a function of much of the discourse of defence intellectuals which has been exposed by Cohn (1987a,b).

21 Kaplan (1984) takes a different position from Knelman, arguing that what was most significant about the Reagan administration was not the quantitative spiralling of the arms race, which had actually started under Carter, but the qualitative dimension. What was shocking and new were Reagan's statements about nuclear war: 'their baldness, the nonchalant innocence with which they were frequently uttered' (Kaplan 1984:390).

22 Davis (1982) develops a historical materialist critique of Thompson which locates the East–West conflict in 'the dynamic of class struggle on a world scale' (1982:42) and

the fundamentally incompatible interests of the two sides. He challenges Thompson's identification of Europe as the pivot of the Cold War, and argues that it is Third World revolutions that are crucial to class struggle.

23 As Campbell (1984) makes clear, much of the history of the US military presence in Britain is shrouded in official secrecy. For instance there are no confirmed figures for the number of US military installations in the country.

24 Luckham is non-committal about the moment of origin of the armament culture (1984:6) and his analysis is disappointingly ahistorical. Nevertheless I consider that the concept is useful, and that the end of détente can be identified as a crucial point in its development.

Chapter 3

1 A similar point is made by Melucci (1989:45).

2 See, for example, Kornhauser (1959), Lang and Lang (1961), Smelser (1962), Gurr (1970), Turner and Killian (1972).

3 See, for example, McCarthy and Zald (1973, 1979), Oberschall (1973, 1980), Jenkins (1983), Klandermans (1984).

4 Some resource mobilization theorists (e.g. Fireman and Gamson, 1979) have since criticized both Olson's negation of the role of collective incentives in mobilization and his suggestion that selective incentives are sufficient for mobilization.

5 This is an argument that has been made by Parkin (1968) about involvement in CND.

6 This problem also exists in the work of Klandermans (1988) and Klandermans and Tarrow (1988), which suggests that mobilization occurs in a far more logical and well-organized manner than is generally the case.

7 Snow and Benford (1988) develop the notion of ideological framing, though in a manner which assumes too high a degree of formal organization.

8 Cook and Kirk (1983:38–9), Jones (1983:79–80), Harford and Hopkins (1984:9–19), Liddington (1989:221–2), A. Young (1990:16–17).

9 A number of writers have recently emphasized the important role of social and political networks, counter-cultural networks or subcultures in interceding between macro-structural changes and individual decisions to participate in social movements. See Melucci (1984, 1988, 1989), Diani and Lodi (1988), della Porta (1988), Klandermans and Tarrow (1988), Kriesi (1988), McAdam (1988). This draws on earlier work in the resource mobilization theory tradition (e.g. Gerlach and Hine, 1970).

10 Folder A, *Women for Life on Earth Papers*, Mid-Glamorgan County Archive, County Hall, Cardiff. Examples of each group: (1) Southern Region Campaign against the Missiles, local branches of CND, END, World Disarmament Campaign, Campaign against the Arms Trade, Medical Campaign against Nuclear Weapons; (2) Women's International League for Peace and Freedom, Feminism and Nonviolence Newsletter, Women Oppose the Nuclear Threat, Mothers for Peace; (3) WIRES – the national women's liberation newsletter, Beyond the Fragments Network – a socialist feminist network; (4) Plaid Cymru, trade union shop stewards.

11 Folder A, ibid. Letters of support were sent by a number of well known women who had been asked to participate, including Sheila Kitzinger, Cleo Laine, Janet Suzman and Glenda Jackson and Margaret Drabble.

12 Klandermans (1988) highlights the role of the media in social movement mobilization, intervening between the macro-structural context and individuals' decision to participate.

13 Document 8 in Folder A, ibid.

14 Thorne (1975) discusses the use of two different strategies by social movements to gain credibility: the minimizing of differences between movement activities and the rest of the world, and the maximizing of differences, to demonstrate participants' commitment.

15 See 13 above.

16 Ibid.

17 Ibid.

18 Ibid.

19 See King (1983).

20 Throughout I give the age of the woman interviewed at the time when she first got involved with Greenham (not at the time of the interview). The designation 'camper', 'stayer', 'visitor' is explained in Appendix II.

21 The *Western Mail* (26 August 1981) carried a pre-march article; the *Wiltshire Gazette and Herald* (3 September 1981) carried a front page photograph of the march arriving in Devizes and an article.

22 A similar opinion is expressed by Ann Pettitt interviewed by Liddington (1989:230).

23 Messages of support were delivered by the postal service from Harrogate Women's Liberation Group, Berkshire Anti-Nuclear Campaign, Isle of Wight CND, Cardigan Peace Group and from a number of individuals (Folder A, ibid.).

24 The camp did, in fact, provide new opportunities for women journalists, particularly on the tabloids, to write major features because news editors had to accept that male journalists would not get 'good copy'.

25 This is an argument that was echoed in the published criticisms of Greenham of a number of feminists. For instance, Eglin (1987), Segal (1987), and Oldfield (1989) argue that women-only peace activism, particularly Greenham, suggests that women have a particular relationship to peace which serves to reproduce rather than challenge the gender relations of militarism; they favour a mixed peace movement. The most critical, Oldfield, argues that separatism is a form of Fascism, and that Greenham was separatist, and therefore Fascist (1989:218). Her position is actually a thinly veiled expression of anti-lesbianism (cf. women living at Greenham were 'unusual' and became 'more and more psychologically entrenched in their female separatism': 217–8). Soper (1985) also expressed opposition to women-only organization within the peace movement.

26 Kriesi's (1989) argument is therefore borne out in the case of Greenham; the women interviewed, whether public or private sector workers, were overwhelmingly 'specialists' rather than 'technocrats'.

27 The term 'housewife' was used by these women to describe themselves and implies that they were financially dependent on their husbands. These women were not 'unemployed' in the sense either of being dependent on state benefits or of looking for paid work.

28 The term 'unemployed' is used to describe women who received unemployment benefit or supplementary benefit in their own right, or, in one case, a woman who was dependent on a man who received it.

29 One of these women was also engaged in a lesbian relationship at the same time, and has

been classified as 'don't know'. For a discussion of the problems attendant on classifying women's sexuality see Appendix II.

30 Women whose problems with childcare hindered their involvement with Greenham significantly were not, of course, likely to be represented in the sample. There were likely to have been many thousands of women who were unable to do more than visit Greenham, if that, because of childcare responsibilities.

31 Of these one woman's youngest child was under five, three had youngest children aged between five and thirteen, and three between thirteen and eighteen.

32 This table does not show involvement with a campaign or movement if that involvement was no more than paper membership; in order to figure in the totals, a woman's involvement had to have included, at least, participation in a demonstration, petitioning or regular attendance at meetings. However, the table does not differentiate between degrees of involvement, so that the level of involvement of, for example, Carol Harwood, who had been imprisoned in the 1960s for peace actions, is not marked out from that of others, who merely attended a few demonstrations.

33 This echoes Evans' (1979) argument that the origins of the women's liberation movement were in the sexism and male domination experienced by women who had been involved in the New Left.

34 'Bridget Evans' is a pseudonym given to this woman who felt that she could not be named. It was also a name frequently used by Greenham women, often *en masse*, when arrested or in dealings with the authorities when they wished to remain anonymous. Women at Seneca called themselves 'Jane Doe'.

35   Saving the world is really fun,
    Doodah
    Saving the world is really fun,
    Doodah, doodah, day . . .
    was an often-sung refrain at Greenham.

36 A similar feature of collective action is discussed by Tiryakian (1988). He draws on the later work of Durkheim to describe revolutions as sacred experiences, involving processes of dedifferentiation and 'creative effervescence'.

Chapter 4

1 However, there is some discussion of principles of action in writings by Greenham women (e.g. Cook and Kirk 1983; Harford and Hopkins 1984).

2 In the first few months of the camp's existence, a number of the women who had been involved in the Cardiff to Greenham walk drew up a list of rules; these included asking for a financial contribution from those staying at the camp and banning the smoking of cannabis. However, the rules were never seriously followed.

3 The exception to this was that on occasions of major actions, such as 11 December 1983, the principles of non-violence, caring for the environment, and valuing the 'non-rational' were set out in a leaflet. However, this leaflet was produced by CND, not by women at the camp. The general informality and lack of codification of principles contrasted with the Seneca Women's Peace Encampment in the US, where a list of 'respected policies' was drawn up and given to women as they arrived. For a discussion of the 'governance' of Seneca and a list of the 'respected policies' decided by national planning meetings and general meetings at Seneca, see Linton (1989).

4 For discussion of the principles of radical feminist practice see Koedt *et al.* (1973), Feminist Practice (1979), Jaggar (1988), Douglas (1990), Rowland and Klein (1990). Anarchism is a diverse body of political thought, with varying attitudes to the use of violence and the organization of revolution; see Woodcock (1962, 1977), Bookchin (1971), Erlich, *et al.* (1979), Quiet Rumours (n.d.), Miller (1984), Goodway (1989). On non-violence, see Sharp (1974), Bruyn and Rayman (1979). On feminist non-violence see Shrew (1978), McAllister (1982), Feminism and Nonviolence Collective (1983), Meyerding and Smith (1984). Eco-feminism encompasses essentialist and social constructionist positions; see Daly (1979), Merchant (1983), Griffin (1978), King (1989), Plant (1989), Diamond and Orenstein (1990), Biehl (1991), Seager (1993).

5 For a discussion of the importance to feminist ethics of the principle that one should monitor whom one is becoming, see Davion (1991).

6 The song refers to the frequent allegations by government ministers and in the press that Greenham (and CND) was in receipt of Soviet money and that there were Soviet agents at work at Greenham. It also comments on the tabloid press coverage of Greenham women as dirty, lesbians, and inadequate mothers, and on the liberal broadsheet coverage of Greenham women as self-sacrificing women suffering for their cause.

7 This is a principle shared with one strand of radical feminism, exemplified in the writing of Griffin (1978) and Daly (1979). See Jaggar (1988:95–6, 366–369) for a discussion. It was also the target of criticism by radical feminists (e.g. Onlywomen Press (1983).

8 See, for example, Spretnak (1982).

9 Melucci (1989:205) argues that this principle is an important characteristic of many contemporary social movements, and one of their distinctively 'new' features.

Chapter 5

1 Peterson (1992) uses the terms 'group level of social action' and 'public level of social action'. My preference is for Offe's terminology rather than Peterson's because the word 'level' implies a layering and a hierarchy of importance, whereas 'mode' suggests merely that the two forms of action can be analysed separately.

2 The importance of the internal workings of social movements is stressed by Melucci (1989). He argues that the latent, submerged networks which are involved in the daily production of alternative frameworks of meaning, and from which periodic visible manifestations of collective action are created are as important as those visible aspects of collective action. Both are forms of resistance and challenge (1989:70–3). However, Melucci's terms, 'latency' and 'visibility', are inappropriate for Greenham, where daily life did not take place in 'submerged' networks, but in publicly visible camps, and where confrontation with and resistance to the nuclear state was inherent in every moment and action of daily living outside the base.

3 For a discussion of the positive aspects of conflict within feminism, see Hirsch and Keller (1991).

4 Freeman (1984:6), in her critique of 'the tyranny of structurelessness' within the women's liberation movement, makes the point that there is no such thing as a 'structureless' group, and that informal structure is inevitable.

5 On another level, the web was a symbol of women's collective power, seemingly fragile, but actually very strong. The spider has traditionally been seen as female.

6 This role was, to some extent, also taken by the London Greenham office, set up by women in London as a base for co-ordinating London activities and for liaising with the press. The office moved a number of times, often occupying houses on short term licenses from Labour-controlled councils. These houses also provided accommodation for women from the camp when they needed a rest, and served as a stopping place for women arriving from abroad.

7 For example, Camden Women for Peace, Hackney Greenham Support Group, West London Greenham Support Group, and Balham Women for Peace/South London Women for Peace.

8 In Nottingham and Leeds there were groups called Women Oppose the Nuclear Threat (WONT) and in Cardiff, Women For Life On Earth, though these later became Women for Peace Groups.

9 Hetherington (1994) resurrects the concept of 'Bund', and applies it to Greenham. He contrasts the elective nature of the Bund, which is rooted in affectual action, with Tönnies' (1955) concept of gemeinschaftlich forms of sociation, which are ascriptive, constraining, and based in traditional social action (Weber 1978:25). He is wrong in its application to Greenham if central to the concept is his assertion that 'the maintenance of the Bund as a group [was] paramount and individual wishes secondary to that', as at Greenham individuals tended to be given priority over and above the needs of the collectivity.

10 The notion of community as a symbolic construction is developed by Cohen (1985).

11 See Caroline, in Harford and Hopkins (1984:31) for a description of the thinking behind this.

12 In Friedan's (1963) now famous dictum, 'housewifery expands to fill the time available'. For discussion of the domestic labour of wives, see Oakley (1974), Hardyment (1988), Delphy and Leonard (1992).

13 'The Sanctuary' was a small, rather swampy and fly-infested piece of land in the woods close to Green Gate, which was privately owned by someone who had no interest in using it or in evicting Greenham women from it. Until it was purchased and donated to the camp in 1988 and occupied by King's Cross women (see later), it was thought unsuitable for living on.

14 This money meeting is documented on the film *Carry Greenham Home* (made by Beeban Kidron and Amanda Richardson).

15 *Daily Express*, 9 April 1984.

16 The International Wages for Housework Campaign is derived from the Marxist economism of dalla Costa and James (1972) and argues that women's oppression should be tackled by paying wages for housework. This position has been rejected by every other feminist group in Britain (see Segal 1987). There is also a history of attempts at 'infiltration' and disruption of feminist campaigns around Britain by the Wages for Housework campaign.

Chapter 6

1 LeBon has been critiqued by, amongst others, Horowitz (1972) and Cloward and Piven (1979).

2 See Olson (1965), Oberschall (1973), and McCarthy and Zald (1977).

3 For example, Turner (1970), Tilly (1978, 1979), Freeman (1979, 1983), Kitschelt (1986), Ennis (1987), Rucht (1990), West and Blumberg (1990), Ryan (1992).

4 I would suggest that the concept of 'strategy' is also inapplicable in many of the other cases where it has been used, especially with respect to the women's movement.

5 Shaw (1990) argues that the concept of 'strategy' as used by sociologists originates in military terminology, and that it should not be used in other contexts. For discussion of the use of the concept in recent British sociology, see Wallace (1993).

6 My rejection of the concept of 'strategy' in the case of Greenham parallels Edwards and Ribbens' (1991) critique of its use in describing women's family lives. They argue that women tend to be concerned with processes rather than goals, and with detail, rather than with 'strategic ends': 'This is not to imply that the public world is rational and the domestic/women are irrational – just that domestic "rationality" has to be understood on its own terms as guided by both emotion and perception, with "goals" that are linked to processes and orientation' (1991:486).

7 The distinction between instrumental and expressive orientations in social movements is made by Gordon and Babchuk (1959), Parkin (1968), and Rucht (1990).

8 Rucht (1990) identifies seven main strategies available to social movements, depending on whether their 'logic of action' is instrumental or expressive. These are, for instrumental movements: political participation, bargaining, pressure and political confrontation. For expressive movements: reformist divergence, subcultural retreatment, and counter-cultural challenge. Whilst he acknowledges that some of the new social movements are both instrumental and expressive, he argues that at any one time a movement tends to prioritize one strategy. Kitschelt (1986) distinguishes between confrontational and assimilative strategies.

9 I use the term 'forms of action', or just 'actions' (which was the term used at Greenham: 'doing an action'), rather than 'tactics', as is more usual in social movements research. 'Tactics', like 'strategy', are part of rational choice and military discourses which are inappropriate to describe Greenham; cf. Rucht's definition of tactics as 'techniques of action' 'based in a situational assessment of available resources as well as of the benefits and costs of various forms of action, both for the actor and its opponent(s)' (Rucht 1990:174).

10 Ennis (1987) argues similarly that 'tactics' are shaped by *external limits* (e.g. lack of resources, repression by opponents etc.), and by the *inner logic* of the movement (i.e. its ideology, organization, and cost–benefit calculations).

11 See Thompson (1966), Rudé (1985) and Tilly (1978, 1979) on the use of pageantry, street theatre, and songs of protest in eighteenth century Britain.

12 This date was chosen because it was the anniversary of NATO's decision to deploy Cruise.

13 Rothenbuhler draws on Turner's (1977) concept of liminality, which refers to ritual 'time-out', in which everyday structures and rules are swept aside.

14 I am grateful to Paul Bagguley for drawing my attention to recent work in the tradition of late Durkheim on the symbolic and 'sacred' aspects of contemporary societies. See, for example, Alexander (1988).

15 The symbol of the dragon, or rainbow serpent, drew upon Chinese, native North American, and Australian Aboriginal mythologies, and represented women's demand for life and peace (Harford and Hopkins 1984:153).

16 Leaflet entitled 'Common Women's Day'. The play on the word 'common' is significant, emphasizing the 'ordinariness' of the women involved (that they were not exceptional martyrs), as well as the location of the camp on common land and invoking the English tradition of commoners' rights.

17 At this stage however, King's Cross women were only making irregular overtures to Greenham, for instance, by sending leaflets to Greenham about their events and inviting Greenham women to speak at them. They had not yet recruited any Greenham women into their organization.

18 The Ten Days action is debated in the Green and Common newsletter, 'more June news issue', 1984.

19 On women's physical embodiment, see Iris Marion Young (1990).

20 For a discussion of the policing of Greenham, see Johnson (1989).

21 However, the level of police violence at Greenham did not match that at Orgreave. See Coulter *et al.* (1984), Lloyd (1985) and Scraton (1985). In part at least this has to be explained by the fact that, unlike some miners, Greenham women did not use violence in response to police violence.

22 This amusing incident is captured on Beeban Kidron and Amanda Richardson's film *Carry Greenham Home* and is described by Kim Smith in Harford and Hopkins (1984:139–40).

23 For a description of the silos action see Harford and Hopkins (1984:97–101).

24 For an exposition of the case for fence-cutting as a non-violent action, see Rebecca Johnson in Harford and Hopkins (1984:40–1).

25 This was such a major breach of security involving a top secret aeroplane that charges against the women were dropped. See Tracy Hammond in Harford and Hopkins (1984: 154–6).

26 Those cases which went to crown court generally did result in conviction (e.g. the women who cut the fence in July 1983). The most severe sentence given to a Greenham woman was that imposed on Ann Francis; she received two one-year sentences to run concurrently, which were reduced to six months on appeal.

27 There has also been a campaign by Newbury residents to retain their 'commoners' rights'.

28 This is inevitably a brief overview of what could be a major study in its own right. See Harford and Hopkins (1984), Hickman (1986), Johnson (1986) and A. Young (1990) for further discussion.

29 In a similar vein, women refused the role of arrestee before reaching court. For instance, women often turned to the policeman who was arresting them, and declared that they were themselves carrying out a citizen's arrest on him, in order to prevent genocide. This was acted out in a spirit of parody.

30 For a description of the silos trial see, Harford and Hopkins (1984:104–6). The theatrical and lively gathering outside the courtroom is shown in *Carry Greenham Home*.

31 Greenham women uncovered case law which allowed a 'McKenzie friend' to accompany and advise an unrepresented defendant, and regularly made use of this. See Nicky Edwards in Harford and Hopkins (1984: 141–4).

32 It is not unlawful in Britain to call oneself by any name one chooses.

33 The MOD and Hampshire police have recently been ordered to pay two women £21,300 for holding them, without charge, in a sunken pit surrounded by barbed wire (*Guardian*, 24 March 1993). Another woman received £10,000 in an out of court settlement over the same incident (*Guardian*, 12 July 1994).

34 *Carry Greenham Home* was first the title of a song written for Greenham by Peggy Seeger, and later the title of Kidron and Richardson's film.

35 The case was eventually dismissed in 1985. See Greenham Common Women Against Cruise Missiles (1984), Hickman (1986), and A. Young (1990) for a more detailed discussion.

36 For a discussion of the connections between animal liberation and women's liberation, see Adams (1990).

37 There were also women's peace camps inspired by Greenham at the Cruise missile base at Comiso, Italy, and at bases in the Netherlands, Denmark, W. Germany, the US, Australia, and Canada.

38 The classic visual coverage of Greenham involved arranging the cosy domestic imagery of the camp – a kettle steaming over the fire, women with mugs in their hands gathered around it, for instance – in the foreground, with the fence and the silos in the background.

39 In recognition of public disquiet about the secrecy surrounding nuclear power, the power station at Sellafield has recently been turned into a free tourist attraction, regularly advertised on television; the aim appears to be to make nuclear power seem less threatening by opening a power station to the public.

Chapter 7

1 For a general discussion of responses to social movements, see Oberschall (1973) and Marx (1979). One area which has received considerable attention, however, is responses to women's movements: see Morrell (1981), Jeffreys (1985), Marshall (1985), Wiltsher (1985), Chafetz and Dworkin (1987), Kimmell (1987), Walby (1988, 1993).

2 See Glasgow University Media Group (1985), Meinhof (1986), Hollingsworth (1986), Jones (1987), and A. Young (1990).

3 In particular, they take issue with the position of those such as Hanmer (1978) and MacKinnon (1983) who suggest that the state is patriarchal and operates in the interests of men. See also Connell (1987, 1990), Walby (1990b) and Marshall (1994) for discussions of the various feminist perspectives on the state. Allen (1990) has even argued that feminists should abandon the notion of the state altogether.

4 I do not wish to imply that there are no laws in existence in Britain which allow this, but merely that those laws were not applicable to the project of removing Greenham.

5 Compare with Walby (1988) on the suffragettes.

6 For a discussion of the history of the US military presence in Britain, see Campbell (1984).

7 See Harford and Hopkins (1984:29–30) for the text of the letter and the camp's response.

8 In January 1985, however, 13 women were struck off the electoral register after objections from local residents (*Guardian*, 26 January 1985).

9 See Randle (1987) on the 1962 Official Secrets trial.

10 Some of these imprisonments were later overturned on appeal.

11 Electromagnetic radiation (EMR) is non-ionizing radiation, unlike nuclear radiation. EMR includes radiofrequency, microwave, and extremely low frequency radiation. See *Peace News*, 20 September 1985; *The Nation*, 14 March 1987.

12 Women at the Seneca Women's Peace Encampment in the United States reported similar symptoms.

13 In 1985 Cathy Massiter, a former MI5 officer, revealed that the telephones of CND had been tapped, and this was later confirmed in court (Carter 1992). On surveillance techniques used by the British state, see Bunyan (1983). For a discussion of those used by the FBI, see Marx (1979).

14 The area was the home of numerous military establishments: in addition to USAF Greenham Common, there was RAF Welford (nuclear and conventional ammunition store), an army depot at Thatcham, the School of Military Survey at Hermitage, and, for the manufacture of nuclear warheads, the Atomic Weapons Research Establishment at Aldermaston and the Royal Ordnance Factory at Burghfield.

15 For an interesting discussion of the relationship between US overseas bases and local communities, see Enloe (1989).

16 This is also illustrated by the fact that two years before the decision to site Cruise at Greenham was announced, there was a proposal to locate 15 KC135 aeroplanes there. These tanker planes aroused enormous local opposition because all they offered the local population was noise and a reduction in house prices. They were eventually sited at RAF Fairford (Lynchcombe n.d.). Lynchcombe, the pseudo-nymous author of a pamphlet describing Newbury's response to Cruise and to the camp, argues that the primary reason for local support for the missiles, and hostility to the women, was material self-interest. He identifies the Newbury Rotary Club, made up of estate agents, builders, and magistrates, as prime movers in campaigns against the camp.

17 See Faslane: Diary of a Peace Camp (1984).

18 Letter from Anthony Meyer to *Newbury Weekly News*, 3 May 1984.

19 Similar points were made by numerous correspondents to the *Newbury Weekly News*, many also suggesting that the police were biased in favour of the Greenham women (e.g. Jocelyne Gardner, *Newbury Weekly News*, 26 April 1984).

20 In an interesting prelude to the sustained newspaper campaign against 'loony left' Labour councils later in the 1980s, the *Newbury Weekly News* carried a large article about the Greater London Council spending 'thousands' on supporting Greenham. This was denied by the GLC, which claimed only to have supported women's peace initiatives in London (*Newbury Weekly News*, 17 May 1984).

21 In addition to the struggle to register to vote in 1983, and the arbitrary refusal of Greenham as an address by a stipendiary magistrate, women had to go to appeal to be granted full householders' entitlement to supplementary benefit, and the post was delivered somewhat sporadically, and envelopes often arrived open and parcels damaged.

22 See letter from Lynette Edwell, press officer for Newbury Against Cruise Missiles, to *Newbury Weekly News*, 24 May 1984.

23 In April 1984 RAGE threatened to picket the Home Office to prevent a group of Spanish women visiting Greenham. The picket was called off when their visit was cancelled, which RAGE claimed was due to unofficial pressure by the British government on the Spanish authorities (*Newbury Weekly News*, 26 April 1984). Accusations of treachery were commonplace against women peace campaigners during the First World War (Liddington 1989:125).

24 *Newbury Weekly News*, 17 November 1983.

25 Edwards (1987) notes how policemen called to incidents of 'domestic' violence frequently make judgements about the validity of the woman's complaint on the basis of

the cleanliness and tidiness of her home; a sink full of unwashed breakfast dishes often leads to no further action being taken.

26 There is a considerable history of the use of violence by men against feminists, notably the suffragettes (Morrell 1981) and women peace campaigners during the First World War (Liddington 1989:121). More recently the mass murder of women engineering students in a Canadian university was explained by the perpetrator as being because he hated feminists (Wise Harris 1991).

27 When numbers of women at the camp were especially low and no women arrived specifically to do the nightwatch, there was none. On such occasions there were often attacks.

Chapter 8

1 This strand of Giddens' work has been criticized by Hay *et al.* (1993/4), who argue that self-growth is an activity of a limited global significance, and is largely the preserve of 'ethnically dominant groupings in the middle classes' (1993/4:75).

2 Exceptions to this include contributors to Westwood and Radcliffe's volume (1993) on women's movements in Latin America, and the phenomenon of women's changed consciousness within mixed movements is recorded by Evans (1979), King (1988), and Blumberg (1990) in the case of the civil rights movement, and by Evans (1979), Freeman (1975) and Thorne (1975) about the New Left. Rucht (1990) notes that, at the collective level, social movements tend to expand their critique over time; he calls this the 'principle of generalization'. Overy (1982) notes that involvement in peace movements often leads to interest in 'broader issues', such as civil liberties, when protesters confront the criminal justice system.

3 Other subjective aspects of involvement in Greenham are explored in earlier chapters, particularly the emotional and affective elements of involvement in actions.

4 'Identity politics' has comparatively few written expressions, being located almost entirely outside the academy. In Britain it was evident, for example, in the politics of the London Women's Liberation Newsletter, in the mid-1980s. For critiques of 'identity politics', see Fuss (1989) and Bourne (1987).

5 A similar argument is made by Kitzinger (1994), though she rejects the label 'poststructuralist'.

6 It was radical feminists, and to a lesser extent socialist feminists, rather than liberal feminists who emphasised the importance of changing consciousness (Jagger, 1988).

7 Both McCarney (1980) and McLellan (1986) have pointed out that Marx himself never actually used the term 'false consciousness'. For a discussion of Marxist debates about the term, see Barrett (1991).

8 This issue is addressed by MacKinnon (1989:50–2).

9 It is not just poststructuralist feminists who have criticized essentialism within feminism; see also Echols (1983), Eisenstein (1984).

10 See Fraser (1992) for a discussion of Kristeva's shift from a 'gynocentric–maternalist essentialism' in her early work to a 'post-feminist anti-essentialism' (1992:67) in 1986, where she rejects any notion of 'woman' as an identity.

11 Riley (1988) expresses the same tension within feminism in terms of that between underfeminizing and overfeminizing women.

12 Smith-Rosenberg (1975), Faderman (1981), Rich (1980), Zimmerman (1985), Fuss (1989), Franklin and Stacey (1988), Jeffreys (1989), Butler (1991), Wittig (1992).

13 As the number of visitors interviewed was small (4), generalizations are difficult to make. However, accounts published in 1983 ('Yorkshire Women go to Greenham') by women who had mostly only visited Greenham suggest that visitors too experienced significant transformations.

14 I take the concept of 'heterorelations' from Raymond (1986): 'in a hetero-relational society [. . .] most of women's personal, social, political, professional, and economic relations are defined by the ideology that woman is for man' (1986:11).

15 This is in contrast to the mainstream media's coverage, particularly television, which rarely even asked why the camp was women-only (Glasgow University Media Group 1985).

16 I am grateful to Nickie Charles for helping me to clarify this point.

17 One of these women was already involved in a relationship with another woman, but was still living with her husband at the time of getting involved; she had been classified as 'don't know' at this time.

Chapter 9

1 In Hungary and Poland the end of Communism proceeded by negotiation between dissident movements and the Communist Party. In East Germany there were huge demonstrations in the autumn of 1989, followed by the opening and dismantling of the Berlin Wall. Czechoslovakia's 'velvet revolution' was similarly led from below, and non-violent. The exception was Romania, where the underground opposition was much weaker and the Communist Party much more determined to try to retain power.

2 This is not to imply that nuclear militarism is a thing of the past; indeed the major nuclear powers still retain 'overkill' quantities of nuclear weapons, and the danger of trade in plutonium from the former Soviet Union must not be underestimated.

3 A few women were still living on the Common (though not outside a gate) at the time of writing; these were women who had been associated with the King's Cross take-over of Yellow Gate, and who had lived separately from the camp for several years.

4 Norden (1985) argues that Greenham became increasingly socialist feminist over time. This is an inappropriate label which misconstrues the consciousness which developed as connections were made between different struggles and issues. These are better understood as a global feminism, with strong ecofeminist and radical feminist influences.

5 It is widely accepted by writers on social movements that movements invariably have a limited life-span, particularly at a high level of mobilization (e.g. Tarrow 1983; Brand 1990).

6 Nigel Young (1990) also makes the important point that the revolutions of 1989 were reported by media commentators as if they came from nowhere; the context of underground dissident peace activism over the preceding decades was largely ignored.

7 Opinion polling is notoriously dependent on the wording of questions, and opposition to Cruise varied according to the degree of emphasis placed on the 'Americanness' of the weapon, and on Soviet deployment of SS-20s (Berrington 1989). A consistent gender gap was reported by opinion polls on the issue of Cruise. For instance, in late 1983 45% of men approved of their siting in Britain, against 29% of women, and the

gender gap continued to fluctuate between 7 and 9% (Berrington 1989:27). Differences in opinion by age existed, with older people more favourable than younger, but the gap was not large (Berrington 1989:28).

8   Randle (1987) makes a similar argument about the impact of the peace movement of the 1950s/1960s.

9   See Kaldor *et al.* (1989) for discussions of this.

10   The *Sun*, 14 December 1982.

11   The cultural impact of social movements is emphasized by Melucci (1989), who argues that their 'hidden efficacy' lies in overturning dominant cultural codes.

12   The notion of the performativity of gender is developed by Butler (1990, 1993).

13   On ACT UP, Outrage and queer politics see Plummer (1992) and Smyth (1992).

14   Section 28 of the Local Government Act 1988 stated that a local authority should not 'promote homosexuality or publish material for the promotion of homosexuality; . . . promote the teaching in any maintained school of the acceptability of homosexuality as a pretended family relationship by the publication of such material or otherwise' (Jeffrey-Poulter 1991:218–19).

References

Acker, J. (1989) The trouble with patriarchy, *Sociology*, 23(2): 235–40.

Adams, C. (1990) *The Sexual Politics of Meat*. Cambridge: Polity Press.

Adler, P. and Adler, P. (1987) *Membership Roles in Field Research*. California: Sage.

Alderson, L. (1983) Greenham Common and all that, in Onlywomen Press (ed) *Breaching the Peace*. London: Onlywomen Press.

Alexander, J. (1982) *Positivism, Presuppositions, and Current Controversies*. Berkeley and Los Angeles: University of California Press.

Alexander, J. (1988) (ed) *Durkheimian Sociology: Cultural Studies*. Cambridge: Cambridge University Press.

Allen, J. (1990) Does feminism need a theory of the state?, in S. Watson (ed) *Playing the State*. London: verso.

Almond, G. and Verba, S. (1963) *The Civic Culture*. Princeton: Princeton University Press.

Amos, V. and Parmar, P. (1984) Challenging imperial feminism, *Feminist Review*, 17: 3–19.

Andersen, K. (1975) Working women and political participation 1952–1972, *American Journal of Political Science*, 19(3): 439–53.

Anderson, P. (1969) Components of the national culture, in A. Cockburn and R. Blackburn (eds) *Student Power*. Harmondsworth: Penguin.

Arditti, R., Duelli-Klein, R. and Minden, S. (eds) (1984) *Test-Tube Women: What Future for Motherhood?* London: Pandora.

Arkin, W. (1982) Nuclear weapons in Europe, in M. Kaldor and D. Smith (eds) *Disarming Europe*. London: Merlin Press.

As, B. (1982) A materialistic view of men and women's attitudes towards war, in *Women's Studies International Forum*, 5(3/4): 355–64.

Bagguley, P. (1992) Social change, the middle class and the emergence of 'new social movements', *The Sociological Review*, 40(1): 26–48.

Banks, O. (1986) *Faces of Feminism: A Study of Feminism as a Social Movement*. Oxford: Martin Robertson.

Barnes, S. *et al.* (1979) *Political Action: Mass Participation in Five Western Democracies*. Beverley Hills: Sage.

Barrett, M. (1980) *Women's Oppression Today*, 2nd edn., London: Verso.

Barrett, M. (1990) *Women's Oppression Today*, 2nd edn., London: Verso.

Barrett, M. (1991) *The Politics of Truth: From Marx to Foucault*. Cambridge: Polity.

Bartky, S.L. (1990) Toward a phenomenology of feminist consciousness, in S. Bartky (ed.) *Femininity and Domination: Studies in the Phenomenology of Oppression*. New York: Routledge.

Bassnett, S. (1986) *Feminist Experiences: The Women's Movement in Four Cultures*. London: Allen and Unwin.

Beales, A. (1931) *The History of Peace: A Short Account of the Organized Movements for International Peace*. London: G. Bell.

Beck, U. (1992) *Risk Society: Towards a New Modernity*. London: Sage.

Bell, D. (1974) *The Coming of Post-Industrial Society*. London: Heinemann.

Bellos, L. *et al.* (1983) Is Greenham feminist? in Onlywomen Press (ed) *Breaching the Peace*. London: Onlywomen Press.

Beneira, L. and Blank, R. (1989) Women and the economics of military spending, in A. Harris and Y. King (eds) *Rocking the Ship of State: Toward a Feminist Peace Politics*. Boulder, Colorado: Westview Press.

Berrington, H. (1989) British public opinion and nuclear weapons, in C. Marsh and C. Fraser (eds) *Public Opinion and Nuclear Weapons*. Basingstoke: Macmillan.

Besley, K. (1986) Zapping information, unpublished paper.

Biehl, J. (1991) *Rethinking Ecofeminist Politics*. Boston: South End Press.

Bishop, J. (1983) Essay, in Onlywomen Press (ed) *Breaching the Peace*. London: Onlywomen Press.

Black, N. (1984) The mothers' international: the women's co-operative guild and feminist pacifism, in *Women's Studies International Forum*, 7(6): 467–76.

Black, N. (1989) *Social Feminism*. Ithaca, NY: Cornell University Press.

Blumberg, R.L. (1990) White mothers as civil rights activists: the interweave of family and movement roles, in G. West and R.L. Blumberg (eds) *Women and Social Protest*. Oxford: Oxford University Press.

Bookchin, M. (1971) *Post-Scarcity Anarchism*. San Francisco: Ramparts Press.

Bordin, R. (1981) *Women and Temperance: The Quest for Power and Liberty*. Philadelphia: Temple University Press.

Bourne, J. (1987) Homelands of the mind: Jewish feminism and identity politics, *Race and Class*, 29(1): 1–24.

Bowles, G. and Duelli Klein R. (eds) (1983) *Theories of Women's Studies*. London: Routledge and Kegan Paul.

Brand, K.W. (1990) Cyclical aspects of new social movements: waves of cultural criticism and mobilization cycles of new middle class radicalism, in R. Dalton, and M. Kuechler (eds) *Challenging the Political Order: New Social and Political Movements in Western Democracies*. Cambridge: Polity.

Brittan, P. (1987) Fighting Fascism in Britain: the role of the Anti-Nazi League, *Social Alternatives*, 6(4): 42–6.

Brock, P. (1972) *Pacifism in Europe to 1914*. Princeton: Princeton University Press.

Brown, W. (1984) *Black Women and the Peace Movement*. London: Falling Wall Press.

Brownmiller, S. (1976) *Against our Will: Men, Women and Rape*. Harmondsworth: Penguin.

Bruyn, S. and Rayman, P.M. (1979) (eds) *Nonviolent Action and Social Change*. New York: Irvington Publishers.

Bryant, C.G. and Jary, D. (eds) (1991) *Giddens' Theory of Structuration*. London: Routledge.

Bryman, A. (1988) *Quantity and Quality in Social Research*. London: Unwin Hyman.

Bulmer, M. (1979) Concepts in the Analysis of Qualitative Data, *Sociological Review*, 27(4): 651–77.

Bunch, C. (1987) *Passionate Politics: Feminist Theory in Action.* New York: St Martins Press.

Bunyan, T. (1983) *The History and Practice of the Political Police in Britain.* London: Quartet.

Burgess, R. (1984) *In the Field: An Introduction to Field Research.* London: Unwin Hyman.

Burke, P. (1988) *The Nuclear Weapons World.* London: Pinter.

Bussey, G. and Tims, M. (1965) *Women's International League for Peace and Freedom.* London: Allen & Unwin.

Butler, J. (1990) *Gender Trouble: Feminism and the Subversion of Identity.* New York: Routledge.

Butler, J. (1991) Imitation and gender insubordination, in D. Fuss (ed.) *Inside/Out.* New York: Routledge.

Butler, J. (1992) Contingent foundations: feminism and the question of 'postmodernism', in J. Butler and J.W. Scott (eds) *Feminists Theorize the Political.* New York: Routledge.

Butler, J. (1993) *Bodies that Matter: On the Discursive Limits of Sex.* New York: Routledge.

Byrd, P. (1985) The development of the peace movement in Britain, in W. Kaltefleiter and R.L. Pfaltzgraff (eds) *The Peace Movements in Europe and the United States.* London: Croom Helm.

Byrne, P. (1988) *The Campaign for Nuclear Disarmament.* London: Croom Helm.

Caedel, M. (1980) *Pacifism in Britain 1914–1945: The Defining of a Faith.* Oxford: Clarendon Press.

Cain, M. (1993) Foucault, feminism and feeling: what Foucault can and cannot contribute to feminist epistemology, in C. Ramazanoglu, (ed) *Up against Foucault: Explorations of Some Tensions between Foucault and Feminism.* London: Routledge.

Cambridge Women's Peace Collective (ed) (1984) *My Country is the Whole World: an Anthology of Women's Work on Peace and War.* London: Pandora.

Campbell, A., Converse, P., Miller, W. and Stokes, D. (1960) *The American Voter.* New York: John Wiley.

Campbell, D. (1984) *The Unsinkable Aircraft Carrier: American Military Power in Britain.* London: Paladin Books.

Carter, A. (1992) *Peace Movements: International Protest and World Politics since 1945.* Harlow: Longman.

Chafetz, J.S. and Dworkin, A.G. (1987) In the face of threat: organized anti-feminism in comparative perspective, *Gender and Society*, 1(1): 33–60.

Chandler, J., Bryant, L. and Bunyard, T. (1992) *Women in Combat.* Paper presented to the British Sociological Association Annual Conference, University of Kent.

Chandler, W. and Siaroff, A. (1986) Postindustrial politics in Germany and the origins of the Greens, *Comparative Politics*, 18(3): 303–25.

Chilton, P. (1987) Metaphor, euphemism and the militarisation of language, *Current Research on Peace and Violence*, X(I): 7–20.

Clesse, A. (1985) The peace movements and the future of West European security, in P. van den Dungen (ed) *West European Pacifism and the Strategy for Peace.* Basingstoke: Macmillan.

Cloward, R.A. and Piven, F.F. (1979) Hidden protest: the channelling of female innovation and resistance, in F.F. Piven and R.A. Cloward (eds) *Regulating the Poor*. New York: Pantheon Books.

CND (1983) *Report of Research*, unpublished paper.

Cockburn, C. (1985) *Machinery of Dominance: Women, Men and Technical Know-how*. London: Pluto Press.

Cohen, A.P. (1985) *The Symbolic Construction of Community*. London: Ellis Horwood.

Cohen, I. (1989) *Structuration Theory: Anthony Giddens and the Constitution of Social Life*. Basingstoke: Macmillan.

Cohn, C. (1987a) Nuclear language and how we learned to pat the bomb, *Bulletin of Atomic Scientists*, 43(9): 17–24.

Cohn, C. (1987b) Sex and death in the rational world of defense intellectuals, *Signs*, 12(4): 687–712.

Cohn, C. (1989) Emasculating America's nuclear deterrent, in A. Harris and Y. King (eds) *Rocking the Ship of State: Toward a Feminist Peace Politics*. Boulder, Colorado: Westview Press.

Cohn, C. (1993) Wars, wimps and women: talking gender and thinking war, in M. Cooke and A. Woollacott (eds) *Gendering War Talk*. Princeton: Princeton University Press.

Coleman, J. (1958) Relational analysis: the study of social organisations with survey methods, *Human Organisation*, 16(4): 28–36.

Connell, R.W. (1987) *Gender and Power*. Cambridge: Polity.

Connell, R.W. (1990) The state, gender and sexual politics: theory and appraisal, *Theory and Society*, 19: 507–44.

Cook, A. and Kirk, G. (1983) *Greenham Women Everywhere: Dreams, Ideas and Actions from the Women's Peace Movement*. London: Pluto Press.

Cotgrove, S. (1982) *Catastrophe or Cornucopia*. Chichester: Wiley.

Cotgrove, S. and Duff, A. (1980) Environmentalism, middle class radicalism and politics, *The Sociological Review*, 28(2): 333–51.

Cotgrove, S. and Duff, A. (1981) Environmentalism, values and social change, *British Journal of Sociology*, 32(1): 92–110.

Coulter, J., Miller, S. and Walker, M. (1984) (eds) *State of Siege: Miners' Strike 1984 – Politics and Policing in the Coal Fields*. London: Canary Press.

Cox, J. (1981) *Overkill*, Harmondsworth: Penguin.

dalla Costa, M. and James, S. (1972) *The Power of Women and the Subversion of the Community*. Bristol: Falling Wall Press.

Dalton, R., Kuechler, M. and Burklin, W. (1990) The challenge of new movements, in R. Dalton, and M. Kuechler (eds) *Challenging the Political Order: New Social and Political Movements in Western Democracies*. Cambridge: Polity.

Daly, M. (1979) *Gyn/Ecology: The Metaethics of Radical Feminism*. London: Women's Press.

Davidoff, L. and Hall, C. (1987) *Family Fortunes: Men and Women of the English Middle Class 1780–1850*. London: Hutchinson.

Davion, V.M. (1991) Integrity and radical change, in C. Card (ed) *Feminist Ethics*. Lawrence, Kansas: University Press of Kansas.

Davis, K. (1991) Critical sociology and gender relations, in K. Davis, M. Leijenaar and J. Oldersma (eds) *The Gender of Power*. London: Sage.

Davis, M. (1982) Nuclear imperialism and extended deterrence, in New Left Review (ed) *Exterminism and Cold War*. London: New Left Books.

della Porta, D. (1988) Recruitment processes in clandestine political organizations: Italian left-wing terrorism, in B. Klandermans, H. Kriesi and S. Tarrow (eds) (1988) *From Structure to Action: Comparing Social Movement Research Across Cultures*, Vol. 1. Greenwich, Connecticut: Jai Press.

Delphy, C. and Leonard, D. (1992) *Familiar Exploitation: A New Analysis of Marriage in Contemporary Western Societies*. Cambridge: Polity.

Diamond, I. and Orenstein, G. (1990) *Reweaving the World: The Emergence of Ecofeminism*. San Francisco: Sierra Club Books.

Diani, M. and Lodi, G. (1988) Three in one: currents in the Milan ecology movement, in B. Klandermans, H. Kriesi and S. Tarrow (eds) *From Structure to Action: Comparing Social Movement Research Across Cultures*, Vol. 1, Greenwich, Connecticutt: Jai Press.

Dobash, R.E. and Dobash, R.P. (1992) *Women, Violence and Social Change*. London: Routledge.

Douglas, C.A. (1990) *Love and Politics: Radical Feminist and Lesbian Theories*. San Francisco: ism Press.

Driver, C. (1964) *The Disarmers: A Study in Protest*. London: Hodder & Stoughton.

Durkheim, E. (1961) *The Elementary Forms of Religious Life*. New York: Collier.

Duverger, M. (1955) *The Political Role of Women*. Paris: UNESCO.

Dworkin, A. (1981) *Pornography: Men Possessing Women*. London: Women's Press.

Early, F.H. (1986) The historic roots of the women's peace movement in North America, *Canadian Woman Studies*, 7(4): 43–53.

Easlea, B. (1983) *Fathering the Unthinkable: Masculinity, Scientists and the Nuclear Arms Race*. London: Pluto Press.

Echols, A. (1983) The new feminism of yin and yang, in A. Snitow, C. Stansell and S. Thompson (eds) *Powers of Desire: The Politics of Sexuality*. New York: Monthly Review Press.

Eckersley, R. (1992) *Environmentalism and Political Theory*. London: UCL Press.

Edwards, N. (1986) *Mud*. London: Women's Press.

Edwards, S.S.M. (1987) 'Provoking her own demise': from common assault to homicide, in J. Hanmer and M. Maynard (eds) *Women, Violence and Social Control*. London: Macmillan.

Edwards, R. and Ribbens, J. (1991) Meanderings around 'strategy': a research note on strategic discourse in the lives of women, *Sociology*, 25: 477–90.

Eglin, J. (1987) Women and peace: from the suffragists to the Greenham women, in R. Taylor and N. Young (eds), *Campaigns for Peace: British Peace Movements in the Twentieth Century*. Manchester: Manchester University Press.

Ehrenreich, B. and English, D. (1979) *For her own good: 150 years of experts' advice to women*. New York: Doubleday.

Eisenstein, H. (1984) *Contemporary Feminist Thought*. London: Unwin.

Elshtain, J.B. (1985) Reflections on war and political discourse: realism, just war and feminism in a nuclear age, in *Political Theory*, 13(1): 39–57.

Elshtain, J.B. (1987) *Women and War*. New York: Basic Books.

Elworthy, S. (1989) Nuclear weapons decision-making and accountability, in C. Marsh and C. Fraser (eds) *Public Opinion and Nuclear Weapons*. London: Macmillan.

Emberley, J. and Landry, D. (1989) Coverage of Greenham and Greenham as 'Coverage', *Feminist Studies*, 15(3): 485–98.

END (1980) Appeal for nuclear disarmament, in E.P. Thompson and D. Smith, *Protest and Survive*. Harmondsworth: Penguin.

Enloe, C. (1981) The military model, in W. Chapkis (ed) *Loaded Questions: Women in the Military*. Amsterdam: Transnational Institute.

Enloe, C. (1983) *Does Khaki Become You: The Militarisation of Women's Lives*. London: Pandora.

Enloe, C. (1989) *Bananas, Beaches and Base: Making Feminist Sense of International Politics*. London: Pandora.

Ennis, J. (1987) Fields of action: structure in movements' tactical repertoires, *Sociological Forum*, 2(3): 520–33.

Erlich, C. (n.d.) Socialism, anarchism and feminism, in *Quiet Rumours: An Anarcha-Feminist Anthology*. London: Dark Star.

Erlich, H., Erlich, C., DeLeon, D. and Morris, G. (1979) (eds) *Reinventing Anarchy*. London: Routledge and Kegan Paul.

Evans, S. (1979) *Personal Politics: The Roots of Women's Liberation in the Civil Rights Movement and the New Left*. New York: Vintage Books.

Evans, J., Hudson, C. and Smith, P. (1985) Women and the strike: it's a whole way of life, in B. Fine and R. Millar (eds) *Policing the Miners' Strike*. London: Lawrence and Wishart.

Eyerman, R. and Jamison, A. (1991) *Social Movements: A Cognitive Approach*. Cambridge: Polity.

Fadermann, L. (1981) *Surpassing the Love of Men: Romantic Friendships and Love Between Women from the Renaissance to the Present*. London: Women's Press.

Faslane: Diary of a Peace Camp (1984) Edinburgh: Polygon Books.

Feminism and Nonviolence Collective (1983) *Piecing It Together: Feminism and Non-violence*. Devon: Feminism and Nonviolence Collective.

Feminist Practice: Notes from the Tenth Year (1979) London: Theory Press.

Finch, J. (1984) 'It's great to have someone to talk to': the ethics and politics of interviewing women, in C. Bell and H. Roberts (eds) *Social Researching: Policies, Problems, Practice*. London, Routledge and Kegan Paul.

Finch, S. (1986) Socialist feminists and Greenham, *Feminist Review*, 23: 93–100.

Fireman, B. and Gamson, W.A. (1979) Utilitarian logic in the resource mobilization perspective, in J.D./McCarthy and M.N. Zald (eds) *The Dynamics of Social Movements*. Cambridge, Massachusetts: Winthrop Publishers.

Flora, C. (1977) Working class women's political participation: its potential in developed countries, in M. Githens and J. Prestage (eds) *A Portrait of Marginality: The Political Behaviour of American Women*. New York: McKay.

Foucault, M. (1984) *The History of Sexuality Vol. 1: An Introduction*. Harmondsworth: Penguin.

Foster, C. (1989) *Women for all Seasons: The Story of the Women's International League for Peace and Freedom*. Georgia: University of Georgia Press.

Franklin, S. and Stacey, J. (1987) Dyke-tactics for difficult times, in C. McEwan (ed) *Out the Other Side: Contemporary Lesbian Writing*. London: Virago.

Fraser, N. (1992) The uses and abuses of French discourse theories for feminist politics, *Theory, Culture and Society*, 9: 51–71.

Freeman, J. (1975) *The Politics of Women's Liberation*. New York: Longman.

Freeman, J. (1979) Resource mobilization and strategy: a model for analyzing social movement organization actions, in J. McCarthy, and M.N. Zald (eds) (1979) *The Dynamics of Social Movements*. Cambridge, Massachusetts: Winthrop Publishers.

Freeman, J. (1983) A model for analyzing the strategic options of social movement organizations, in J. Freeman (ed) *Social Movements of the Sixties and Seventies*. New York: Longman.

Freeman, J. (1984) The tyranny of structurelessness, in *Untying the Knot: Feminism, Anarchism and Organisation*. London: Dark Star Press and Rebel Press.

Friedan, B. (1963) *The Feminine Mystique*. Harmondsworth: Penguin.

Fuchs, C. (1991) In Praise of Women Warriors, *Dissent*, Summer: 421–22.

Fuss, D. (1989) *Essentially Speaking: Feminism, Nature and Difference*. New York: Routledge.

Gamble, A. (1988) *The Free Economy and the Strong State*. London: Macmillan.

Gerlach, L.P. and Hine, M.M. (1970) *People, Power, Change: Movements of Social Transformation*. Indianapolis: Bobbs-Merill.

Gerson, J.M. and Peiss, K. (1985) Boundaries, negotiation, consciousness: reconceptualizing gender relations, *Social Problems*, 32(4): 317–31.

Giddens, A. (1976) *New Rules of Sociological Method*. London: Hutchinson.

Giddens, A. (1977) *Studies in Social and Political Theory*. London: Hutchinson.

Giddens, A. (1984) *The Constitution of Society*. Cambridge: Polity.

Giddens, A. (1990) *The Consequences of Modernity*. Cambridge: Polity.

Giddens, A. (1991) *Modernity and Self-Identity: Self and Society in the Late Modern Age*. Cambridge: Polity.

Giddens, A. (1992) *The Transformation of Intimacy*. Cambridge: Polity.

Giddens, A. and Turner, J. (1987) *Social Theory Today*. Cambridge, Polity.

Gilligan, C. (1982) *In a Different Voice: Essays on Psychological Theory and Women's Development*. Cambridge, Massachusetts: Harvard University Press.

Glaser, B. and Strauss, A. (1967) *The Discovery of Grounded Theory*. Chicago: Aldine Publishing.

Glasgow University Media Group (1985) Breaching the peace at Greenham Common, in Glasgow University Media Group (eds) *War and Peace News*. Buckingham: Open University Press.

Gledhill, C. (1992) Pleasurable negotiations, in F. Bonner, L. Goodman, R. Allen, L. Janes and C. King (eds) *Imagining Women: Cultural Representations and Gender*. Cambridge: Polity.

Gleditsch, N.P. (1990) The rise and decline of the new peace movement, in K. Kodama and U. Vesa (eds) *Towards a Comparative Analysis of Peace Movements*. Dartmouth: Gower.

Goodway, D. (ed) (1989) *For Anarchism: History, Theory and Practice*. London: Routledge.

Gordon, C. and Babchuk, N. (1959) A typology of voluntary associations, *American Sociological Review*, 24: 1049–81.

Greed, C. (1990) The professional and the personal: a study of women quantity surveyors, in Stanley, L. (ed.) *Feminist Praxis: Research, Theory and Epistemology in Feminist Sociology*. London: Routledge.

Green, F. (1983) Not weaving but frowning, in Onlywomen Press (ed.) *Breaching the Peace*. London: Onlywomen Press.

Greenham Women Against Cruise Missiles (1984). New York: Center for Constitutional Rights, Legal Education Pamphlet.

Griffin, S. (1978) *Women and Nature*. New York: Harper & Row.

Griffin, S. (1989) Ideologies of madness, in D. Russell (ed) *Exposing Nuclear Phallacies*. New York: Pergamon Press.

Griffin, G., Hester, M., Rai, S. and Roseneil, S. (1994) (eds) *Stirring It: Challenges for Feminism*. London: Taylor and Francis.

Gurr, T.R. (1970) *Why Men Rebel*. Princeton: Princeton University Press.

Habermas, J. (1963) *Theory and Practice*. London: Heinemann.

Habermas, J. (1981) New social movements, *Telos*, 49: 33–7.

Habermas, J. (1987a) *The Theory of Communicative Action*, Vol. 2. Cambridge: Polity.

Habermas, J. (1987b) *The Philosophical Discourse of Modernity*. Cambridge: Polity.

Halfpenny, P. (1982) *Positivism and Sociology: Explaining Social Life*. London, Allen & Unwin.

Hall, S. and Jacques, M. (1983) (eds) *The Politics of Thatcherism*. London: Lawrence & Wishart.

Hall, M. and Jacques, M. (1989) *New Times*. London: Lawrence and Wishart.

Halliday, F. (1982) The sources of the new cold war, in New Left Review (ed) *Exterminism and Cold War*. London: New Left Books.

Hammersley, M. (1984) The researcher exposed: a natural history, in R. Burgess (ed) *The Research Process in Educational Settings: Ten Case Studies*. London: Falmer Press.

Hammersley, M. and Atkinson, P. (1983) *Ethnography: Principles in Practice*. London: Tavistock.

Hanmer, J. (1978) Violence and the social control of women, in G. Littlejohn, B. Smart, J. Wakeford and Nira Yuval-Davis (eds) *Power and the State*. London: Croom Helm.

Hannam, J. (1985) Usually neglected in standard histories, in D. Farran, *et al. Writing Feminist Biography*, Studies in Sexual Politics, Nos. 13/14. Manchester: University of Manchester.

Haraway, D. (1988) Situated knowledges: the science question in feminism and the privilege of partial perspective, *Feminist Studies*, 14(3): 575–99.

Harding, S. (1986) *The Science Question in Feminism*. Buckingham: Open University Press.

Harding, S. (1991) *Whose Science? Whose Knowledge?* Buckingham: Open University Press.

Hardyment, C. (1988) *From Mangle to Microwave*. Cambridge: Polity.

Harford, B. and Hopkins, S. (1984) *Greenham Common: Women at the Wire*. London: Women's Press.

Harris, A. and King, Y. (1989) (eds) *Rocking the Ship of State: Towards a Feminist Peace Politics*. Boulder, Colorado: Westview Press.

Hartsock, N. (1989) Masculinity, heroism, and the making of war, in A. Harris and Y. King (eds) *Rocking the Ship of State: Towards a Feminist Peace Politics*. Boulder, Colorado: Westview Press.

Hartsock, N. (1990) Foucault on power: a theory for women?, in L. Nicholson (ed) (1990) *Feminism/Postmodernism*. London: Routledge.

Hastings, E.H. and Hastings, P.K. (1982) (eds) *Index to International Public Opinion 1978–1980*. Westport, Connecticut: Greenwood Press.

Hastings, E.H. and Hastings, P.K. (1984) (eds) *Index to International Public Opinion 1982–1983*. Westport, Connecticut: Greenwood Press.

Hay, C., O'Brien, M. and Penna, S. (1993/4) Giddens, modernity and self-identity: the 'hollowing out' of social theory, *Arena Journal*, 2: 45–75.

Hayano, D. (1983) *Poker Faces: The Life and Work of Professional Card Players*. London: University of California Press.

Hetherington, K. (1994) The contemporary significance of Schmalenbach's concept of the bund, *Sociological Review*, 42(1): 1–25.

Hirsch, M. and Keller, E.F. (1991) (eds) *Conflicts in Feminism*. New York: Routledge.

Hickman, J. (1986) Greenham women against cruise missiles and others versus Ronald Reagan and others, in J. Dewar, A. Paliwala, S. Picciotto and M. Ruete (eds) *Nuclear Weapons, the Peace Movement and the Law*. London: Macmillan.

Hoagland, S.L. (1989) *Lesbian Ethics: Towards New Value*. Palo Alto, California: Institute of Lesbian Studies.

Hobbs, D (1988) *Doing the Business: Entrepreneurship, the Working Class and Detectives in the East End of London*. Oxford: Oxford University Press.

Hobhouse, E. (1902) *The Brunt of War and Where it Fell*. London: Methuen.

Hollingsworth, M. (1986) *The Press and Political Dissent*. London: Pluto.

Horowitz, I. (1972) Social deviance and political marginality, in I. Horowitz (ed.) *Foundations of Political Sociology*. New York: Harper & Row.

Ingelhart, R. (1977) *The Silent Revolution: Changing Values and Political Styles among Western Publics*. Princeton: Princeton University Press.

Inglehart, R. (1989) Values, ideology, and cognitive mobilisation in new social movements, in R. Dalton and M. Kuechler (eds) *Challenging the Political Order: New Social and Political Movements in Western Democracies*. Cambridge: Polity.

Jackson, S. (1994) *Heterosexuality as a Problem for Feminist Theory*. Paper presented to the British Sociological Association Annual Conference, University of Central Lancashire, Preston.

Jaggar, A. (1988) *Feminist Politics and Human Nature*. Totowa, New Jersey: Rowan & Littlefield.

Jahn, E. (1989) The role of governments, social organizations and peace movements in the new German and European peace process, in M. Kaldor, G. Holden, and R. Falk (eds) *The New Detente*. London: Verso.

Jeffrey-Poulter, S. (1991) *Peers, Queers and Commons: The Struggle for Gay Law Reform from 1950 to the present*. London: Routledge.

Jeffreys, S. (1985) *The Spinster and Her Enemies: Feminism and Sexuality 1880–1930*. London: Pandora.

Jeffreys, S. (1989) Does it matter if they did it?, in Lesbian History Group (ed) *Not a Passing Phase: Reclaiming Lesbians in History 1840–1985*. London: Women's Press.

Jenkins, J. (1983) Resource Mobilization and the Study of Social Movements, *Annual Review of Sociology*, 9: 527–53.

Jenness, V. (1992) Coming out: Lesbian identities and the categorization problem, in K. Plummer (ed.) *Modern Homosexualities*. London: Routledge.

Johnson, R. (1986) Alice through the fence: Greenham women and the law, in J. Dewar, A. Paliwala, S. Picciotto and M. Ruete (eds) *Nuclear Weapons, the Peace Movement and the Law*. London: Macmillan.

Johnson, R. (1989) Greenham women: the control of protest, in C. Dunhill (ed) *Boys in Blue*. London: Virago.

Jones, L. (1983) On common ground: the women's peace camp at Greenham Common, in L. Jones (ed.) *Keeping the Peace*. London: Virago.

Jones, L. (1987) Perceptions of 'peace women' at Greenham Common 1981–1985, in S. MacDonald, P. Holden and S. Ardener (eds) *Images of Women in Peace and War: Cross Cultural and Historical Perspectives.* Basingstoke:Macmillan.

Joppke, C. (1991) Social movements during cycles of issue attention: the decline of the anti-nuclear movements in West Germany and the USA, *British Journal of Sociology,* 42(1): 43–60.

Kaldor, M. (1982) *The Baroque Arsenal.* London: Deutsch.

Kaldor, M. and Smith, D. (eds) (1982) *Disarming Europe.* London: Merlin Press.

Kaldor, M., Holden, G. and Falk, R. (1989) (eds) *The New Détente.* London: Verso.

Kaplan, F. (1984) *Wizards of Armageddon.* New York: Simon & Schuster.

Kaplan, T. (1982) Female consciousness and collective action: the case of Barcelona, 1910–1918, *Signs,* 7: 545–66.

Kelly, L., Regan, L. and Burton, S. (1994) *The Victim/Survivor Dichotomy: Beyond an Identity Defined by Violation.* Paper presented to the British Sociological Association Annual Conference, University of Central Lancashire, Preston.

Kelly-Gadol, J. (1976) The social relations of the sexes: methodological implications of women's history, *Signs,* 1(4): 809–23.

Kimmel, M. (1987) Men's responses to feminism at the turn of the century, *Gender and Society,* 1(3): 261–83.

King, D. (1988) Multiple jeopardy, multiple consciousness: the context of black feminist ideology, *Signs,* 14: 42–72.

King, Y. (1983) All is connectedness: scenes from the women's Pentagon action USA, in L. Jones (ed.) *Keeping the Peace.* London: Virago.

King, Y. (1989) Healing the wounds: feminism, ecology and nature/culture dualism, in A. Jaggar and S. Bordo (eds) *Gender/Body/Knowledge: Feminist Reconstructions of Being and Knowing.* New Brunswick, New Jersey: Rutgers University Press.

Kirk, G. (1989a) Our Greenham common: feminism and nonviolence, in A. Harris and Y. King (eds) *Rocking the Ship of State: Towards a Feminist Peace Politics.* Boulder, Colorado: Westview Press.

Kirk, G. (1989b) Our Greenham Common: not just a place but a movement, in A. Harris and Y. King (eds) *Rocking the Ship of State: Towards a Feminist Peace Politics.* Boulder, Colorado: Westview Press.

Kitschelt, H. (1986) Political opportunity structures and political protest: anti-nuclear movements in four democracies, *British Journal of Political Science,* 16: 58–85.

Kitzinger, C. (1994) Experiential authority and heterosexuality, in G. Griffin (ed) *Changing Our Lives: Doing Women's Studies.* London: Pluto.

Kitzinger, J. (1984) *The Social Construction of Gender: A Case Study of the Women's Peace Movement.* BA dissertation, New Hall College, University of Cambridge.

Klandermans, B. (1984) Mobilization and participation: social psychological expansions of resource mobilization theory, *American Sociological Review,* 49: 583–600.

Klandermans, B. (1988) The formation and mobilization of consensus, in B. Klandermans, H. Kriesi and S. Tarrow (eds) (1988) *From Structure to Action: Comparing Social Movement Research Across Cultures,* Vol. 1. Greenwich, Connecticut: Jai Press.

Klandermans, B. and Tarrow, S. (1988) Mobilization into social movements: synthesizing European and American approaches, in B. Klandermans, H. Kriesi and S. Tarrow (eds) (1988) *From Structure to Action: Comparing Social Movement Research Across Cultures,* Vol. 1. Greenwich, Connecticut: Jai Press.

Klandermans, B, Kriesi, H. and Tarrow, S. (eds) (1988) *From Structure to Action: Comparing Social Movement Research Across Cultures*, Vol. 1. Greenwich, Connecticut: Jai Press.

Knelman, F. (1985) *Reagan, God and the Bomb: From Myth to Policy in the Nuclear Arms Race*. Toronto: McClelland & Stewart.

Koedt, A., Levine, E. and Rapone, A. (1973) *Radical Feminism*. New York: Quadrangle.

Koonz, C. (1988) *Mothers in the Fatherland: Women, the Family and Nazi Politics*. London: Methuen.

Kornhauser, W. (1959) *The Politics of Mass Society*. Glencoe, Illinois: Free Press.

Krass, A. and Smith, D. (1982) Nuclear strategy and technology, in M. Kaldor and D. Smith, *Disarming Europe*. London: Merlin Press.

Krieger, S. (1983) *The Mirror Dance: Identity in a Women's Community*. Philadelphia: Temple University Press.

Krieger, S. (1985) Beyond 'subjectivity': the use of self in social science, *Qualitative Sociology*, 8: 309–24.

Kriesi, H. (1988) Local mobilization for the people's social petition of the Dutch peace movement, in B. Klandermans, H. Kriesi and S. Tarrow (eds) (1988) *From Structure to Action: Comparing Social Movement Research Across Cultures*. Vol. 1. Greenwich, Connecticut: Jai Press.

Kriesi, H. (1989) New social movements and the 'new class': the class base of the mobilisation potential of Dutch new social movements in 1986, *American Journal of Sociology*, 94(5): 1078–116.

Kristeva, J. (1986) *The Kristeva Reader*, translated by Toril Moi. New York: Columbia University Press.

Lang, K. and Lang, G. (1961) *Collective Dynamics*. New York: Crowell.

Lash, S. and Urry, J. (1987) *The End of Organised Capitalism*. Cambridge: Polity.

de Lauretis, T. (1990) Upping the anti [*sic*] in feminist theory, in M. Hirsch and E.F. Keller (eds) *Conflicts in Feminism*. New York: Routledge.

Laws, S. (1983) Support these women for their children's sake, in Onlywomen Press (ed) *Breaching the Peace*. London: Onlywomen Press.

LeBon, G. (1969) *The Crowd*. New York: Viking Press. (Originally published in 1895).

Liddington, J. (1983) The women's peace crusade, in D. Thompson (ed.) *Over Our Dead Bodies*. London: Virago.

Liddington, J. (1989) *The Long Road to Greenham: Feminism and Anti-Militarism in Britain since 1820*. London: Virago.

Linton, R. (1989) Seneca women's peace camp: shapes of things to come, in A. Harris and Y. King (eds) *Rocking the Ship of State: Towards a Feminist Peace Politics*. Boulder, Colorado: Westview Press.

Linton, R. and Whitham, M. (1982) With mourning, rage, empowerment and defiance, *Socialist Review*, 12(3–4): 11–36.

Lloyd, C. (1985) A national riot police: Britain's 'third force'?, in B. Fine and R. Millar (eds) *Policing the Miners' Strike*. London: Lawrence and Wishart.

Lloyd, G. (1984) *The Man of Reason: 'Male' and 'Female' in Western Philosophy*. Minneapolis: University of Minnesota Press.

Lodgaard, S. (1982) Theatre nuclear weapons: the NATO doctrine, in M. Kaldor and D. Smith (eds) *Disarming Europe*. London: Merlin Press.

Lofland, J. (1971) *Analyzing Social Settings*. New York: Wadsworth.

London Feminist History Group (eds) (1983) *The Sexual Dynamics of History*. London: Pluto Press.

Lorde, A. (1984) *SisterOutsider*. Trumansburg, New York: Crossing Press.

Lovenduski, J. and Randall, V. (1993) *Contemporary Feminist Politics*. Oxford: Oxford University Press.

Luckham, R. (1984) Of arms and culture, *Current Research on Peace and Violence*, VII(1): 1–64.

Lynchcombe, (n.d.) *At Least Cruise is Clean*. Niccolo Press.

Lyotard, J-F. (1978) *The Postmodern Condition: A Report on Knowledge*. Minneapolis: University of Minnesota Press.

McAdam, D. (1988) Micromobilization Contexts and Recruitment to Activism, in B. Klandermans, H. Kriesi and S. Tarrow (eds) *From Structure to Action: Comparing Social Movement Research Across Cultures*, Vol. 1. Greenwich, Connecticut: Jai Press.

McAllister, P. (ed.) (1982) *Reweaving the Web of Life: Feminism and Nonviolence*. Philadelphia: New Society Publishers.

McCarney, J. (1980) *The Real World of Ideology*. Brighton: Harvester.

McCarthy, J. and Zald, M.N. (1973) *The Trend of Social Movements in America: Professionalization and Resource Mobilization*. Morristown, New Jersey: General Learning Press.

McCarthy, J. and Zald, M.N. (1977) Resource mobilisation and social movements: a partial theory, *American Journal of Sociology*, LXXXII: 1212–41.

McCarthy, J. and Zald, M.N. (eds) (1979) *The Dynamics of Social Movements*. Cambridge, Massachusetts: Winthrop Publishers.

McDonagh, C. (1985) The women's peace movement in Britain, *Frontiers*, VIII(2): 53–8.

MacKinnon, C. (1981) Feminism, marxism, method and the state: an agenda for theory, in N.O. Keohane, M.Z. Rosaldo and B.C. Gelpi (eds) *Feminist Theory: A Critique of Ideology*. Chicago: Chicago University Press.

MacKinnon, C. (1983) Feminism, Marxism, method and the state: towards a feminist jurisprudence, *Signs*, 8: 635–58.

MacKinnon, C. (1989) *Towards a Feminist Theory of the State*, Cambridge, Massachusetts: Harvard University Press.

McLellan, D. (1986) *Ideology*. Buckingham: Open University Press.

McNeil, M. (1991) Making and not making the difference: the gender politics of Thatcherism, in S. Franklin, C. Lury, and J. Stacey (eds) *Off-Centre: Feminism and Cultural Studies*. London: Harper Collins.

Mahoney, M.A. and Yngvesson, B. (1992) The construction of subjectivity and the paradox of resistance: reintegrating feminist anthropology and psychology, *Signs* 18(1): 44–73.

Mann, M. (1987) War and social theory: into battle with classes, nations and states, in C. Creighton and M. Shaw (eds) *The Sociology of War and Peace*. Basingstoke: Macmillan.

Marcus, S. (1992) Fighting bodies, fighting words: a theory and politics of rape prevention, in J. Butler and J. Scott (eds) *Feminists Theorize the Political*. New York: Routledge.

Marshall, B. (1994) *Engendering Modernity: Feminism, Social Theory and Social Change*. Cambridge: Polity.

Marshall, S.E. (1985) Ladies against women: mobilization dilemmas of antifeminist movements, *Social Problems*, 32(4): 348–62.

Marx, G.T. (1979) External efforts to damage or facilitate social movements: some patterns, explanations, outcomes, and complications, in J.D. McCarthy, and M.N. Zald (eds) *The Dynamics of Social Movements*. Cambridge, Massachusetts: Winthrop Publishers.

Mattausch, J. (1987) The Sociology of CND, in C. Creighton and M. Shaw, *The Sociology of War and Peace*. Basingstoke: Macmillan.

Mattausch, J. (1989) *A Commitment to Campaign: A Sociological Study of CND*. Manchester: Manchester University Press.

Maynard, M. (1990) The re-shaping of sociology? trends in the study of gender, *Sociology*, 24(2): 269–90.

Meinhof, U. H. (1986) Revolting women: subversion and its media representation in West Germany and Britain, in S. Reynolds (ed) *Women, State and Revolution*. Brighton: Wheatsheaf.

Melucci, A. (1984) 'An end to social movements?', *Social Science Information*, 23(4/5): 819–35.

Melucci, A. (1985) The symbolic challenge of contemporary movements, *Social Research*, 52: 789–816.

Melucci, A. (1988) Getting involved: identity and mobilization in social movements, in B. Klandermans, H. Kriesi and S. Tarrow (eds) (1988) *From Structure to Action: Comparing Social Movement Research Across Cultures*, Vol. 1. Greenwich, Connecticut: Jai Press.

Melucci, A. (1989) *Nomads of the Present: Social Movements and Individual Needs in Contemporary Society*. London: Hutchinson Radius.

Merchant, C. (1983) *The Death of Nature: Women, Ecology and the Scientific Revolution*. San Francisco: Harper & Row.

Meyerding, J. and Smith, R. (1984) (eds) *We are All Part of One Another: A Barbara Deming Reader*. Philadelphia: New Society Publishers.

Miles, A. (1989) Introduction, in A. Miles and G. Finn (eds) *Feminism: From Pressure to Politics*. Montreal: Black Rose Books.

Miles, M.B. and Huberman, A.M. (1984) *Qualitative Data Analysis: A Sourcebook of New Methods*. London: Sage.

Miller, D. (1984) *Anarchism*. London: Dent.

Mills, C.W. (1958) *The Sociological Imagination*. New York: Oxford University Press.

Minnion, J. and Bolsover, P. (eds) (1983) *The CND Story*. London: Allison & Busby.

Mohin, L. (1983) Is Greenham feminist? in Onlywomen Press (ed) *Breaching the Peace*. London: Onlywomen Press.

Moraga, C. (1983) *Loving in the War Years*. Boston: South End Press.

Morgan, R. (1977) Going Too Far: The Personal Chronicle of a Feminist. New York: Random House.

Morrell, C. (1981) *'Black Friday' and Violence against Women in the Suffragette Movement*. London: Women's Research and Resources Centre.

Mouzelis, N. (1989) Restructuring structuration theory, *Sociological Review*, 37: 613–35.

Murray, R. (1988) Life after Henry (Ford), *Marxism Today*, October: 8–13.

Nedelmann, P. (1984) New political movements and changes in processes of intermediation, *Social Science Information*, 23(6): 1029–48.

Norden, B. (1985) Many hands, many visions, *Spare Rib*, September: 6–8.

Oakley, A. (1974) *The Sociology of Housework*. Oxford: Martin Robertson.

Oakley, A. (1981) Interviewing women: a contradiction in terms, in H. Roberts (ed.) *Doing Feminist Research*. London, Routledge and Kegan Paul.

Oberschall, A. (1973) *Social Conflict and Social Movements*. Englewood Cliffs, New Jersey: Prentice-Hall.

Oberschall, A. (1980) Loosely structured collective conflicts, in L. Kriesberg (ed.) *Research in Social Movements, Conflict and Change*, Vol. 5. Greenwich, Connecticut: Jai Press.

Offe, C. (1985) *Disorganised Capitalism*. Cambridge: Polity.

Offe, C. (1987) Challenging the boundaries of institutional politics: social movements since the 1960s, in C. Maier (ed.) *Changing Boundaries of the Political: Essays on the Evolving Balance Between the State and Society, Public and Private in Europe*. Cambridge: Cambridge University Press.

Oldfield, S. (1989) *Women against the Iron Fist: Alternatives to Militarism 1900–1989*. Oxford: Blackwell.

Olson, M. (1965) *The Logic of Collective Action*. Harvard: Harvard University Press.

Onlywomen Press (ed.) (1983) *Breaching the Peace*. London: Onlywomen Press.

Overy, B. (1982) *How Effective Are Peace Movements?* London: Housmans/Bradford University School of Peace Studies.

Pankhurst, S. (1977) *The Suffragette Movement: An Intimate Account of Persons and Ideals*. London: Virago.

Papadakis, E. (1993) Interventions in Social Movements, in *Social Research: Philosophy, Politics and Practice*. London: Sage.

Parkin, F. (1968) *Middle Class Radicalism: the social bases of CND*. Manchester: Manchester University Press.

Pateman, C. (1988) *The Sexual Contract*. Cambridge: Polity.

Pateman, C. (1989) Feminist critiques of the public/private dichotomy, in C. Pateman (ed.) *The Disorder of Women*. Cambridge: Polity.

Perkins Gilman, C. (1903) *The Home: its Work and Influence* (reprinted (1972)). Urbana: Illinois Press.

Peterson, A. (1992) *Women as Collective Actors: A Case Study of the Swedish Women's Peace Movement*. Goteborg: Research Report, Department of Sociology, University of Gothenburg.

Plant, J. (1989) *Healing the Wounds: The Promise of Ecofeminism*. Philadelphia: New Society Publishers.

Plant, S. (1992) *The Most Radical Gesture: the Situationist International in a Postmodern Age*. London: Routledge.

Plummer, K. (ed) (1992) *Modern Homosexualities*. London: Routledge.

Portnoy, A. (1986) *The Little School: Tales of Disappearance and Survival in Argentina*. Pittsburgh: Cleis Press.

Pringle, R. and Watson, S. (1992) 'Women's Interests' and the Post-Structuralist State, in M. Barrett and A. Phillips (eds) *Destabilizing Theory: Contemporary Feminist Debates*. Cambridge: Polity.

Quiet Rumours: An Anarcha-Feminist Anthology, (n.d.) London: Dark Star.

Radcliffe, S. and Westwood, S. (eds) (1993) *'Viva': Women and Popular Protest in Latin America*. London: Routledge.

Ramazanoglu, C. (ed.) (1993) *Up against Foucault: Explorations of Some Tensions between Foucault and Feminism*. London: Routledge.

Randle, M. (1987) Non-violent direct action in the 1950s and 1960s, in R. Taylor and N. Young, *Campaigns for Peace: British Peace Movements in the Twentieth Century*. Manchester: Manchester University Press.

Raymond, J. (1986) *A Passion for Friends: Towards a Philosophy of Female Affection*. London: Women's Press.

Redstockings (1970) Redstockings manifesto, in R. Morgan (ed) *Sisterhood is Powerful*. New York: Random House.

Rich, A. (1980) Compulsory heterosexuality and lesbian existence', *Signs* 5(4): 631–60.

Riemer, J. (1977) Varieties of opportunistic research, *Urban Life*, 5(4): 467–77.

Riley, D. (1988) *Am I that Name? Feminism and the Category of 'Women' in History*. London: Macmillan.

Roach Pierson, R. (1987) (ed) *Women and Peace: Theoretical, Historical and Practical Perspectives*. Beckenham: Croom Helm.

Rochon, T.R. (1990) The West European peace movement and the theory of new social movements, in R. Dalton, and M. Kuechler (eds) *Challenging the Political Order: New Social and Political Movements in Western Democracies*. Cambridge: Polity.

Rootes, C. (1989) The Campaign for Nuclear Disarmament: from moral crusade to mobilisation of anxiety, in C. Marsh and C. Fraser (eds) *Public Opinion and Nuclear Weapons*. Basingstoke: Macmillan.

Rootes, C. (1991) The new politics and the new social movements: accounting for British exceptionalism. Paper given to UK Political Studies Association Conference, Lancaster.

Roseneil, S. (1993) Greenham revisited: researching myself and my sisters, in D. Hobbs and T. May (eds) *Interpreting the Field*. Oxford: Clarendon Press.

Roseneil, S. (1994a) Gender, in M. Haralambos (ed.) *Developments in Sociology*. Ormskirk: Causeway Press.

Roseneil, S. (1994b) *Feminist Political Action: A Case Study of the Greenham Common Women's Peace Camp*. Unpublished PhD thesis, London School of Economics and Political Science.

Roseneil, S. (1995) The coming of age of feminist sociology: some issues of theory and practice for the next twenty years, *British Journal of Sociology*, 46(2): 191–205.

Rothenbuhler, E.W. (1988) The liminal fight: mass strikes as ritual and interpretation, in J. Alexander (ed.) *Durkheimian Sociology: Cultural Studies*. Cambridge: Cambridge University Press.

Rowbotham, S. (1973) *Woman's Consciousness, Man's World*. Harmondsworth: Penguin.

Rowbotham, S. (1981) The trouble with patriarchy, in Feminist Anthology Collective (ed.) *No Turning Back*. London: Women's Press.

Rowbotham, S. (1989) *The Past is Before Us: Feminism in Action since the 1960s*. Harmondsworth: Penguin.

Rowland, R. and Klein, R.D. (1990) Radical feminism: critique and construct, in S. Gunew (ed.) *Feminist Knowledge: Critique and Construct*. London: Routledge.

Rucht, D. (1990) The strategies and action repertoires of new movements, in R. Dalton, and M. Kuechler (eds) *Challenging the Political Order: New Social and Political Movements in Western Democracies*. Cambridge: Polity.

Ruddick, S. (1990) *Maternal Thinking: Towards a Politics of Peace*. London: Women's Press.

Rude, G. (1985) *The Crowd in History*. London: Lawrence and Wishart.

Russell, D. (1989) Introduction, in D. Russell (ed.) *Exposing Nuclear Phallacies*. New York: Pergamon Press.

Ryan, B. (1992) *Feminism and the Women's Movement: Dynamics of Change in Social Movement Ideology and Activism*. New York: Routledge.

Salomon, K. (1986) The peace movement – an anti-establishment movement, *Journal of Peace Research*, 23(2): 115–27.

Sanders, J. (1983) *The Peddlers of Crisis: The Committee on the Present Danger and the Politics of Containment*. Boston, Massachusetts: South End Press.

Sassoon, A.S. (1987) *Women and the State: the Shifting Boundaries of Public and Private*. London: Routledge.

Schell, J. (1982) *The Fate of the Earth*. London: Picador.

Schott, L. (1985) The women's peace party and the moral basis for women's pacifism, in *Frontiers*, VIII(2).

Schreiner, O. (1911/1978) *Woman and Labour*. London: Virago.

Schutz, A. (1967) *The Phenomenology of the Social World*. Evanston: Northwestern University Press.

Schuyf, J. (1992) The company of friends and lovers: lesbian communities in the Netherlands, in K. Plummer (ed.) *Modern Homosexualities*. London: Routledge.

Scott, A. (1990) *Ideology and the New Social Movements*. London: Unwin Hyman.

Scott, J.W. (1988) *Gender and the Politics of History*. New York: Columbia University Press.

Scott, J.W. (1992) 'Experience' in J. Butler and J.W. Scott (eds) *Feminists Theorize the Political*. New York: Routledge.

Scott, J.W. (1993a) Women's history, in L.S. Kauffman (ed.) *American Feminist Thought at Century's End*. Cambridge, Massachusetts: Blackwell.

Scott, J.W. (1993b) The evidence of experience, in H. Abelove, M.A. Barale and D.M. Halperin (eds) *The Lesbian and Gay Studies Reader*. New York: Routledge.

Scraton, P. (1985) From Saltley Gates to Orgreave: a history of the policing of recent industrial disputes, in B. Fine and R. Millar (eds) *Policing the Miners' Strike*. London: Lawrence and Wishart.

Seager, J. (1993) *Earth Follies: Feminism, Politics and the Environment*. London: Earthscan Publications.

Segal, L. (1987) *Is the Future Female: Troubled Thoughts on Contemporary Feminism*. London: Virago.

Sharp, G. (1974) *The Politics of Nonviolent Action*. Boston: Porter Sargent.

Shaw, M. (1990) Strategy and social process: military context and sociological analysis, *Sociology*, 24: 65–74.

Shaw, M. (1991) *Post Military Society*. Cambridge: Polity.

Shrew (1978) 'Neither victim nor assassin: feminism and nonviolence', *Shrew*, special issue.

Smelser, N. (1962) *Theories of Collective Behaviour*. London: Routledge & Kegan Paul.

Smith, D and Smith, R. (1980) British military expenditure in the 1980s, in E.P. Thompson and D. Smith (eds) *Protest and Survive*. Harmondsworth: Penguin.

Smith-Rosenberg, C. (1975) The female world of love and ritual: relations between women in 19th century America, *Signs*, 1(1): 1–29.

Smyth, C. (1992) *Lesbians Talk Queer Notions*. London: Scarlet Press.

Snitow, A. (1985a) Holding the line at Greenham, *Mother Jones*, February/March: 30–47.

Snitow, A. (1985b) Pictures for 10 million women, *Frontiers*, VIII(2): 45–9.

Snitow, A. (1990) A gender diary, in M. Hirsch and E.F. Keller (eds) *Conflicts in Feminism*. New York: Routledge.

Snow, D.A. and Benford, R.D. (1988) Ideology, Frame Resonance and Participant Mobilization in B. Klandermans, H. Kriesi and S. Tarrow (eds) *From Structure to Action: Comparing Social Movement Research Across Cultures*, Vol. 1. Greenwich, Connecticut: Jai Press.

Soper K. (1985) Missing the mark? *Journal of European Nuclear Disarmament*, No. 5, April/May: 32.

Spretnak, C. (1982) (ed.) *The Politics of Women's Spirituality: Essays on the Rise of Spiritual Power within the Feminist Movement*. Garden City, New York: Anchor/Doubleday.

Stacey, J. (1988) Can there be a feminist ethnography? *Women's Studies International Forum*, 11(1): 21–7.

Stanko, E.A (1990) *Everyday Violence*. London: Pandora.

Stanley, L. (1985) Biography as microscope or kaleidoscope? in D. Farran *et al. Writing Feminist Biography*, Studies in Sexual Politics, Nos. 13/14. Manchester: University of Manchester.

Stanley, L. and Wise, S. (1983) *Breaking Out: Feminist Consciousness and Feminist Research*. London: Routledge and Kegan Paul.

Stanley, L. and Wise, S. (1990) Method, methodology and epistemology in feminist research processes, in L. Stanley (ed.) *Feminist Praxis: Research, Theory and Epistemology in Feminist Sociology*. London: Routledge.

Stanley, L. and Wise, S. (1993) *Breaking Out Again: Feminist Ontology and Epistemology*. London: Routledge.

Strachey, R. (1978) *The Cause: A Short History of the Women's Movement in Great Britain*. London: Virago.

Summers, A. (1988) *Angels and Citizens: British Women as Military Nurses 1854–1914*. London: Routledge.

Swerdlow, A. (1989) Pure milk, not poison: Women Strike for Peace and the Test Ban Treaty of 1963, in A. Harris and Y. King (eds) *Rocking the Ship of State: Toward a Feminist Peace Politics*. Boulder, Colorado: Westview Press.

Tarrow, S. (1983) *Struggling to Reform: Social Movements and Policy Change During Cycles of Protest*. Ithaca, New York: Cornell University (Western Societies Paper No.15).

Taylor, R. (1988) *Against the Bomb: The British Peace Movement 1958–1965*. Oxford: Clarendon Press.

Taylor, R. and Pritchard, C. (1980) *The Protest Makers: The British Nuclear Disarmament Movement of 1958–65, Twenty Years On*. Oxford: Pergamon Press.

Taylor, R. and Young. N. (1987) (eds) *Campaigns for Peace: British Peace Movements in the Twentieth Century*. Manchester: Manchester University Press.

Thompson, E.P. (1966) *The Making of the English Working Class*. Harmondsworth: Penguin.

Thompson, E.P. (1982a) Notes on exterminism, the last stage of civilisation, in New Left Review (ed) *Exterminism and Cold War*. London: New Left Books.

Thompson, E.P. (1982b) 'Beyond the Cold War', in E.P. Thompson (ed.) *Zero Option*. London: Merlin Press.

Thompson, P. (1988) *The Voice of the Past: Oral History*. Oxford, Oxford University Press.

Thomson, A. and Eichler, M. (1985) The impact of labour force attachment on political participation: a reconsideration, *International Political Science Review*, 6(3): 367–81.

Thorne, B. (1975) Protest and the problem of credibility: uses of knowledge and risk-taking in the draft-resistance movement of the 1960s, *Social Problems*, 23: 111–123.

Tilly, C. (1978) *From Mobilization to Revolution*. Reading, Massachusetts: Addison-Wesley.

Tilly, C. (1979) Repertoires of contention in America and Britain, 1750–1830, in J.D. McCarthy and M.N. Zald (eds) *The Dynamics of Social Movements*. Cambridge, Massachusetts: Winthrop Publishers.

Tilly, C., Tilly, L. and Tilly, R. (1975) *The Rebellious Century*. Cambridge, Massachusetts: Harvard University Press.

Tiryakian, E. (1988) From Durkheim to Managua: revolutions as religious revivals, in J. Alexander (ed) *Durkheimian Sociology: Cultural Studies*. Cambridge: Cambridge University Press.

Tobias, S. (1985) Toward a feminist analysis of defence spending, in *Frontiers*, VIII(2): 65–8.

Tönnies, F. (1955) *Community and Association*. London: Routledge and Kegan Paul.

Touraine, A. (1971) *The Post-Industrial Society – Tomorrow's Social History: Classes, Conflicts and Culture in the Programmed Society*. New York: Random House.

Touraine, A. (1981) *The Voice and the Eye: An Analysis of Social Movements*. Cambridge: Cambridge University Press.

Touraine, A. (1983) *Anti-Nuclear Protest*. Cambridge: Cambridge University Press.

Touraine, A. (1985) An introduction to the study of social movements, *Social Research*, 52(4): 749.

Turner, R.H. (1970) Determinants of social movement strategies, in T. Shibutani (ed.) *Collective Behaviour*, annual publication. Englewood Cliffs, New Jersey: Prentice-Hall.

Turner, V. (1977) *The Ritual Process: Structure and Anti-Structure*. Ithaca, New York: Cornell University Press.

Turner, R.H. and Killian, L.M. (1972) *Collective Behaviour*, annual publication Englewood Cliffs, New Jersey: Prentice-Hall.

Vellacott, J. (1993) A place for pacifism and transnationalism in feminist theory: the early work of the Women's International League for Peace and Freedom, *Women's History Review*, 2(1): 23–56.

Vicinius, M. (1985) *Independent Women: Work and Community for Single Women, 1820–1920*. London: Virago.

Walby, S. (1988) Gender politics and social theory, *Sociology*, 22(2): 215–32.

Walby, S. (1989) Theorizing patriarchy, *Sociology*, 23(2): 213–34.

Walby, S. (1990a) From public to private patriarchy: the periodisation of British history, *Women's Studies International Forum*, 13(1/2): 91–104.

Walby, S. (1990b) *Theorizing Patriarchy*, Oxford: Blackwell.

Walby, S. (1992) Post-post-modernism? Theorizing social complexity, in M. Barrett and A. Phillips (eds) *Destabilizing Theory: Contemporary Feminist Debates*. Cambridge: Polity Press.

Walby, S. (1993) 'Backlash' in historical context, in M. Kennedy, C. Lubelska and V. Walsh (eds) *Making Connections*. Basingstoke: Falmer Press.

Walker, M. (1993) *The Cold War and the Making of the Modern World*. London: Fourth Estate.

Walker, R.B.J. (1987) Culture, discourse and insecurity, *Current Research on Peace and Violence*, X(I): 50–64.

Wallace, C. (1993) Reflections on the concept of 'strategy', in D. Morgan and L. Stanley (eds) *Debates in Sociology*. Manchester: Manchester University Press.

Wallsgrove, R. (1983) Greenham Common – so why am I still ambivalent? *Trouble and Strife*, 1: 4–6.

Waters, M. (1989) Patriarchy and viriarchy, *Sociology*, 23(2): 193–211.

Weber, M. (1978) *Economy and Society*, Vol.1. Berkeley: University of California Press.

Weedon, C. (1987) *Feminist Practice and Poststructuralist Theory*. Oxford: Blackwell.

Welch, S. (1977) Women as political animals, *American Journal of Political Science*, 21(4): 711–30.

West, G. and Blumberg, R.L. (1990) Reconstructing social protest from a feminist perspective, in G. West and R.L. Blumberg (eds) *Women and Social Protest*. Oxford: Oxford University Press.

Westwood, S. and Radcliffe, S. (1993) *'Viva': Women and Popular Protest in Latin America*. London: Routledge.

Wheelwright, J. (1989) *Amazons and Military Maids: Women who Dressed as Men in the Pursuit of Life, Liberty and Happiness*. London: Pandora.

Wheelwright, J. (1992) 'A brother in arms, a sister in peace': contemporary issues of gender and the military, in G. Kirkup and L. Smith Keller (eds) *Inventing Women: Science, Technology and Gender*. Cambridge: Polity.

Wilkinson, S. and Kitzinger, C. (1993) *Heterosexuality: A Feminism and Psychology Reader*. London: Sage.

Wiley, N. (1990) The history and politics of recent sociological theory, in G. Ritzer (ed.) *Frontiers of Social Theory: New Syntheses*. New York, Columbia University Press.

Wilton, T. (1993) Queer subjects: lesbians, heterosexual women and the academy, in M. Kennedy, C. Lubelska and V. Walsh (eds) *Making Connections*. London: Taylor and Francis.

Wiltsher, A. (1985) *Most Dangerous Women: Feminist Peace Campaigners of the Great War*. London: Pandora.

Wise, S. (1987) A framework for discussing ethical issues in feminist research: a review of the literature, in *Writing Feminist Biography 2: Studies in Sexual Politics*, No. 19, University of Manchester, pp. 47–88.

Wise Harris, D. (1991) Keeping women in our place: violence at Canadian Universities. *Canadian Woman Studies*, 2(4): 37–41.

Wittig, M. (1992) *The Straight Mind and Other Essays*. Hemel Hempstead: Harvester Wheatsheaf.

Wittner, L. (1988) The transnational movement against nuclear weapons 1945–1986: a preliminary summary, in C. Chatfield and P. van den Dungen (eds) *Peace Movements and Political Cultures*. Knoxville: University of Tennessee Press.

Wolffensperger, J. (1991) Engendered structure: Giddens and the conceptualization of gender, in K. Davis, M. Leijenaar and J. Oldersma (eds) *The Gender of Power*. London: Sage.

Woodcock, G. (1962) *Anarchism*. Harmondsworth: Penguin.

Woodcock, G. (1977) (ed.) *The Anarchist Reader*. Glasgow: Fontana.

Woolf, V. (1982) *Three Guineas*. Harmondsworth: Penguin.

York, J., Leonard, D., Liensol, C., Chester, G., Warrick, J., Sebestyen, A., Henderson, R. and Pachachi, R. (1979) We are the feminists that women have warned us about, reprinted in S. Gunew (1991) (ed.) *A Reader in Feminist Knowledge*. London: Routledge.

Yorkshire Women Go To Greenham (1983) (eds) *You Can't Kill the Spirit*. Wakefield: Bretton Women's Book Fund.

Young, A. (1990) *Femininity in Dissent*. London: Routledge.

Young, I. M. (1990) Throwing like a girl: a phenomenology of feminine bodily comportment, motility and spatiality, in *Throwing Like a Girl and other Essays in Feminist Philosophy and Social Theory*. Bloomington: Indiana University Press.

Young, N. (1990) *Peace Movements as Actors in the European Process of Change*, unpublished paper.

Yuval-Davis, N. (1994) Identity politics and women's ethnicity, in V.M. Moghadam (ed.) *Identity Politics and Women: Cultural Reassertions and Feminisms in International Perspective*. Boulder, Colorado: Westview Press.

Zimmerman, B. (1985) What has never been: an overview of lesbian feminist literary criticism, in E. Showalter (ed.) *The New Feminist Criticism: Essays on Women, Literature and Theory*. New York: Pantheon Books.

Zimmerman, D.H. and Wieder, D.L. (1977) The diary: diary interview method, *Urban Life*, 54.

Index

Aboriginal land rights, 144
ACT UP, 172
actions
    being there, 114–17
    blockades, 20, 75, 76, 104–6
    courtroom, 108–10
    gatherings/demonstrations, 100–4
    incursions, 106–8
    monitoring, 111–12
    roving, 112–14
activation, 31, 51–3
Addington, C., 78, 102, 145–6, 147, 150
affective bonds/relations, 69, 74, 77, 98
age, 45, 79, 80, 81, 84, 175
agency, 1, 2, 30, 66, 84, 139, 142, 156–7,
    163, 168, 172, 180 ns4, 5, 181 n7
Aldermaston
    marches, 20, 36
    to Burghfield chain, 106
Alderson, L., 63
Alexander, J., 190 n14
Allen, K., 73, 146, 153, 154–5, 156
AMNLAE, 144
anarchism/anarchist, 20, 62, 66, 70, 98
ANC, 64, 144, 149
Andropov, Y., President, 27
animal rights, 113, 172
anti-communism, 23, 25, 28, 130

anti-hierarchical, 64–5
anti-lesbianism, 129, 130, 131, 132, 186
    n25
anti-militarism, 4–7, 17, 19
    feminist, 4, 5–7, 34–5, 36
    materialist, 4, 5, 34, 35, 37
    maternalist, 4–5, 34–6, 37
Anti-Nazi League, 20, 48, 49
anti-nuclear power, 16, 21, 22, 113
    movement, 32, 99, 104
anti-roads movement, 172
anti-Vietnam war movement, 20, 104
Arkin, W., 24
Armstrong, A., 52, 56, 102, 147, 151, 154
arrest, 100, 107, 120
Ashworth, G., 108
Atkinson, P., 12, 183 n33

Bagguley, P., 183 n4
Banks, O., 116, 180 n4
Barnes, S. et al., 170
Barrett, M., 137, 180 n1
Bartky, S., 140, 141
Bassnett, S., 21
Beck, U., 16
being there, 114–17
Bell, D., 15
Bellos, L., 171

Beneria, L., 5
Benford, R.D., 34, 35
Benham, S., 50, 57, 61, 74–5, 94, 160
Berkshire Anti-Nuclear Campaign, 33
Berkshire County Council, 119, 123
Berrington, H., 195–6 n7
Besley, K., 127
Bestic, P., 43, 58, 59, 61, 94, 126, 148
Bishop, J., 63
black feminism
  and Greenham, 95–6
Black, N., 181 n15
Blank, R., 5
blockades, 20, 75, 76, 104–6
Bond, S., 93
Bookchin, M., 69
Booth, G., 68
Brittan, P., 20
Brown, W., 95–6
Brownmiller, S., 6
Bund, 189 n9
Burgess, R., 9
Burklin, W., 14
Burton, J., 37
Butler, J., 141, 142, 180 ns4, 7, 196 n12
by-laws, 108, 122
Byrne, P., 16, 177

Cadden, C., 51, 53, 55, 80, 102, 143
Caedel, M., 168, 181 n13
Campaign for Nuclear Disarmament
  (CND), 20, 23, 28, 33, 36, 37, 39, 51,
  52, 53, 54, 55, 74, 106, 114, 135, 145,
  149–50, 169
Campbell, D., 183 n23
capitalism
  changes in, 15–17
caring work
  women's, 34, 44
Carter, A., 168
Carter, J., President, 22, 23
Catholicism, 51
Chandler, W., 16
Chester, G., 62, 64, 66, 67
Chevaline programme, 22, 25
childcare, 36, 45–6
children, 5, 34, 36, 45, 54, 86–7
Chilton, P., 27–8

Citadel locks action, 106
civil defence, 25
class, 15, 17, 41, 65, 79, 80, 81, 91, 103–4,
  177–8
  and the new politics, 183 n5
Clause 28, 172
Clesse, A., 25
Close the Base, 51, 105, 122
cognitive praxis, 2, 31–2, 60–70,
  137
Cohn, C., 6, 182 n19
Cold War, 22–8
  end of, 164
collective identity, 2, 29, 30, 31, 35, 37,
  61–2, 87–8, 90, 104, 135
collectivity, 64–5
Committee of 100, 20, 49
Committee on the Present Danger, 23,
  25
Common Women's Days, 103
communality, 66, 82, 85, 86, 92
Communist Party, 48, 86
conflict, 3
  about class, 91, 103–4
  about hierarchy, 64, 74–5, 93–5, 95–6,
    103–4
  about Kings Cross, 95–6
  about lesbianism, 116
  about money, 90–2
  about New York Supreme Court case,
    113
  about power and resources, 82, 90–3,
    93–5, 95–6
  about race, 95–6
  about women-only policy, 39–40
  about Yellow Gate, 82, 91
consciousness, 136, 137, 138, 139–41
  about criminal justice system, 153, 154,
    155
  about environment, 147–8
  false, 5
  feminist, 1, 11, 139–41, 163
  global, 144, 148–9
  about lesbianism, 147
  raising, 31, 138, 139–40, 144
  about the state, 153, 154–5
  transformations in, 67, 74, 143–55, 163
  about violence against women, 152–3

of women's oppression/male
domination, 145–6, 152–3
Cook, A., 3
Cotgrove, S., 16, 177
courtroom, 108–10
Cox, J., 24, 28
criminal justice system, 108, 108–10, 122,
123, 153, 154, 155
criticisms of Greenham
by feminists, 2–3, 8, 186 n25
see also Onlywomen Press
Cruise missiles, 1, 23–4, 28, 33, 34, 35, 53,
55, 56, 57, 59, 88, 98, 99, 103, 107,
111–12, 115, 148, 164, 165, 166, 168
Cruisewatch, 111

Dalton, R., 15
Daly, M., 7, 22, 67
dancing, 102
date of first involvement, 175
Davidoff, L., 4
Davis, M., 184–5 n22
de Beauvoir, S., 4
de Lauretis, T., 141
decision-making, 61, 64–5, 67, 103–4
about money, 91–2
dedifferentiation, 101
defence and foreign policy, 5, 22–3
delegates, 94, 95
Delphy, C., 4, 189 n12
Department of Transport, 119, 120, 121–4
Derbyshire County Council, 135
DHSS, 121, 129, 165
difference/diversity between women, 35,
45, 65, 78–82, 84, 91–2, 103, 104, 110,
143
Direct Action Committee (DAC), 20
dirt, 130, 131
discursive framing, 32, 33–6, 37, 118
discursive reversal, 129–30
documentary sources, 11
domestic labour, 40, 63, 66, 82–8
Dragon Festival, 103
Duff, A., 16, 177
Dworkin, A., 6–7, 22

Easlea, B., 182 n19
ecofeminism, 21, 62, 67

education, 179
Edwards, N., 181 n10
Edwards, R., 190 n6
Edwards, S., 47, 48–9, 102, 125
Eglin, J., 186 n25
El Salvador, 144
electro-magnetic radiation, 126–7, 165
Elshtain, J.B., 3, 4
Elworthy, S., 22, 23
Embrace the Base, 7, 51, 101–2, 122
emotion, 69
empowerment, 1, 2, 40, 98, 156–7
see also agency
Enloe, C., 3, 5, 6, 119
Ennis, J., 190 n10
environment, 16, 67, 162
environmental movement, 16, 20, 21
epistemological issues, 8
Erlich, C., 20
essentialism, 3, 141–2
ethical/political issues, 11–13
ethnicity, 179
ethnography, 2, 7–8, 10, 11–12
ethos, 60–70
formation of, 60–2
Greenham network, 74
European Nuclear Disarmament (END),
28, 169
Evans, B., 50, 79, 110, 117, 156
Evans, S., 187 n33
evictions, 89, 120–4
experience, 7, 136, 138–9, 155
exterminism, 16
external mode of action, 71, 97–117
and transformations in consciousness,
149–55
Eyerman, R., 2, 31, 60

Fadermann, L., 18, 19
family background, 50–1
Faslane, 74, 129, 193 n17
femininity
Greenham's challenge to, 58, 83,
116–17, 131, 155–7
feminist
anti-militarism, 4, 5–7, 34–5, 36
consciousness, 1, 11, 139–41, 163
criticisms of Greenham, 2–3, 8, 186 n25

lesbian, 79
liberal, 34–5
poststructuralism, 118, 138–9, 141–3
radical, 6–7, 21, 22, 62
theories of the state, 118–19
fence-cutting
debate, 106–7
first wave feminism, 18, 19
Foster, C., 5
Foucault, M., 180 n7
fractured foundationalism, 8, 140
Franklin, S., 141, 195 n12
Fraser, N., 194 n10
Freedom Association, 130
Freeman, J., 41, 188 n4
friendship, 10, 11–12, 31, 56, 73, 78, 146
and getting involved, 40, 52
fun, 57–9, 67–9
see also humour
Fuss, D., 138, 141, 194 n4, 195 n12

Galst, L., 54, 87, 161
Gamble, A., 24
Gandhi, M., 63
gates, 9, 75–82, 176
management of difference, 78–82
naming, 75–6
as small group structure, 77–8, 92
gatherings/demonstrations, 100–4
Gay Liberation Front, 20
GCHQ, 22
gender identities, 137, 141, 142
see also identity of 'woman'
geopolitical
context, 22–8
privacy, 22–3
Gerlach, L., 72
getting involved, 36–7, 41–59
context of, 41–51
routes to, 51–3
reasons, 53–9
Giddens, A., 2, 15, 16, 137, 180 n6, 182
n24
Glaser, B., 11–12, 182 ns30, 31
Glasgow University Media Group, 195 n15
Gleditsch, N., 168
global economy, 15, 16
globalization, 15

Goldman, E., 67, 70
Gorbachev, M., President, 164, 168, 169
Greed, C., 8
Green, F., 171
Greenham
beginnings, 32–7
creation/re-creation, 40–1, 82–8
establishment of, 37–9
ethos, 60–70
end of, 164–7
legacy, 172
network, 72–5
organizational structure, 67, 72–82
women-only decision, 39–40
Greenham Common Women Out, 129,
131, 134
Greenham women
as communists/foreigners, 130
as hysterical/mad, 130, 131
Greenham Women against Cruise, 113
Griffin, S., 22, 67, 69
Guardian, The, 33, 36, 130
Gulf War, 167
Gulliver, P., 49, 55–6, 58, 61, 86, 125, 146,
148, 152–3, 158, 159–60
Gwedhen, R., 44, 56–7, 58, 78, 122, 153–4,
160–1

Habermas, J., 15, 16, 17
Hall, C., 4
Hall, S., 15, 24
Halliday, F., 26–7
Hallowes, F., 5
Hammersley, M., 12, 183 n33
Haraway, D., 8
Harding, S., 17
Harford, B., 3, 37, 39, 101, 115, 129
Hartsock, N., 180 ns4, 7, 182 n20
Harwood, C., 49, 145, 158
Hastings, E.H., 169
Hastings, P.K., 169
Hayano, D., 8
Henderson, R., 62, 64, 66, 67
Heron, J., 52–3, 86, 94, 95, 132, 145, 157,
162
Heseltine, M., 108
heterorelations, 146, 155
heterosexual

contexts, 44–7
women, 44–7, 80
women becoming lesbians, 161–2
women's partners and Greenham, 46–7,
    150–2
Hetherington, K., 189 n9
hierarchy, 64, 74–5, 93–5, 95–6, 103–4
    and level of involvement, 64, 74–5, 94
higher education, 15, 16, 51
Hine, V., 72
Hoagland, S.L., 68, 180 n4
Hobhouse, E., 5
Holloway Prison, 113
Holy Loch, 20
Home Office, 119
homosexuality, male, 6
Hopkins, S., 3, 37, 39, 101, 115, 129
Huberman, A.M., 12
Hudson, C., 167
humanism, 141
humour, 67–8, 79–80, 134, 170
Hutcheon, A., 131
Hutchinson, J., 108

identity, 136, 137, 138, 141–3
    of 'lesbian', 142, 157–62
    politics, 138
    transformations in, 67, 155–63
    of 'woman', 141–2, 155–7, 162
    see also collective identity
imprisonment, *see* prison
incursions, 106–8
individuality, 65
    see also difference/diversity between
        women
Inglehart, R., 16
injunctions against Greenham women,
    121–2
Intermediate Nuclear Forces Treaty, 111,
    164
internal mode of action, 71–96, 188 n2
    and transformations in consciousness,
        144–9
International Fellowship of Reconciliation,
    21
International Marxist Group, 48, 49
international relations discourse, 168
interviews, 9–11

intuition, 69, 98

Jacques, M., 15, 24
Jaggar, A., 139, 194 n6
Jahn, E., 169
Jamison, A., 2, 31, 60
Jeffrey-Poulter, S., 20
Jenness, V., 142
John, H., 36, 38, 84–5, 157, 162
Jones, H.M., 55, 150, 152
Jones, L., 131, 181 n10
July blockades, 105, 106

Kaldor, M., 16, 26, 27, 184 n19
Kaplan, F., 22, 23, 184 n21
Kaplan, T., 5
Kelly-Gadol, J., 18
KGB, 27
King, C., 157
King, Y., 22
Kings Cross Women's Centre, 95–6, 103,
    191 n17
Kirk, G., 3, 64
Kitschelt, H., 97
Kitzinger, C., 178, 194 n5
Kitzinger, J., 181 n10
Klandermans, B., 185 ns3, 6, 186 n12
Knelman, F., 25, 184 n21
Koonz, C., 3
Krass, A., 24
Kriesi, H., 177, 183 n5, 186 n26
Kristeva, J., 142, 194 n10
Kuechler, M., 15

Labour Party, 22, 24, 25, 50
Lamb, S., 54, 154
Lash, S., 15
Laws, S., 171
leaders, 61, 64–5, 93–5, 145
leadership, 61, 66, 96, 97, 145
Leah, E., 37
Learoyd, J., 130
leaving Greenham, 165–7
LeBon, G., 97
length of involvement
    and hierarchy, 94
Leonard, D., 4, 62, 64, 66, 67, 189 n12
Lesbian Avengers, 172

lesbian community, 56–7
lesbian feminism, 79
lesbian sex, 79, 158, 159, 161
lesbianism, 1, 18
  conflict about, 116
lesbians, 2, 44, 45, 56–7, 79, 80, 114,
  116–17, 129, 130, 131, 147, 157–62,
  170, 172
level of involvement, 9, 43–4, 45, 46, 47,
  176
  and hierarchy, 64, 74–5, 94
Lewis, M., 36, 37–8, 81, 156
liberal feminism, 34–5
Liddington, J., 3, 4, 5, 6, 21, 22, 28, 32, 33,
  176, 181 n14
Liensol, C., 62, 64, 66, 67
liminal experience, 101
liminality, 2, 143
Linda, 117
Linton, R., 22
List, J., 50, 52, 57, 79–80, 157, 159
Little Chef, 131
Lloyd, G., 69
local response
  anti-Greenham, 121, 128–35, *see also*
    Newbury
  pro-Greenham, 33, 38, 39
Lodgaard, S., 23
Logan, N., 47–8, 86
Lovenduski, J., 3
Luckham, R., 27, 185 n24
Lukes, A., 81
Lynchcombe, 193 n16
Lyotard, J–F., 15

MacKinnon, C., 140, 141, 192 n3
macro-structural context, 15–19, 28–9
magic, 134
Maitland, Lady O., 134
making connections, 112–14
male domination
  in political groups, 21, 37, 49
Mann, M., 22, 184 n10
Marshall, B., 137, 192 n3
martyrdom, 52, 67–9, 106
marxism, 136–7, 140
masculinity, 2–3, 9
materialism, 4, 5, 34, 35, 37, 54

maternalism, 3, 4, 5, 34, 35, 36, 37, 54,
  157, 162
Mattausch, J., 16, 41, 177, 181 n13, 183 n5
Maynard, M., 1
McCarthy, J., 37, 41, 47, 183 ns1, 2, 185
  n3
McNair Wilson, M., MP, 129
McNeil, M., 129
means/ends relationship, 69–70
media, 33, 38–9, 52, 68, 76, 93, 94, 115,
  122, 130, 170, 195 n15
meetings, 38, 60, 91–2
Melucci, A., 14, 15, 16, 31, 32, 137, 185
  n1, 188 ns2, 9
Menwith Hill, 167
meso-level context, 19–28, 29
methodological issues, 7–13
Meyer, A., 129, 130
MI5, 22, 127–8
MI6, 22
Miles, M., 12
militarism, 1, 2, 3–7, 21
  challenge to, 167–70
  and gender, 3–7, 34–5, 40
  nuclear, 53–5
military discourse, 6, 70
military exercises, 111–12
Mills, C.W., 8
miners' strike, 3, 89, 106
minions, 94, 95
Ministry of Defence, 22, 106, 112, 119,
  120, 125, 127, 133, 164
  MOD building, 112
  MOD police, 133
mobilization, 30, 31, 33–4, 51, 52,
  53
modernity, 17
Mohin, L., 63, 171
Molesworth, 129
money, 19, 65, 88, 89, 90–2, 165
  meetings, 91–2
monitoring, 111–12
Moraga, C., 138
Morgan, R., 11
motherhood, 4
mothering, 4
Mouzelis, N., 181 n8
Murray, R., 15

Namibia, 113
native Americans, 149, 167
NATO, 2, 23, 24, 26, 103, 111, 119, 168
  policy, 164, 168, 169
Nedelmann, P., 137
network
  anti-nuclear, 32, 36
  Greenham, 9, 10, 101, 103–4
  peace, 28
networks, 33, 37, 39, 172, 185 n9
neutron bomb, 23
New Left, 20, 21
new politics, 15–16, 183 n5
New Right, 24–5, 130
new social movements, 14–17, 30–1, 137
New York Supreme Court Case, 113
Newbury, 116–17, 128, 129, 130, 131, 132
Newbury against the Missiles, 38
Newbury District Council, 119, 120–4, 164
Newbury magistrates court, 108–10
Newbury Weekly News, 129, 130, 131, 132
Nicaragua, 6, 26, 64, 144
nightwatch, 133–4
nimbyism, 128, 129
nonviolence, 21, 40, 62, 63–4, 106–7
nonviolent direct action, 20, 104
  see also actions
Norden, B., 195 n4
Northern Ireland, 50
nuclear
  fear, 28, 54, 55
  war, 28, 34
  weapons/militarism, 2, 16, 22–5, 34,
    35–6, 53–5

Oakley, A., 183 n34
October 29 action, 107
Offe, C., 15, 16, 41, 51, 71, 137, 177, 179
Official Secrets Act, 122
Oldfield, S., 186 n25
Olson, M., 31, 183 n1
Onlywomen Press, 3, 135
organizational structure, 67, 72–82, 96, 104
Overy, B., 194 n2

Pacific Islands, 144
  women's network for Nuclear Free and
    Independent Pacific, 166, 167

Pactriachi, R., 62, 64, 66, 67
paid employment
  and Greenham, 41–4
  and politics, 184 n9
  women's, 16–17, 18
Paris, P., 46–7, 49, 50, 54, 86–7, 151–2,
  162
Parkin, F., 16, 177, 181 n13, 185 n5
Pateman, C., 71, 119
patriarchy, 1, 2, 18, 70, 180 n1
  challenge to, 170–2
  changes in, 18–19
Presidential Directive 59 (PD–59), 24
peace camps, 74, 129, 193 n17
peace movement, 19, 20, 28, 104, 114
  hostility to Greenham, 114, 140–50
  support for Greenham, 33, 135
Peace News, 33
Perkins Gilman, C., 83
Pershing II, 23–4, 28
personal responsibility, 61, 66, 67, 84–5,
  86, 98, 104, 110
Peterson, A., 188 n1
Pettitt, Ann, 32–3, 40, 54
Plaid Cymru, 43, 48–9
Plant, S., 20
police, 37, 104, 105, 106, 107, 109, 111,
  119, 120, 133, 152, 153, 154
policing
  of Greenham, 104, 105–6, 122–3, 127–8
political, the, 181 n9
political and social orientations, 47–51
political environment, 19–22
politics
  male domination, 145–6
  women's exclusion, 34–5
Porton Down, 113
postmodernity, 15
poststructuralism, 118, 138–9, 141–3
poverty, 5
practice/theory
  relationship, 60–2
Pringle, R., 118, 119
prison, 120, 154–5
Pritchard, C., 16, 177, 180 n13, 184 n11
Protestantism, 50
public opinion
  about Cruise, 168, 169, 170

about Greenham, 169–70

race, 65, 95–6, 179
Radcliffe, S., 180 n4, 194 n2
radical feminism, 6–7, 21, 22, 62
RAGE, Ratepayers against Greenham
    Encampments, 129–30, 131, 132
RAND Corporation, 22
Randall, V., 3
Randle, M., 20, 104, 168, 169, 184 n11,
    196 n8
Rape Crisis, 166
rational choice theory, 31, 97
rationality, 69, 97–8
Rawson, B., 42, 56, 146, 149, 154, 156
Raymond, J., 2, 19, 146, 195 n14
Reagan, R., President, 24, 25, 26, 55, 113,
    168
Redstockings, 138
reflexivity, 67, 95, 98, 137
region, 179
repertoire of action, 99–100
resource mobilization theory, 14, 30–2, 97
resources
    activation of, 39
    collective resources, 88–90
    conflict about, 82, 90–3, 93–5, 95–6
    discursive, 2, 142–3, 163
    donation of, 33, 39, 88–90
    financial, 19, 65, 88, 89, 90–2, 165
    mobilization of, 33
    personal resources, 88
    time, 41
retrospective auto-ethnography, 7–8
Ribbens, J., 190 n6
Riemer, J., 8, 10
Riley, D., 195 n11
risk society, 16, 17
Rochon, T.R., 169
Rootes, C., 169, 179, 183 n7
Roseneil, S., 8, 180 n3, 182 ns21, 25, 28
Rothenbuhler, E.W., 190 n13
roving, 112–14
Rowbotham, S., 3, 180 n1
Rucht, D., 190 ns8, 9, 194 n2
Ruddick, S., 4–5, 182 n16
Rumbold, A., M.P., 134
Russell, D., 7

sabotage, 107
SALT II, 23
sample, 9, 175–6
Sandinistas, *see* Nicaragua
Sassoon, A.S., 118
Scandinavian Women for Peace Walk, 28,
    32
Schell, J., 16
Schutz, A., 8
Schuyf, J., 142
Scott, A., 15, 31, 137, 183 n7
Scott, J., 138–9, 141, 181 n9, 184 n8
Scull, Mr & Mrs, 128, 134
Sebestyan, A., 62, 64, 66, 67
Secretary of State for Defence, 38, 108
Segal, L., 3, 186 n25, 189 n16
sexual harassment, 125
sexual identities, 141, 142, 157–62
    see also identity of 'lesbian'
sexuality, 1, 10, 44–7, 65, 129, 130, 131,
    132, 178, 186 n25
    see also heterosexual; lesbian/ism
Shaw, M., 168–9, 190 n5
Shedden, S., 131, 134
Siaroff, A., 16
silos action, 106–7
singing, 66, 83
sit-downs, 20
situationism, 20
skills, 84
Smith, B., 138
Smith, D., 24
Smith, K., 49, 105, 145
Smith, R., 24
Snitow, A., 142, 181 n10
Snow, D.A., 34
social constructionism, 63, 64, 141–2
social movements
    construction of, 30–2
    gender ignorance in theories of, 3, 14–17
    new social movements theory, 14–17,
        30–1
    rational choice theory, 31
    resource mobilization theory, 14, 30–2,
        97
    social psychological theories of, 30–1
Socialist Workers' Party, 52
soldiers, 3, 6

at Greenham, 107, 119, 120, 125–6, 152–3
Solsbury Hill, 172
South Africa, 64, 144, 149
Spanish Civil War, 48
speaks, 114
Spinsters, 22
spirituality, 59, 69, 80, 81
Stacey, J., 141, 195 n12
standpoint theory, 4
Stanley, L., 8, 11, 140–1, 182 n27
state
    consciousness about, 153, 154–5
    feminist theories of, 118–19
    response to Greenham, 118–28, 135, 170
state benefit, 19, 89, 165
Stoker, L., 37
Strategic Defense Initiative (SDI), 27
strategy, 31, 97–9, 190 ns4, 5, 6
Strauss, A., 11–12, 182–3 n30, 183 n31
structuration theory, 2, 139
subjectivity, *see* consciousness; identity
suffrage campaign, 1, 18, 39, 50, 180 n2
Sunday Times, 33
surveillance
    of Greenham, 122, 127–8
Swanwick, H., 5
SWAPO, 64
Swerdlow, A., 4

Tarrow, S., 47, 185 n6
Taylor, R., 16, 177, 180 n13, 184 n11
Teddy Bears' picnic action, 106
Ten Days action, 103–4
Thalmann, L., 50, 53, 57, 58–9, 85, 146, 147, 152, 161, 167
Thatcher, M., 24–5, 26, 129
theory/practice
    relationship, 60–2
third world, 26
Thompson, E.P., 9–10, 16, 26, 27, 184–5 n22
Thorne, B., 186 n14
Tilly, C., 99, 183 n3
Tiryakian, E., 101–2, 187 n36
Tobias, S., 5
Touraine, A., 15, 16, 183 n32
transport, 81, 89, 90, 92–3

Trina, 50
Trisha, 50, 148–9
Turner, V., 190 n13
twin track decision, 23–4, 27
Twyford Down, 172

unemployment
    and Greenham, 43–4
    and social movement participation, 41
United States
    Air Force, 1, 20, 27, 111–12, 113, 115, 120
    bombing Libya, 167
    defence policy, 22–8
    imperialism, 20
    National Security Agency, 167
    nuclear policies, 2
    military/defence establishment, 4, 6
Upper Heyford, 129
uranium mining, 113
Urry, J., 15
USSR
    break-up, 164
    conventional weapons, 24
    defence/foreign policy, 23–8
    nuclear weapons, 23, 24, 164

veganism, 79
vehicles, 81, 89, 90, 92–3
Vicinius, M., 19
Vietnam war, 20, 26
vigilantism, 132–4
violence, 40, 61
    against Greenham women, 105, 106, 107, 123, 125–6, 132–4, 152–3
    against women, 1, 6–7, 35, 152–3
    see also nonviolence
Voice of Women, 4, 34

Wages for Housework Campaign, 95, 103
Walby, S., 18–19, 134, 155, 180 n1, 183 n7, 192 ns3, 5
Walker, M., 27
Walker, R.B.J., 27–8
war, 3, 4, 5, 6
War Resisters International (WRI), 21
Warr, B., 132
Warrick, J., 62, 64, 66, 67

Watson, S., 118, 119
web; as symbol, 72, 103
Weedon, C., 137, 139, 141
Weinberger, C., 113
Westwood, S., 180 n4, 194 n2
Whitham, M., 22
Wilkinson, S., 178
Wilkinson, Simone, 54, 127–8
Wiltsher, A., 4
Wise, S., 8, 11, 140–1, 183 ns34, 36
Wittner, L., 168
Women against Pit Closures, 113
Women and Families for Defence, 134
Women for Life on Earth march/walk,
    32–7, 61, 101
  mobilizing statement, 34–6
Women for Peace
  Nottingham, 46
  Merseyside, 74
  Scandanavian, 28, 32
  South London, 74
women-only, 2, 21, 39–40, 55–6, 61, 62–3,
    74, 79, 149–50, 170–1
  men's response to, 40
  opposition to, 39–40
Women Oppose the Nuclear Threat
    (WONT)
  Cambridge, 33
  Leeds, 28

Women's Aid, 42, 49, 166
women's bodies, 100, 104, 105, 106
women's history, 1, 32
Women's International League for Peace
    and Freedom, 4, 5, 33
women's liberation movement, 20–1, 22,
    23, 47, 61, 62
women's peace movement, 22, 28
Women's Peace Party, 4
Women's Pentagon Action, 22, 35,
    67
Women's Pit Camps, 172
Women's Strike for Peace, 4, 34
Woolf, V., 5, 182 n18
world war one, 5, 6
world war two, 18
Wright, V., 43, 56

xenophobia, 130

York, J., 62, 64, 66, 67
Young, A., 130, 131, 176
Young, N., 168, 195 n6
Yugoslavia, former, 4, 6, 167
Yuval-Davis, N., 137

Zald, M.N., 37, 41, 47, 183 ns1, 2,
    185 n3
zapping, *see* electro–magnetic radiation

GENDERED WORK
SEXUALITY, FAMILY AND THE LABOUR MARKET

Lisa Adkins

Gendered Work contributes to current debates on the labour market via an exploration of the significance of sexual and family relations in structuring employment. Through detailed studies of conditions of work in the British tourist industry, it shows how men and women are constituted as different kinds of 'workers' in the labour market not only when segregated in different occupations but also when they are nominally located in the same jobs.

This differentiation is shown to be connected to two key processes: the sexualization of women workers which locates women as sexual as well as 'economic' workers, and the operation of family work relations within the sphere of employment when women work as wives rather than waged-labourers in the context of the contemporary labour market. These two processes are then drawn together to show the ways in which labour market production is gendered. This book therefore makes an important contribution to the growing feminist literature which is exposing the deep embeddedness of gender within labour market processes and practices.

Special Features
- New empirical material on the terms and conditions of typical contemporary jobs for women.
- New ways of understanding the gendered structure of the labour market.
- Reviews a range of analyses (feminist and sociological) in a constructively critical way to throw light on change and continuity in employment in the consumer society.

Contents
Introduction – Sexuality and the labour market – Family production and the labour market – Sexual servicing and women's employment – The condition of women's work – References – Index.

192pp   0 335 19296 3 (Paperback)   0 335 19297 1 (Hardback)

MAKING VIOLENCE SEXY
FEMINIST VIEWS ON PORNOGRAPHY

Diana E.H. Russell (ed.)

A crucially important collection of feminist voices challenging the pornocrats. Even if you read nothing else on the subject, read this.

(Robin Morgan)

Making Violence Sexy is a courageous book that chronicles women's resistance to pornography over the last twenty years. It does this in a collection of feminist articles, including testimonies by victims/survivors of pornography that together make a convincing case for the view that pornography (as distinct from erotica) causes harm to women, including acts of violence.

This book will appeal to students and lecturers of women's studies and sociology, political activists, public officials, social scientists, legal and medical professionals – those who consider it a form of discrimination against women. Women's studies teachers will find it a welcome addition to their required reading lists, and those working against sexual violence will appreciate it as a primary, up-to-date, and comprehensive source and inspiration.

Contents
Introduction – Part I: Survivors of pornography – Part II: Overview – Part III: Feminist research on pornography – Part IV: Feminist strategies and actions against pornography – Notes – References – Index.

320pp   0 335 19200 9 (Paperback)